PAUL MASON is the economics editor of the BBC's flagship current affairs programme *Newsnight* and was recently short-listed for an Emmy with *BBC World News America*. Mason has covered globalization and social justice stories from locations around the world, including Latin America, Africa and China. His previous book, *Live Working, Die Fighting*, was longlisted for the *Guardian* First Book Award; his blog, Idle Scrawl, was shortlisted for the 2009 Orwell Prize: www.bbc.co.uk/blogs/newsnight/paulmason

MELTDOWN

The End of the Age of Greed

Paul Mason

VERSO

London • New York

For Jane

First published by Verso 2009
This updated edition published by Verso 2010
© Paul Mason 2010
All rights reserved

The moral rights of the author have been asserted

3 5 7 9 10 8 6 4 2

Verso
UK: 6 Meard Street, London W1F 0EG
US: 20 Jay Street, Suite 1010, Brooklyn, NY 11201
www.versobooks.com

Verso is the imprint of New Left Books

ISBN-13: 978-1-84467-653-8

British Library Cataloguing in Publication Data
A catalogue record for this book is available from the British Library

Library of Congress Cataloging-in-Publication Data
A catalog record for this book is available from the Library of Congress

Typeset by Hewer Text UK Ltd, Edinburgh
Printed by Scandbook AB, Sweden

Contents

Introduction

WE HAVE LIVED through an event that most of us thought we would never see. In October 2008, free-market capitalism, on the edge of collapse, was rescued by the state. The alternative was oblivion. One year on, it is clear that the state bit off more than it could chew. As the eighteen-month respite bought by fiscal and monetary stimulus falters, we are entering a third, decisive phase of the meltdown.

By spring 2010, the same poison that took down banks was beginning to take down states: now the spectre of debt restructuring and default has spread from Greece to Portugal and Spain. As a result of the euro bailout, austerity programmes not seen for a generation are being imposed. Two years of competitive devaluation have failed to rebalance the world's currencies or world trade; the acid of competitive routes out of the crisis is still corroding the globalised economy, albeit under a veneer of diplomatic niceties. Meanwhile, the unrestrained tendency to create speculative bubbles has – at the very pit of the crisis – enriched the selfsame financial elite that caused it.

I wrote the first edition of *Meltdown* in the months after September 2008, while the financial system was still in chaos. Beginning after midnight on the day Lehman Brothers collapsed, I completed it in February 2009 – that is, after the second British bank bailout but before the turn to quantitative easing in London and Washington.

Inevitably, then, the first edition was always going to be an interim report, and I summarise below the facts unknown to me at the time and where I think they enrich or contradict my initial analysis. Leaving intact the original narrative – chapters 1–8 – I have added two new chapters at the end. The first covers the period from March 2009, with the turn to quantitative easing, to the Greek crisis, the euro-bailout and the British emergency budget of June 2010. This entire period now seems like a fourteen-month Phase Two of the crisis, marked by stimulus moves and weak recovery. Phase Three poses the threat of a double-dip recession, with some countries facing a deflationary spiral and a renewed competitive scramble towards an exit route that would break up globalisation.

I found myself in the right place to report the events of September 2008 and have barely paused for breath since then. On the weekend Lehman slid into bankruptcy I was interviewing Ford workers who had lost their jobs and homes amid the surreal Art Deco wreckage of Detroit. I spent the next week in New York and Washington, DC, then trod the subterranean passageways of Whitehall, witnessing the first British bailout, before returning to Washington for the G20 summit in November.

Between then and now I've toured Eastern Europe as parts of it collapsed; I've stood on the streets of Athens with striking workers; I've witnessed the heroic switch from exports to heavy infrastructure spending in China – meeting a railway carriage full of migrant workers travelling from the Shenzhen factories to build railway tunnels in Inner Mongolia, without a break to return home to Gansu province to see their kids.

I was there at the inauspicious birth of the G20 – shunted into a basement at a State Department with scrawled signs Sellotaped to the walls explaining the imminent transition process from Bush to Obama. In London, Pittsburgh and Toronto, I have watched the G20 grow into an ad-hoc replacement for the various defunct multilateral treaties that were supposed to govern the world economy.

I've seen the economics establishment throw up its hands in disbelief, the free-market right bury its head in denial, and the crude Keynesian solutions thrown at the crisis run into dead ends that would have been entirely predictable to J. M. Keynes himself.

In the introduction to the first edition of this book I wrote: 'The choice facing the developed world is this: either the rapid and decisive nationalisation of the banks, combined with a massive fiscal stimulus led by public spending and job creation; or the recession turns into a prolonged global slump.'

Things turned out differently. The US did unleash a massive fiscal stimulus; China's was even bigger. But what really changed the game was the turn to quantitative easing – a massive monetary stimulus running to $1.75 trillion in the US and £200 billion in the UK, which is, at time of writing, still filtering through the banking system into the wider economy.

If I underplayed the possibility of a turn to quantitative easing (QE) in the first edition it was because the political auguries for it were not good. Alistair Darling, then British Chancellor, told me in late December 2008 that if the UK did go down the quantitative easing route it would be a political decision, but that he was undecided; we now know that the Bank of England had only then begun studying the technical options. In mid-January 2009, Federal Reserve chief Ben Bernanke travelled all the way to the London School of Economics to advise an audience of esteemed British policymakers not to do QE, and said that he would not himself be doing it. But in March 2009, after the first edition went to press, both governments opted for QE. I explore the impact and the pitfalls of this move in Chapter 9.

By early summer 2009, it had become clear that the policy elites of the US and the UK had stemmed the crisis by splitting the difference between nationalisation and slump. Outright nationalisations had been rare. The pattern – with RBS, HBOS, AIG, Citigroup and Bank of America – came to be quasi-nationalisations, in which the state took a decisive equity stake and assumed all the downside while the bankers enjoyed all the indemnity. There would be a severe recession but by 2010 most economies were technically out of it, albeit with some flat-lining in terms of recovery.

During this hiatus policymakers began to flatter themselves that they had saved the world. But we now know at what cost. China had revived demand at the cost of a massive switch to internal consumption: its 'fiscal stimulus' was nothing of the sort – two thirds of new spending being fuelled by uncontrolled bank lending. America had revived at the cost of a $1.4 trillion deficit, a $14 trillion debt and a $16 trillion exposure to the stricken financial system. Europe – where no country had opted for massive discretionary fiscal stimulus – simply transferred the stress into ill-designed single currency arrangements, with the result that Greece almost went bankrupt, the eurozone rules were shattered and austerity was imposed on southern Europe.

All over the world we saw stress within the system transferred from the banks to the state. But stress transferred is stress only partly dissipated. After the Lehman crisis its explosive power was absorbed by the US taxpayer, the state, future generations, other countries. Some of the damage – as we now know – was hidden. But the system cannot absorb another blow like Lehman, and meanwhile, new problems are building up.

We now face a period of stress between currencies, between rival trading blocks, between governments and their taxpayers, between social classes. The Doha trade round, ailing at the start of the crisis, is widely described in private by participants as dead; the much-trumpeted COP15 summit in Copenhagen produced nothing, either. All permanent solutions to the banking crisis imply some new global agreement on banking regulation; on the record of Doha and Copenhagen, it does not look promising.

Because political elites all over the world chose to transfer the stress out of the banking system and into the sphere of public spending and sovereign debt, we had a pause. During that pause, cappuccinos were ordered, notebook computers bought and the iPhone conquered the trendy world. Four billion dollars was spent on iTunes and one billion cell phone handsets were sold. It was a slump during which nobody had the will to impose the social costs on workers or consumers.

But Phase Three is payback time. Countries with huge budget deficits face two simple options: impose the cost on their own population, through tax rises and spending cuts, or impose them on somebody else, through currency devaluation and inflating away their debts. One route leads to class struggle, the other to intra-country friction. That is the phase we're entering as I write in June 2010.

We're also entering the world of retribution. In the first edition of *Meltdown* it was necessary to take at face value the accounts and justifications given by politicians. The dominant narrative was of economic crisis: a housing crisis that became a global liquidity crisis, taking down otherwise solvent banks because of the sheer complexity of the products that had grown up during the bubble. A giant accident.

But now another narrative strand has emerged – that of malfeasance. The Madoff scandal, which shocked and embarrassed America's elite investors, revealed that a $65 billion Ponzi scheme – the financial equivalent of pyramid selling – had been going on under the noses of the regulators. Then came the Valukas Report, which revealed the alleged balance sheet manipulation at the heart of Lehman's operation, known as Repo 105. It emerged that off-balance-sheet finance lay at the root of Lehman's demise: the company had possibly not been solvent at all during the crisis of 2008, but insolvent and hiding its liabilities. Then came the SEC's decision to charge Goldman Sachs with civil fraud, following the allegation that it had defrauded its own clients by selling them a package of subprime debt effectively designed by a hedge fund manager who wanted to bet they would lose money.[1]

In many cases those seeking a venue to push the boundaries of regulation came to London. Lehman had turned to British law firm Linklaters to certify its balance sheet practices:

Unable to find a United States law firm that would provide it
with an opinion letter permitting the true sale accounting
treatment under United States law, Lehman conducted its . . .
programme under the aegis of an opinion letter the Linklaters
law firm in London wrote . . . under English law.[2]

Meanwhile, Bernie Madoff's London operation was, the us
government alleged, crucial to his money laundering activities.
Fabrice Tourre, a London trader for Goldman Sachs, said the SEC
had been at the centre of the bank's alleged civil fraud, writing in
an e-mail:

> More and more leverage in the system. The whole building is
> about to collapse anytime now . . . Only potential survivor,
> the fabulous Fab[rice Tourre] . . . standing in the middle of all
> these complex, highly leveraged exotic trades he created
> without necessarily understanding all of the implications of
> those monstrosities!!!

When it comes to misbehaviour, we learned, states, too, are
capable of mis-stating their liabilities: the incoming social-
democratic government in Greece was forced to restate the
country's deficit from 6 per cent to 13 per cent. Under the
very eyes of the Brussels bean-counters, the former centre-right
government had been allowed, repeatedly, to cook the books.
Plus we learned that states are capable of welching on their debts.
The €3 billion imposed by Britain and the Netherlands as the
price for bailing out Iceland's banks was rejected by Iceland's
people in a referendum.

We also learned that − at any given stage in the crisis −
government response is a mixture of the known and the secret.
The RBS and HBOS episode of October 2008 (described in
Chapter 3) now has to be seen in light of the fact, revealed a
year later, that the British government had secretly lent the two
banks a combined £62 billion. At the time of their part-

nationalisation, the value of these banks was a fraction of that sum: they had been effectively nationalised twice over, even as the politicians protested that nationalisation was undesirable.[3]

Because this book is essentially a work of journalism rather than of theory, I have avoided the temptation to tinker with the text of the first edition. As a result the chronological account of the crisis now exists in two parts: chapters 1–3 cover events from the Lehman collapse to the nationalisation of the banks; Chapter 9 covers the period from March 2009 to the present. Chapters 4–6 outline the back plot: the rise of the investment banks; the scandal of subprime lending; and then the crazy year beginning in September 2007 when subprime lending collapsed and commodity inflation took off. Chapter 7, which contains a highly critical account of neo-liberalism, was seen by some as harsh at the time of publication. I believe it has been vindicated by everything since revealed about the behaviour of the power elite during the crisis. Chapter 8, which tried to situate the crisis within a long-wave theory of capitalism, was nothing more than a first stab at understanding these events.

The new material in this book is contained in chapters 9 and 10. Since on the day this book goes to the printers the British government has announced a budget demanding £113 billion of tax rises and spending cuts, I hope you will take this as just a second stab. The definitive history and theory of this crisis will have to be written when it's over. And it is not over.

London, 22 June 2010

1. Midtown Meltdown

The Collapse of Free-Market Capitalism

I T'S 5AM ON Monday 15 September 2008. I'm at Washington's Union Station, and have slept about four hours. Lehman Brothers is about to go bust. Its European arm, based in London, has already been put into administration. If the train is on time I will get to Wall Street in time to witness the markets open and a whole era of financial hypocrisy come to a close.

Twelve hours ago I was in Detroit, finding out how the credit crunch has impacted on the lives of car workers, out-of-work Starbucks baristas and dollar-store owners. By now I can sum it up in one word: catastrophically. But it's dawning on me that the real catastrophe begins today. The phrase 'credit crunch' has been around for more than a year but, it turns out, that was just the prologue.

In London it's already 10AM, and harassed traders at Lehman's Canary Wharf HQ, a thirty-two-storey skyscraper from whose top floor everybody else in the world looks powerless, are leaving the building clutching cardboard boxes filled with their possessions. 'What have you been told?' a TV reporter asks; 'To look for a new job,' replies one. Another holds up a self-help book called *What to Do When the Shit Hits the Fan*.

I stumble aboard the train. As it speeds through Maryland, I try to follow the news via guerrilla log-ons to wi-fi networks as we pass through stations: Baltimore, Philadelphia, Newark. The Susquehanna river flashes past, shimmering in the dawn. The herons, gliding low across the water, were here long before investment banks. What nobody on earth has yet realised is that, within seven days, there will still be herons but no more investment banks.

*   *   *

Lehman Brothers' New York HQ is not on Wall Street anymore: that is, not downtown in the financial district. After 9/11 the bank moved into a modest skyscraper on Seventh Avenue fronted by a massive, immodest LCD display screen. This plays, over and over, Valkyrie-cam point-of-view shots: swooping across a tossing ocean, passing a bridge at sunset, surfing a desert canyon. Welcome to the Martini-ad reality of investment banking.

Whenever I see this video on the front of the Lehman building I think of a rock star outliving the dream: an ageing guitar hero with lizard-leather shoes, stubble and a medallion. Now, as I scramble out of the taxi just before the markets open, I get a shock: the rock star has entered self-destruct mode and is surrounded by paparazzi ready for the Sid-and-Nancy style denouement.

At least thirty camera crews crowd the pavement. The swing doors of the building are patrolled by the kind of men who swarm out of the back rooms of a Las Vegas casino if a customer gets physical. A nose-to-tail line of satellite trucks forms a white tunnel through which Lehman's employees have to pass. Behind them, blocking Seventh Avenue, is a line of dark-window Lincoln 'executive cars', each with a heavily built driver leaning on the open door, chewing gum, whispering into his Bluetooth headset.

A woman at a window five floors up blows a forlorn kiss to a colleague in the deli on the corner of 50th Street. A few young guys from the trading floor pull stupid faces at the TV crews, their eyes bugging out with adrenaline. By now another group has formed on the opposite sidewalk: people from nearby banks and offices snapping photographs with their Nokias and iPhones. They have a look on their faces that reminds me of Richard Dreyfuss in *Close Encounters of the Third Kind* when the spaceship lands. Some Lehman employees, emerging now from Lehman's front door, have the same stunned look as the long-lost Navy pilots who come out of that spaceship: the world they're stumbling into has travelled decades in a single weekend. Everything they thought was certain has disintegrated.

Meanwhile a man has appeared in front of the Lehman building. He is tall, unkempt and bearded, and is carrying a red flag. 'Fuck Lehman Brothers', he shouts, 'Fuck capitalism. You're all doomed. We've been taken for a ride by Wall Street. Fuck Lehman, fuck Merrill Lynch, fuck AIG, man.'

The cameras swarm around him, greedily capturing – but, I notice later, not televising – this nemesis figure straight out of central casting. By midweek some bloggers will be calling this country the United Socialist States of America. But that's later. It's only just gone 9AM. Lehman is officially bankrupt. Now details have begun to emerge of what's been going on during the past forty-eight hours.

Lehman had been in trouble for more than a year, but only in August 2008 did its situation become critical. The bank, short of capital, had tried to persuade the state-owned Korean Development Bank to bail it out.

Looking back, this was a harbinger of the changing power balance in the world – from banks to states – but Wall Street, trapped by its own narcissism, missed the moment. Since New York investment banks are effectively controlled by their managers, not their shareholders, the Koreans were expected to behave as they do at London's Chelsea Football Club, where Samsung is a major sponsor: sit in the stands quietly, respect the local customs and fork out their cash.

Instead, the Koreans walked away. One Lehman insider told me that in August 2008 the Korean Development Bank had offered $27 per share to acquire the bank. But chief executive Dick Fuld, who had built Lehman into the fourth-largest bank on Wall Street, was determined to play hardball. When the Koreans pulled out, on 9 September, Lehman's share price fell by 45 per cent in a single day. Jeremy Isaacs – the bank's European boss, who had tried to engineer the Korean deal – quit. Then, as

Lehman put itself up publicly for sale or breakup, its shares collapsed again by a further 40 per cent. Lehman insiders told me there was a widespread view among the top managers that Fuld's brinkmanship was the product of 'incredible arrogance, a detachment from reality'.

At 6PM on Friday 12 September, the players gathered for the poker game that would ruin Wall Street, at the mock-Renaissance sandstone fortress that houses New York's Federal Reserve. The hosts were the politicians: Henry Paulson, the US Treasury Secretary, flanked by New York Fed chief Tim Geithner and Christopher Cox, the boss of the Securities and Exchange Commission. Around the table were thirty people who, until then, had run the global finance system.

First there were the chief executives of the 'pure' investment banks, otherwise known as broker-dealers.[1] John Thain of Merrill Lynch, the highest-paid boss in America, was present, as was John Mack of Morgan Stanley. A driven competitor, Mack's slogan on the way to the top had been: 'There's blood in the water, let's go kill someone.' Lloyd Blankfein, recently installed as the boss of Goldman Sachs, was also at the table. Missing was Dick Fuld himself: his firm was the prize they were all gambling for.

Did the players expect to wield political influence? Well, Thain had just handed John McCain a $28,000 donation;[2] Mack had sprayed $49,000 at George W. Bush's 2004 campaign, but had then swung behind Hillary Clinton, and was said to have been her nominee to replace Paulson;[3] Blankfein's money had mostly gone to the Democrats – $28,000 to senators preparing to fight the 4 November election, plus a specific donation of $2,300 to Chris Dodd, the senator in charge of overseeing the banking industry.[4]

Then there were the bosses of the big, diversified US commercial banks: Vikram Pandit of Citigroup, and Jamie Dimon of JP Morgan Chase. Dimon is one of the world's 100 most influential people, according to *Time* magazine: six months previously, he had helped Paulson with the rescue of Bear Stearns, the first investment bank to fail. In a conference call back then he'd ordered Pandit to 'stop jerking around': that's the way people talk to each other while they are carving up billion-dollar companies. Also present were the American plenipotentiaries of Credit Suisse and UBS, the two giant institutions at the heart of the impenetrable Swiss banking system. The only missing player among this group was Kenneth Lewis, the boss of a third major US banking group, Bank of America (BOA).

Around this table, in other words, were men of huge wealth, colossal power and acknowledged political influence. They functioned as a tightly knit network. They mostly knew each other, had worked in each other's firms, even poached each other earlier in their careers. Paulson, too, was a former boss at Goldman Sachs. These guys, in the parlance, had 'juice'.

To understand 'juice', you can take as a case study the example of Morgan Stanley boss John Mack. In 2005 he 'had a conversation' with the boss of a hedge fund called Pequot. All the quotes that follow are from a Congressional minority report.[5] Following the conversation, Pequot engaged in 'highly suspicious' trades in advance of a takeover: the allegation was insider trading. At the SEC a lawyer called Gary Aguirre tried to subpoena Mack to give evidence in the case. Aguirre's supervisor warned him that he would not be able to question Mack due to his 'very powerful political connections'. When Aguirre complained about this he was sacked. John Mack, Aguirre was told, would have direct access to the law enforcement officers of the SEC. He would, said the email, have 'juice'.

We will come back to the concept of juice: it's not corruption, it's influence based on a shared belief system. Suffice to say, as dusk fell on Friday 12 September, there was juice aplenty flowing around that table. The bankers had every reason to expect that the US government would underwrite a bailout of Lehman, probably by Bank of America, which had money to spare:

indeed, BOA's boss had stayed away out of decorum, in anticipation of the deal.

All week BOA had been lining up to buy Lehman, but now it was not so sure: the bad loans on Lehman's books meant that it was probably worth less than nothing. What the assembled chiefs of Wall Street wanted was government cash to sugar-coat the takeover. But they were in for a shock.

Tim Geithner kicked off the proceedings. 'There is no political will for a Federal bailout', he said. 'Come back in the morning and be prepared to do something.'[6] Everybody is exposed, Paulson reasoned: you should get together and take a stake in Lehman's bad debts, creating a new institution known as the 'bad bank', in which the company's toxic debts would be buried for decades, like nuclear waste hidden in a landfill site.

The next day the bankers reassembled, black limousines blocking the narrow streets around the Fed and disturbing the Saturday morning quiet. They broke into task groups. One group explored the 'bad bank' option, another explored a takeover of the remaining profitable parts of the business. As the day wore on, BOA became cooler about the bailout. The UK banking group Barclays sniffed the opportunity to buy part of Lehman briefly, but was warned off by its own regulator – on the instructions of the UK Treasury – and walked away. It was turning, one participant joked, into 'the world's biggest game of poker'.

Then, amid muttered conversations in the men's lavatory, and a frenzy of Blackberry messages from the smokers' huddle in the street, there was drama: a major player had stacked their cards. Merrill Lynch, which had been at the table as part of the collective salvage effort, had quietly contacted Bank of America: would BOA, instead of buying Lehman, be prepared to acquire Merrill itself? Within hours the deal was done. But now the giant insurance group AIG contacted Paulson to reveal that its finances were shot to pieces and it needed an immediate $40 billion loan to avoid going bust.

Amid the wreckage of takeaway lasagne cartons, Paulson broke the news: Lehman would go bust, Merrill would disappear inside Bank of America – and the bankers now had to go through the whole process one more time to stop AIG going bankrupt. The mood, those close to the talks briefed journalists, was 'sombre'.

Tuesday 16 September

The newspapers are calling yesterday 'Meltdown Monday'. In midtown Manhattan, where I am seated in a Times Square diner, the atmosphere is oppressively humid – and it's only 8.45AM. From the walls, cartoon caricatures of Einstein, Arnold Schwarzenegger and Bette Midler are glaring down at me. So is a waiter. Do I want cheesecake? I have just eaten corned beef hash and eggs – so, no, I do not need cheesecake, but probably high-dose statins. But what I need above all is information.

My editors want to know 'what's the story'. The problem is, nobody knows. The bankruptcy of Lehman has sent shares sliding all over the world, but Paulson and Geithner have done what they aimed to do. They have put an end to 'moral hazard'.

And what is moral hazard? Only by understanding moral hazard can you understand what is about to happen, how within a month the situation will degenerate rapidly, how America's free-market elite will be forced against its will to inaugurate a full-blown regime of state capitalism, and how moral hazard – having previously been deemed a bad thing – will be embedded into the global finance system for a generation. And to understand moral hazard, we have to perform a flashback, and tell the story of Jimmy Cayne.

Jimmy Cayne is a mean bridge player. So mean that when not selling scrap metal and photocopiers, he spends most of his time in bridge tournaments, playing for money. This is in 1969, the year fellow bridge enthusiast Alan 'Ace' Greenberg recruits him as a bond trader at a bank called Bear Stearns. At this point Bear Stearns is a classic 'white shoe' bank, making leisurely millions out of managing the money of rich people, so there is plenty of time for bridge. By 1993 Cayne, as is the way of the world in banking, has become both the chief executive of Bear Stearns and – more important – an American Grand Life Master at bridge.

Fast-forward to July 2007. Cayne, now aged seventy-two, was in Nashville at a bridge tournament, when he got a call saying $3 billion worth of Bear Stearns–affiliated hedge funds were in trouble. His response was to remain at the bridge tournament for ten days, with only sporadic access to email or a mobile phone.[7] The hedge funds collapsed, and this became the first big event of the credit crunch. Later the man in charge of the hedge funds was indicted for conspiracy, fraud and insider trading.

Bear Stearns itself lost $1.6 billion in the fiasco. By March 2008 the whole bank was going down the tubes, with its total exposure to bad debts calculated at $220 billion. By now Cayne had stepped down as CEO, but was still chairman of the board. During the crucial days, as investors began to pull their money out, Cayne was again at a bridge tournament, this time in Detroit.

On Sunday 16 March, Hank Paulson and Tim Geithner were forced to engineer the takeover of Bear Stearns by JP Morgan at $2 a share (one year before, the shares had been priced at $170). To facilitate this deal the US government had to underwrite $30 billion worth of bad debts run up under the stewardship of Jimmy Cayne, and manoeuvre with JP Morgan to avoid rules that stipulated the government should never bail out investment banks.

One week later, an outcry among shareholders forced JP Morgan to up its price to $10 a share. For Cayne, that meant the difference between his personal shareholding being left at $12 million or $60 million. Seizing the microphone at a shareholder meeting, Cayne shouted: 'That which doesn't kill you makes you stronger. And at this point we all look like Hercules. Life goes on.'[8] He cashed in his chips a few days later, to the disgust of fellow Bear executives.

After the Bear Stearns debacle, all across Manhattan there was talk of 'moral hazard'. Moral hazard, as the dictionaries put it, is the idea that some investors believe they are 'too big to fail' and take reckless risks accordingly. The Fed-inspired bailout of Bear Stearns saved the system from collapse, but left every executive on Wall Street with the distinct impression that, should their own card-playing distractions cause them inadvertently to destroy a major bank, there would always be Paulson and Geithner on the other end of a phone, ready to engineer a bailout. It was a textbook case of moral hazard, and it galled Paulson all summer. And it was to kill off this spectre of moral hazard that Paulson and Geithner had pulled the plug on Lehman. That was how it seemed on Monday night. But now, on Tuesday 16 September, moral hazard was set to make a spectacular comeback.

By midday, though there are still crowds and sat-trucks stationed outside Lehman, it's clear that the story is AIG. AIG has asked for $40 billion, but the wires are reporting that there is an $85 billion bailout in the offing from, once again, the generous Jamie Dimon of JP Morgan Chase. Given what happened with Jimmy Cayne and Bear Stearns, it is inevitably assumed that Dimon will be backed by money from the Federal Reserve.

But there's an anomaly here: why would Paulson and Geithner go to the trouble of sinking Lehman to make a point, but then revert to a state-backed private bailout in the case of AIG? Answer: AIG is not Lehman. Its turnover is $110 billion a year, and its assets total $1 trillion. It is the world's biggest insurer. AIG really is too big to fail.

But how did it get in so much trouble in the first place? AIG is an insurer; insurers are supposed to understand risk, parcel it up, buy it, sell it. If it is now at risk of crashing like an investment bank, what has the regulator been doing? Why is one of the world's supposedly safest companies on the brink of collapse? Time for another flashback (and another, different, guy called Greenberg).

The American International Group (AIG) once stood as a symbol of the deal capitalism made with the American people after 1945. During the post-war boom, the savings of the middle class were mobilised as investments in big business through the banking and insurance system – not, as now, through individual share portfolios. There was no Bloomberg Channel, no day trading, no spread betting: you put your savings into the bank and they grew. The insurance industry played a vital part in the system. While health insurance functioned as a kind of private welfare state, life insurance became a means of long-term saving. Without ever having to see or hear about an individual share price, the middle class could participate in the investment process and watch their money grow.

By excelling at this business AIG assumed a central place in America's financial system, and then the world's. In 1984, under the leadership of its boss Maurice 'Hank' Greenberg, AIG was floated on the stock exchange. Over the next twenty-one years the company's share price grew on average by 24 per cent a year.

What AIG traded on was its size, stability and safety. AIG's aircraft-leasing subsidiary ILFC, for example, was able to run a fleet of airliners worth $55 billion simply because it could borrow money more easily and insure the planes more cheaply than any airline. Eventually it became Boeing's biggest customer.

At the heart of AIG's business model was its credit rating. Everybody has a credit rating. Sitting on a computer somewhere in the world is a credit score on you: a record of your health, wealth, and trustworthiness, and of all your missed payments. Companies, too, have credit scores, drawn up by a small club of three elite institutions called credit rating agencies. AIG's entire success depended on its gold-plated, 'triple-A' credit rating. Once you've insured something with AIG, so the theory ran, it is as safe as AIG itself – and AIG is 100 per cent safe.

How could anything go wrong? Well, sometime during the early 1990s AIG grasped that, if you could make the formula work with a Boeing 737, you could make it work with complex financial products as well. You could take an apparently risky financial deal, insure it, and instantly turn it into a safe financial deal: the dealmakers pocketed high returns, so did AIG. By September 2000, at the height of the dotcom bubble, AIG was making about 15 per cent of its profits from insuring financial speculation, and its shares were trading at a spectacular thirty-seven times the value of its earnings (for a normal company, a factor of sixteen is considered good). As one industry insider observed: 'To justify its current valuation, AIG must compound its earnings at a breathtaking rate for a long period − a feat that becomes increasingly difficult with size.'[9]

To achieve this, AIG took on bigger and bigger risks. Instead of just insuring lives and jumbo jets, it began to insure a large chunk of the high-risk speculation described in Chapter 5 of this book. At the same time, it began to transgress the law.

In 2005 AIG admitted that $500 million worth of business with other companies 'resulted from transactions which appear to have been structured for the sole or primary purpose of accomplishing a desired accounting result'. That is, they had been faked to fool the auditors.[10] It transpired that another $3 billion of income had been 'misclassified' to boost the company's reported profits.

AIG did a deal with New York attorney general Eliot Spitzer, paying fines of $1.6 billion and forcing Hank Greenberg to retire with nothing but a Van Gogh from his office wall. Spitzer continued to pursue Greenberg, claiming: 'The former top management routinely and persistently resorted to deception and fraud in an apparent effort to improve the company's financial results.'[11]

Soon it became clear that AIG had bigger problems than billion-dollar fines. All through the housing boom, AIG subsidiaries had been lending to 'subprime' homeowners who were now falling into arrears. But it had done more: it had offered these risky homeowners insurance against default; and it had bought into the financial speculation surrounding the mortgage market, whereby risky debt had been bundled up and marketed as safe.[12] Finally, it had taken its customers' insurance premiums and invested them in the speculative bubble.

Early in 2008 AIG was forced by its auditors to reveal the scale of its losses. Analysts discovered that its exposure to bad debt had mushroomed in just two months from $350 million to $6 billion. A new round of management sackings followed. Greenberg, still fighting to regain control of AIG, was elated to find his nemesis Spitzer forced to resign after allegedly being caught by Federal agents in the act of wiring money to a high-class prostitution ring.[13]

Then, on the day Lehman Brothers went bust, AIG suffered the ultimate blow: its credit rating – already diluted after the accounting scandal – was slashed.

Suddenly all its risks looked riskier: and these were risks affecting the whole financial world. If I have a bad debt insured with a good insurer, I am OK and the insurer takes the hit. If I have a bad debt with an insurer whose own debts are suddenly reclassified as risky – we're all in trouble. This is the impetus behind AIG's urgent demand for a $40 billion government loan – a request still pending by the time I arrive outside the company's iconic Pine Street building at 1PM.

Somewhere high above is hazy sunlight. Down here there is only the sweat of security guards, the reek of gasoline dripping from the exhausts of armoured vans and the blinding beauty of AIG's art deco skyscraper. I cut loose from my cameraman and try to walk as far into the building as I can.

The skyscraper tells its own story. At street level it is plated with layer upon layer of aluminium deco friezes and shields. Inside the lobby the glow from Bakelite lampshades bounces off polished brass; angular Aztec maidens guard the silver-steel doors of the elevators. And that's only what I manage to see before the security guard throws me out. One thousand feet above, on the sixty-sixth floor, there is an open-air balcony built in the days before health and safety laws, from which executives can contemplate the world.

Greenberg bought this giant brick phallus to symbolise the massive economic and political power the company wielded. But that power is ebbing away. One money manager warns: 'Its collapse would be as close to an extinction-level event as the financial markets have seen since the Great Depression. AIG does business with virtually every financial institution in the world.'[14]

AIG has provided $447 billion of guarantees on the debts of other global companies that are now worthless. In London, one analyst discovers that $307 billion of this business is with Europe, and 'for the purpose of providing regulatory capital relief rather than risk mitigation'.[15] This means that European banks have been taking high risks but passing them off to their regulators as low risks, simply because they were insured by AIG.

Now, more reporters start to gather outside AIG, frantically quizzing startled secretaries and doormen about the whereabouts of half a trillion dollars. Inside, discussions are taking place with customers and politicians to avoid the 'extinction-level event'. I hang around for an hour, but the event does not take place. I am on deadline. I go back to the studio still convinced Paulson will persuade a consortium of US banks to bail it out. Greenberg has just been on CNBC, pleading: 'It's in our national interest to prevent this from happening. This is beyond a company and beyond its shareholders. It's in our national interest.'[16]

As I prepare to go live on *Newsnight*, I plug in my earpiece and stare into the camera lens. Echoing through the earpiece is the voice of a journalist from another network having an eerie, puzzled run-through with their editor: 'Con-serv-ator-ship? Do I have to say that? Isn't there a simpler term? OK. The troubled insurance company AIG is said tonight to be on the brink of con-serv-ator-ship . . .'

I rush back into the newsroom and see some people rushing around madly and others shouting 'what, what?'. The Bloomberg newswire has just reported that AIG is about to be 'taken into conservatorship' – a move akin to nationalisation. In a few seconds the value of AIG shares has halved. I go on air and report what the wires are saying, but by midnight it turns out to be more complicated.

In a stunning gambit the government has agreed to bail out AIG with an $85 billion loan. But in return it is taking an 80 per cent stake in the company: the management is sacked and the new one must now begin to unpick a skein of complex deals without crashing the world economy. AIG is now effectively in the hands of the US government, and all this happened during that fetid hour when I was skulking outside the building.

Monday was the day that detonated the crisis; Tuesday has been the first day of state capitalism. Few people at this point understand – but Hank Greenberg does: 'I just think it is disgusting,' he rages; 'this is not American.'[17]

On reflection it's clear that, for the whole of Tuesday, the greatest systemic risk since the 1930s hung over the financial sector. It was hard to report this, because nothing was happening; I started telling people to stop watching the financial channels: they were no longer a guide to reality. Only the sudden, sporadic and unpredictable action of the lawmakers was what mattered in these few days.

Meanwhile, in London, a new threat was becoming obvious: one of Britain's biggest banks was collapsing. The contagion was going global.

Wednesday 17 September

'HBOS has gone!' What do you mean HBOS has gone? 'It's gone. It's been taken over by Lloyds TSB. Gordon Brown's brokered the deal.' These are weird words to hear at 5AM, when you only went to sleep at 2AM. It is my news editor, in London, where by now there's a full-scale drama under way. During Monday and Tuesday a stock market slide has been gathering momentum, with all financial companies thought to be exposed to toxic debt getting hammered. That's normal, to be expected.

But nobody expected the venerable banking group Halifax Bank of Scotland (HBOS) to collapse: this is a bank whose Scottish subsidiary literally has a licence to print money – its own sterling banknotes – and the nationalist administration in the Scottish Parliament has HBOS earmarked as the post-independence central bank. Now the BBC has broken the story of a forced merger between HBOS and its rival Lloyds TSB. To make this possible, the British government has unilaterally suspended its competition rules: the merged bank will control one-third of the mortgage market.

Cries of hurt are coming from politicians that HBOS is victim of short selling – a financial tactic that takes advantage of a downward trend in a company's shares to make a profit. But the problem goes deeper. HBOS has fatally exposed itself to the same poison that brought down Lehman and AIG: for every £1 on deposit, it has lent out £1.78 – and the only source of that missing 78 pence was going to be the rest of the banking system. But now that system is freezing over, closing up, shutting down. Hours before its collapse, the ratings agency Standard & Poor's (S&P) had downgraded HBOS, adding that, despite its precarious loan book, 'the outlook is stable'.[18]

Now Lloyds TSB, with the backing of the British government, moves in for the kill. In a marathon overnight meeting, it will get the HBOS management to sell the company for £12 billion. This looks like a good deal, because one year previously the company was worth £36 billion. But a month later the total value of its shares will be just £4 billion, and Lloyds TSB will have collapsed in value and stand on the brink of part-nationalisation itself.

Meanwhile, back in the US, the market turmoil is gathering pace. The last two broker-dealers, Morgan Stanley and Goldman Sachs, are seeing billions of dollars' worth of business unsentimentally yanked away by worried investors. Ten per cent of the money on Morgan Stanley's books has been withdrawn since Monday, and the share price of both companies is sliding. John Mack fires an email to his workforce: 'What's happening out there? It's very clear to me. We're in the midst of a market controlled by fear and rumours, and short-sellers are driving our stock down.'

Mack and Blankfein make frantic calls to Paulson, and soon news filters out that a ban on short selling is being designed. Next, Mack calls the boss of Wachovia – a big high-street bank that is equally deep in trouble – and they discuss a merger. But the shares continue downwards. By the time the markets close, Goldman has lost 20 per cent and Morgan 30 per cent – and the Dow itself has lost 4 per cent.

But that's not the whole story. While the cameras have been trained on Wall Street, ordinary Americans have been pulling their money out of so-called money-market funds. These have grown up as a seemingly risk-free alternative to bank accounts, and with better interest rates: you put your money into a fund, it invests in low-risk securities – bonds issued by the government or blue-chip firms – and it tweaks the investments around to maintain the value of every dollar invested at precisely $1.

On Tuesday, facing losses from transactions with Lehman Brothers, Reserve Primary Fund, the oldest fund in the business, 'broke the buck': that is, the value of every dollar invested actually fell to 97 cents. Since the total number of dollars invested in this sector was over $2 trillion, savers are beginning to get very nervous.

By close of business on Wednesday, $173 billion has been pulled out of money-market funds: 7 per cent of the total invested. All the black humour of the past two days – 'at least there's been no run on the banks' – turns out to be misplaced. There is a run, only it's silent and invisible because people are moving money around through internet accounts.

This immediately freezes up access to short-term loans for ordinary companies. It's by issuing short-term IOUs known as commercial paper that firms such as airlines, supermarkets, and automobile manufacturers actually finance their day-to-day operations. By the end of Wednesday there is $52 billion worth less commercial paper available to companies than there was a week ago.[19]

Thursday 18 September

I'm in Washington: the action seems to have moved here, and so have I. It's Day Four of state capitalism, and policymakers of the world are staring into the abyss. They thought they'd established a pattern: let Lehman die, spend $85 billion to save AIG; meanwhile pump $180 billion of short-term loans into the banking system overnight. But it hasn't worked.

Market data is signalling a catastrophe, and it's got nothing to do with the Dow Jones. In just three days inter-bank lending – the deep, arterial life-source of modern capitalism – has dried up. The gap between what it costs a bank to borrow and what it costs the US government to borrow has suddenly shot up to an all-time high: it's called the 'TED spread' and now stands at 3.02 percentage points. Though this does not sound much, the gap is usually 0.3 points – so borrowing for banks now costs ten times more than normal. Because banks do not announce how much they are borrowing overnight, the TED spread is the most reliable indicator of the collapse in inter-bank lending. Over the next weeks this figure will become as mesmerising as the Dow Jones index was to crash-watchers in 1929.[20] Meanwhile, the cost of borrowing for non-financial firms has shot up from 2 per cent to 8 per cent.[21]

Money is rushing out of the world of speculation and out of the grasp of non-financial companies; it is instead being lent to governments at an almost zero interest rate. In fact, once you allow for inflation, the banks are now effectively paying the US government to keep hold of their money overnight. It's the opposite of capitalism, but right now it's a good idea.

All the first three days of frantic improvisation have done is to prevent the 'extinction-level' collapse of AIG; but now the financial equivalent of an Ice Age is spreading inexorably from Wall Street to London and beyond. It's all the more eerie because, while you can see stock markets gyrate live on television, you can only measure the onset of this freeze-up once a day, against the TED spread and other esoteric numbers. The graph of disaster will be plotted over weeks, not seconds.

At this point it goes political: Paulson and Federal Reserve Chairman Ben Bernanke realise that only the government can save the situation. At 8.30AM Paulson convenes a conference call with Geithner, Cox and Bernanke. Behind Paulson's desk are four plasma screens buzzing red with market data. Bernanke, a man who's made a whole academic career out of studying the Wall Street Crash, leans into his speaker phone: 'The normally mild-mannered economics professor said loudly and forcefully that the government must buy up troubled mortgage debt if there was any hope of bringing stability to the world financial system.'[22]

As the hazy Washington afternoon wears on, most people in this city are still operating on political clock time, in an alternative universe where the single most important person is Sarah Palin. I am eavesdropping on a couple of thirty-something women discussing senators and poll ratings at a sidewalk café table, when news comes over the café's radio that senators are discussing some form of comprehensive bailout.

One of my City contacts rings me from a London pub: the British government has just banned short-selling. 'They're mad!' he shouts. 'This is like admitting your entire financial system is on a par with Nigeria's! There'll be fucking chaos tomorrow. People are stunned. It's desperation.'

'What are they worried about?' I shout back.

'Corporates. Non-financial companies: if this credit freeze spills over into corporates then it's fucking curtains!' And he names certain British companies he believes could be bankrupted if they can't get access to short-term credit. Two months later, two stalwart companies on the list – Woolworths and MFI – will go into administration.

Meanwhile, on the rumour of a government bailout, the Dow Jones has soared, making back the full 4 per cent it lost on Wednesday.

At 7PM Paulson and Bernanke hastily convene with party leaders on Capitol Hill. The room is flooded with light from a golden sunset. They sit around a long, wooden conference table, across which Bernanke lays out the hard facts:

> Despite our actions over the past several months, investors are still losing confidence. There's a run on the money-market funds. The last two big investment banks are under siege. The situation is severe and the Fed is out of tools. If the problem isn't corrected, the United States could enter a deep multi-year recession akin to Sweden or Japan in the early 1990s. We are headed for the worst financial crisis in the nation's history. We're talking about a matter of days.[23]

There are no details of the bailout, but everybody is Googling around to find out how this has worked before – in the 1930s, when the Home Owners Loan Corporation (HOLC) bought about 40 per cent of America's bad mortgage debt; and in the 1980s, when a smaller bailout of failed mortgage lenders created the Resolution Trust Corporation (RTC).

I go live on the BBC World News America bulletin at 10PM, by now well informed about HOLC and RTC but with only the sketchiest of details about the Paulson plan. 'Will the taxpayer lose out?' the anchorwoman asks me. 'Not necessarily', I answer: I confidently explain that with HOLC and RTC the taxpayer made money by buying up the distressed loans at rock-bottom prices and selling them in the recovery. 'Paulson and Bernanke are in a strong position – they'll buy 'em cheap!' I predict.

This shows how wrong you can go by studying history. It will soon be clear that Paulson's strategy is not to buy up Wall Street's debts on the cheap: it is to buy them as expensively as he can get away with – and with no strings attached. Because to buy the debts cheap will penalise Wall Street, but Paulson does not want to do that; he wants to make the crisis go away by throwing as much money as possible at Wall Street. It is this essential problem that will paralyse the Fed, the Bush Administration and Congress in a week of fatal indecision, with terrible consequences not just for America's economy but its standing in the world.

Friday 19 September

I am stretched full-length across three seats in the near-deserted economy cabin of a British Airways jet that has landed at Heathrow. I wake up to quizzical looks from other passengers. I'm the only person in Economy Class wearing a suit, lying amid strewn pages from the *Wall Street Journal* and empty plastic whisky miniature bottles – maybe they think I'm a washed-up Wall Street trader? The pilot thanks us in a voice full of emotion, 'for flying with us in these worrying economic times'. The plane is about a quarter full.

I go straight from Heathrow onto *Newsnight* to talk about Paulson's plan. As my Blackberry chirps into life I discover more details about the bailout: it's big – $700 billion dollars. Billions more will be used to bail out the money-market funds and stem the panic.

Rushing into the studio I see the words 'After The Crash' back-projected in giant letters. 'That's a bit premature', I joke with the cameramen – but the markets disagree: the FTSE 100 has reversed all its losses on the week, closing 8.8 per cent higher than it opened – the biggest one-day rise in its history. The Dow has added another 3.5 per cent, also cancelling out the entire week's losses.

In just five days the wheel has turned full-circle: instead of spending, say, $30 billion to save Lehman Brothers, the Treasury and the Fed will now have to spend upwards of $700 billion to save the whole of Wall Street. The principle is the same: the toxic debts will be buried inside a 'bad bank', like toxic waste; the institutions will survive, though chastened. A 'voluntary self-regulation' agreement with the Wall Street banks, allowing them to amplify their risks, has been summarily withdrawn. Meanwhile the last two broker-dealers standing – Goldman and Morgan Stanley – are getting ready to change their status from investment banks into regulated commercial banks, so they can qualify for a Federal bailout.

Moral hazard is back on an unthinkable and explicit scale: every money-market saver and every bank will be rescued by the state. All that risk-taking, all that adrenaline and testosterone expended daily on the trading floors for more than two decades, turns out to have been a con. There was always a safety net. The giants of the financial system could gamble, lose everything, and yet walk away solvent.

The front pages of the UK's Saturday newspapers, humming out of the studio laser printer, betray euphoria: 'Share Boom Sensation' (*Express*); 'After The Crash – A Record Bounce' (*Guardian*); 'Sickening Slump Gives Way to Euphoria' (*The Times*); 'Global markets roar in approval' (*Financial Times*). The City editor of *The Times* writes: 'After several false dawns, the events of the past week should help to bring the nightmare of the credit crunch to an end.'[24]

Only the TED spread is sceptical: though it's fallen, it still stands at 2.3 per cent – more than seven times higher than normal. This Geiger counter of market fear is still quietly trembling – and it turns out to be a better measure of systemic risk than every newspaper and every stock market in the world.

2. Hyperdrive Blitzkrieg

Wall Street Hubris Kills the Bailout, Enrages America

THE WASHINGTON LOBBYING industry had kicked into action, armed with hyperbole and a lot of money. 'This is a hyperdrive-blitzkrieg, no-huddle situation', Scott Talbot told reporters, invoking American football tactics. Talbot was one of a dozen lobbyists from the Financial Services Round-table whose job it was to make sure that the conditions attached to the $700 billion bailout were minimal; in fact, if possible, zero. Funded by AIG, Bank of America and Merrill Lynch, among others, he had been blitzing lawmakers with suggestions 'to shape several aspects of the proposal': 'Among [our] chief goals is to prevent the legislation from limiting executive compensation at firms that participate in the bailout.'[1] The multimillion dollar bonuses of men who had destroyed major banks were not to be touched.

Hank Paulson too was engaged in a version of football's 'hurry-up offense'. The former All–Ivy League offensive lineman had drawn up a three-page plan, of which only two half-sentences mattered: that $700 billion figure – written out in full with eleven zeros – and the assurance that it would be spent 'on such terms and conditions as determined by the Secretary'.[2]

The Secretary himself now intended to get this through Congress in the way any good offensive lineman would: a half-second sprint at your opponent, crunch him in the face, then jog to the sidelines to breathe oxygen. But as he sat down in front of the Senate Banking Committee to present the Troubled Assets Relief Program (TARP), Paulson's face took the colour and shape of a bottle of sterilised milk.

On the podium were the venerable and aged senators who are supposed to police the US banking system. Some had hearing problems, above all problems hearing the twenty-first century; some even had problems turning up on time. One by one they read out eight-minute statements rubbishing Paulson's plan, barely pausing to glance at him over their bifocals.

Senator Chris Dodd, the committee chairman, had already drafted his own version of the plan, which ran to thirty-six pages of punitive conditions to be imposed on the banks. But as the gavel banged and the camera shutters clicked, Paulson's biggest problem was not the Democrats and their conditions; it was the Republicans and their principles. He knew the political party that he had served since the Nixon era was about to make him eat shit. In fact the entire Bush administration was about to be taught a lesson in the principles of financial conservatism.

The essence of the TARP was to take $700 billion of US taxpayers' money and buy the toxic debts of Wall Street banks, holding the bad loans 'to maturity', just like you store nuclear waste until its half-life is spent. Paulson, Bernanke and the SEC's boss, Christopher Cox, all made statements. Their main demand was that the bad debts be bought for more than they were actually worth. There was no intention to demand a government stake in the banks as quid pro quo. Bernanke was explicit: if the government paid 'fire-sale prices' for these debts it would bankrupt Wall Street. So he proposed to pay above-market prices. He would do it through a 'reverse auction' – though on the details of how it would work he was unforthcoming: it would, he said, be 'designed by experts'.

Republican senator Jim Bunning summed up the conservative objection in a Kentucky drawl: 'We cannot make the losses that our financial institutions are facing go away. Someone must take those losses . . . It's financial socialism, and it's un-American.'[3] Evan Bayh, a Democrat, summed up the liberal objection: 'If we're paying above-market prices, well, what do the taxpayers receive in return? If equity is the answer, that's one thing. If it's not equity, then, we have to ask, why not?'[4]

What was striking, as the hearing streamed live for nearly six hours, was this fixation with market forces. Each faction was trying to establish a market logic for actions that would, essentially, suppress market forces at the heart of global finance. The taking of losses, the equity-for-debt, the reverse auction – described like some kind of financial triple salchow, the coolest move on the ice rink – it was all the product of denial.

In fact it was evidence of a profound cognitive dissonance affecting the US political elites. They had accepted the fact of market breakdown but could not adjust their belief systems in this short time. This was the root cause of the policy paralysis that now kicked in, even as the financial tsunami gathered strength.

For the senators to accept the TARP, Bernanke and Paulson had to convince them that catastrophe was imminent and that only immediate action, with a sketchily improvised plan, could stop it. The problem was, they had been here before. In 2003 the Bush administration had gone to war with Iraq on the excuse that it was supplying weapons of mass destruction (WMD) to terrorists. It had gone to war with no plan for reconstruction – only untrammelled executive power and a belief in market forces. One congressman watching the hearing told reporters:

'This is eerily similar to the rush to war in Iraq. We have been told repeatedly by this administration that the economy is fundamentally sound, and then all of a sudden they say the economy is going to collapse.'[5]

The scepticism was not confined to Capitol Hill. Former British central banker Willem Buiter blogged that night: 'No administration that brought us WMD in Iraq and the torture camps of Guantanamo Bay and Abu Ghraib should expect anything but hysterical giggles in response to such a request.'[6]

In the committee room nobody was laughing. Asked what had caused the disaster, Paulson waved his arms about and railed against the regulatory system:

> After about several months on the job I was shocked, absolutely shocked to find that it wasn't deregulation or too much regulation, it was just a flawed regulatory structure. It was built for a different model, for a different financial system. The financial system changed, the regulatory system didn't change.[7]

Bernanke, sitting next to him, stared glumly at the desk. Just a year before, in a lengthy speech affirming the impossibility of financial crisis in America, he had stated that the system was brilliant: 'In the United States, a deep and liquid financial system has promoted growth by effectively allocating capital and has increased economic resilience by increasing our ability to share and diversify risks both domestically and globally.'[8]

'Does Wall Street owe the people of America an apology?' one senator demanded. Bernanke fidgeted: Wall Street is 'an abstraction' he replied, adding: 'I'm a college professor. I was criticized for taking this job without having worked on Wall Street.'[9]

Meanwhile the markets had begun to drum their fingers with annoyance: they'd expected the bailout, no questions asked. This was beginning to look bad. The Dow slid 1.5 per cent and the FTSE 2 per cent; both indexes were now back where they had closed on the day Lehman went bust. Overnight, the TED spread shot back above 3 per cent. And the Fed announced that the supply of credit to ordinary businesses had fallen by a further $61 billion in the week since AIG was rescued.[10]

The hyperdrive blitzkrieg hadn't worked. To get the TARP through Congress would involve accepting four key Democrat conditions: limits on executive pay; a cap on dividends; a slowdown on foreclosures; and the right of government to take stakes in the stricken banks. This would test to the limit how much cognitive dissonance the Republican Party – and its mass base in small-town America – could stand.

Karl Marx on Wall Street

Around 4PM on 25 September, protesters swarmed over the statue of George Washington on Wall Street, just where the crowds had thronged during the great panics of 1907 and 1929. This was the first financial crash to generate protesters instead of bystanders. The revolt had been building for days, if you knew where to look – in the email inboxes of lawmakers. Candice Miller, a conservative member of the House for Michigan, received many like this: 'I am a registered Republican. I will vote and campaign hard against you if we have to subsidize the very people that have sold out my country.'[11] California senator Barbara Boxer had already received 17,000 email messages opposed to the bailout, and 918 telephone calls, only one of which was in favour.

What catalysed the revolt was a call from a left-liberal NGO called TrueMajority (founded by the Ben Cohen of Ben & Jerry's fame) for demonstrations against the TARP. Around 250 protests took place nationwide, mainly at the end of the working day on 25 September. They were, even in a city the size of Chicago, tiny. But they were televised. Above all, the colourful demo by about 1,000 people on Wall Street got onto the national network news.

The demonstrators were spiky-haired leftists, and they were not in favour of imposing conditions on the $700 billion – they were against spending it full stop. They carried banners saying 'Greed is Evil'; one held up a picture of Karl Marx. They dumped their own junk on the steps of the New York Stock Exchange and stuck arbitrary price labels on it, to emphasise their point.

By the weekend America's talk radio and TV channels were being cluster-bombed with messages against the TARP. No party was coordinating the protests; none of the usual pressure groups took part. This was a spontaneous digital revolt, elbowing its way into the consciousness of the bank bosses, journalists and politicians who, up to now, had treated the crisis as their private property. By the weekend the letters pages of the regional newspapers were full of venom for the TARP and its authors:

> Is it just me, or is the Wall Street mess that we're being asked to fix just another WMD fiasco designed to pad a few people's pockets with sacrifices from the rest of us? (*Minneapolis Star-Tribune*, 28 September 2008)

> Do not bailout companies that have been raped by thieves or managed poorly so they can continue their poor business practices in the future, especially do not use taxpayers' dollars to bail them out. (*Cincinnati Inquirer*, 28 September 2008)

> The truck driver, the policeman, the salesman – all of us ordinary citizens – now will pay for a lot of the good times had by all those people . . . whose greed caused the problems. (*St Louis Post-Dispatch*, 28 September 2008)

In the vast majority of these letters the driving sentiment was conservative. Bush was accused of inaugurating socialism. But this hailstorm of opposition from the free-market plebeian right would have an unintended consequence: it would first delay the passage of the TARP, then ensure that it could only pass with all kinds of liberal-inspired conditions attached.

While protesters buzzed around Wall Street on the afternoon of 25 September, George W. Bush was holding the ring at an even rowdier event at the White House. He had called senior Republicans and Democrats together to try to get cross-party agreement on the TARP. The setting was the Roosevelt Room – the political symbolism softened by the fact that, since 2004, Bush had cleared the room of all graven images of FDR.

Here, for the first time together in the crisis, were Obama and McCain. Obama spelled out the Democrats' conditions for the bailout. When asked to respond, McCain seemed unable to make his mind up. He had responded to AIG with the slogan 'No More Bailouts'. His presidential campaign had promised to balance the Federal Budget – but the TARP would double the budget deficit overnight. Now McCain stood back, deferring to the Republicans' senate leader – who promptly rejected the TARP and spelled out an alternative plan. That was when the shouting started, prompting Bush to state, famously and accurately: 'If we don't loosen up some money into the system this sucker could go down!'[12] But it was already going down.

At that very moment, Washington Mutual's (WaMu) chief executive was in the air between New York and the bank's headquarters in Seattle. WaMu's shares, which had already fallen by more than 80 per cent in a year, fell by a further 25 per cent that day. Since the collapse of Lehman, savers had withdrawn $17 billion from WaMu bank accounts. By the time its CEO landed in Seattle, the bank's assets had been seized by the Federal government and sold immediately to JP Morgan Chase. WaMu had become the biggest American bank in history to go bust.

WaMu's bankruptcy was a sign that the real economy could not survive long without some form of system-wide bailout. Firms like Caterpillar, John Deere and General Electric were now scrambling to roll over short-term loans in a market where new lending was scarce.

The long weekend

By now the global finance system was limping towards the second weekend of the crisis, which most insiders knew would see the collapse of the weakest institutions. Bradford & Bingley (B&B), Britain's one true subprime-focused bank, saw its share price collapse to 20 pence; two years before it had been 536 pence. Ominously, three other massive UK banks reliant on the frozen money markets also saw their shares begin to slide: HBOS, its supposed rescuer Lloyds TSB, and the Royal Bank of Scotland (RBS).

Meanwhile shares in the giant Dutch–Belgian bank Fortis were under pressure: it had lost 21 per cent of its value on the Thursday and another 20 per cent by the end of Friday. Its chief executive assured the media there was 'not a single chance' the bank would go bankrupt. Then, as soon as the markets closed on Friday evening, he was sacked without explanation. In Germany, shares in a bank called Hypo Real Estate, one of the top thirty companies, slid 4.2 per cent. Hypo's problem was that it had acquired an Irish bank called Depfa, which was heavily reliant on short-term credit from the money markets. Now Depfa was in trouble, and so was Hypo.

The rising stress within the European banking system was driven by two problems: first, many of the biggest banks with operations in America were having to borrow dollars in a market where there were now very few available. Though banks like UBS and Deutsche had a large depositor base at home, that was of no use to their operations in the US. Second, some banks were directly exposed to the bad debts of AIG and Lehman Brothers.

Now European politicians began to hurl derision at the US. German finance minister Peer Steinbrueck slammed the US Congress for inaction, and predicted: 'The US will lose its status as the superpower of the global financial system, not abruptly but it will erode. The global financial system will become more multipolar.'[13] Meanwhile, French president Nicolas Sarkozy addressed a rally in Toulon. The man who had been derided as Monsieur Thatcher by the French left slammed the Anglo-Saxon model: 'The idea that markets were always right was mad . . . The present crisis must incite us to refound capitalism on the basis of ethics and work . . . Laissez-faire is finished. The all-powerful market that always knows best is finished.'[14]

On Friday night the crisis managers set to work. During that weekend Bradford & Bingley, Hypo Real Estate and Fortis all collapsed. B&B was nationalised, its operations swiftly sold to the Spanish bank Santander, and its £50 billion debts absorbed by the UK government. Hypo Real Estate was bailed out by the German government, which organised a consortium of private banks to provide a €35 billion loan. Fortis was given €11 billion by the governments of Belgium and the Netherlands, each of which took a 49 per cent stake.

Then, as these three bailouts dominated the morning news agenda across Europe, an Icelandic bank called Glitnir was nationalised. This fact, like Iceland itself, twinkled and sparkled on the edge of Europe's consciousness all day but then faded from view: all eyes were turned to Congress, which was about to vote on the Paulson plan.

The Bernanke doctrine

The impact of the Wall Street Crash of 1929 is engraved in the minds of economists as a series of stunning figures. It is worth recalling some of the most dramatic. In 1929 the number of Americans in work totalled 31 million; by 1932 there were just 24 million – one out of every four adults was on the dole. Gross Domestic Product (GDP) was $103 billion in 1929; by 1933 it had fallen to $56 billion – that is, in nominal terms it had halved.[15] The Dow Jones peaked at 352 points in October 1929; by 8 July 1932 it has collapsed to 42 points – it would not reach 352 points again until the autumn of 1954, almost a quarter-century later.[16]

But these are just the figures. The human cost was that tens of millions of people were scarred for life by the experience, both mentally and physically.

So, inevitably, once the 2008 crisis started, the shadow of 1929 loomed darkly across it. But the shadow didn't quite fit. This crash had not begun in the stock markets, but in the banks themselves; if there were elements similar to 1929 – like the house-price bubble and a recent interest-rate hike – then they were lost within a historical remix few people understood. One man, however, had made a career out of studying 1929: luckily he was the man in charge of the us financial system.

During a lifetime of academic study Ben Bernanke had come to a profound conclusion about the Great Depression. It was not, as capitalism's critics had propounded, the inevitable result of a stock market bubble that burst. It was simply the result of stupid policy decisions at the Federal Reserve. In fact, he had written: 'Without these policy blunders by the Federal Reserve, there is little reason to believe that the 1929 crash would have been followed by more than a moderate dip in us economic activity.'[17]

What were these blunders whose effects had proved so far-reaching? First, the Fed had focused on maintaining the value of the dollar instead of stabilising the us economy. To keep the dollar strong it raised interest rates, even as the effects of the crash were unfolding; raising interest rates is a sure-fire way of cooling down demand, but doing it when you're in the middle of a crash is never a great idea. Thus the Fed 'contributed to soaring unemployment and severe price deflation'.[18]

Second, it had failed to stop the collapse of the banking system, which began in earnest with the failure of the Bank of the United States in December 1930. Then, too, there had been a meeting of Wall Street grandees, who had decided to make an example of the failing bank and let it go. Bernanke's predecessor Andrew Mellon believed the crisis would weed out the weakest banks, allowing the strongest to survive.

Finally, as a result of tighter interest rates and failing banks, the Fed had allowed the money supply of America to dry up: it fell by one-third. For every $100 in circulation in 1929, there were, by 1933, only $66. In fact, Bernanke said, when you examined the Fed's actions, it had probably caused the Wall Street Crash by tightening up its lending to the banks too fast in the months before the collapse.

Bernanke did not originate this doctrine. The whole thesis had been laid out by conservative economists Milton Friedman and

Anna Schwartz in the 1960s. What Bernanke did was to improve our understanding of the financial system as the transmission mechanism for the pain caused by the contracting money supply. This is the debt-deflation theory, which asserts that there are (as Bernanke said in a prescient 2002 speech) 'connections between violent financial crises, which lead to 'fire sales' of assets and falling asset prices, with general declines in aggregate demand and the price level'.[19]

In plain English, Bernanke believed the primary transmitter of financial crisis into the real world economy in the early 1930s had been the 'fire sale' of stocks and shares. This had not only caused deflation, but created a feedback loop in which people's property declines in value, as do their wages, but not their debts. People consequently stop spending, businesses go under, and this feeds even more deflation. This is the debt-deflation theory.

J. K. Galbraith, the historian who fixed the 1929 crash in the modern consciousness, said theories such as this had originally sprung from a desire to 'give Wall Street an alibi'. Indeed, the debt-deflation theory's originator, Irving Fisher, is pilloried by Galbraith for confidently predicting, on the day the 1929 crash began, that 'stock prices have reached what looks like a permanently high plateau'.[20] But by 2008 Galbraith's work had been eclipsed by economists of the Bernanke school. Even though, in all other matters of policy, the monetarists who advised Thatcher and Pinochet in the late 1970s had been sidelined, George Bush had picked a Friedmanite fundamentalist to run the Fed. And Bernanke was determined not to repeat the mistakes of 1929.

In response to the first phase of the credit crunch, in 2007, Bernanke had slashed interest rates; then he had engineered the bailout of Bear Stearns, bending the rules to prevent a bank failure. And he was now determined to prevent a 'fire sale' of Wall Street debts. This was more than pragmatism: it was personal. Bernanke was engaged in a battle to defend his entire belief system. Six years before, on the occasion of Milton Friedman's ninetieth birthday, Bernanke had eulogised his teachers: 'Let me end my talk by abusing slightly my status as an official representative of the Federal Reserve System. I would like to say to Milton and Anna: Regarding the Great Depression. You're right, we did it. We're very sorry. But thanks to you, we won't do it again.'[21]

That is what was at stake as Congress prepared to vote on Paulson's plan: the entire belief system of the elite that rules America.

Neoliberalism is ripped apart

Public scepticism was spreading fast, but the US national newspapers and the TV networks couldn't see how strong or widespread it was. Nor could the global media. In London, on Monday 29 September, I had hit the ground running to report the Bradford & Bingley nationalisation – a story full of political overtones. What had the regulator been doing? Was this the end of the buy-to-let housing boom? As the US Senate had already passed the TARP legislation on the Sunday, we decided to report its final passage through the House of Representatives as an 'American politics' story. But American politics were to prove unpredictable.

Only the local American newspapers and talk-radio shows had a real handle on what was happening: the accidental synergy between right-wing populist opposition to the bailout and the left-liberal stance. One letter-writer to the *Los Angeles Times* summed up the anger: 'It is time for the free market to be free, and let the chips fall where they may. Taxpayers cannot be expected to bail out yet another bunch of white-collar crooks because their get-rich schemes finally hit the wall.'[22] Another correspondent to the *New Orleans Times-Picayune* proposed: 'The resolution for this problem is very simple . . . Arrest all senior level staff involved in this fiasco.'[23]

One emerging problem was the complexity of the deal. From Paulson's original three pages, and Dodd's thirty-six, the draft posted on the internet on Sunday 28 September now ran to 110 pages. Despite this, the one provision on which grassroots voters on both sides were fixated – giving the courts the right to prevent foreclosure against struggling homeowners – was missing.

As the day wore on in Washington, Congressional Representatives – all of whom were painfully aware of the upcoming elections on 4 November – were deluged with calls and emails. Walter Jones, a Republican from North Carolina, took forty calls personally before casting his vote against. 'You can't do this to the American people – it's unfair,' Jones said, adding, 'I'm at peace with my God'.[24]

In London, mid-evening, I was suddenly aware of many pairs of eyes staring transfixed across the *Newsnight* newsroom: dumbstruck, the programme's editor flapped her hand towards a TV screen. It was a wide shot of the House of Representatives with real-time voting results superimposed, like cricket scores. Voting had finished: the bailout plan had been defeated.

That day, the world's decision-makers had planned a coordinated assault on the crisis: a massive injection of short-term cash into the banking system by central banks – $800 billion, dwarfing every other liquidity shot; four bank bailouts in Europe; plus, in the US, a government-brokered shotgun wedding between Citigroup and the ailing retail bank Wachovia, with a $12 billion stake for the taxpayer. All this plus the $700 billion TARP. But the TARP had fallen. It was like a coordinated military assault in which the spearhead unit fails to turn up.

What had turned up instead, on the floor of Congress, was the voice of the American people. One-hundred and thirty-three Republicans – two thirds of the entire party – had voted against, plus ninety-five Democrats who could not stomach the half-hearted conditions placed on the bailout. Grassroots radicalism in America has been divided since the Civil War between a plebeian, white, religious conservatism, on the one hand, and an urban, multi-racial leftism on the other. On 29 September these two demographics – at odds with each other on almost every other issue — pressured their elected representatives to kill the bailout.

With hindsight it is clear that they killed the McCain–Palin presidential campaign as well. McCain's instinct had been to reject the bailout. But by the time of the TARP vote realpolitik had kicked in, and he reluctantly supported it. The Republicans never recovered from the hit their poll ratings took as a result: it has been put down to lack of clarity, or the economy 'not being McCain's issue'. But it was more fundamental: millions of American conservatives believed the bailout was morally wrong and could summon no enthusiasm for a candidate who, however reluctantly, backed it.

The defeat of the TARP sent the Dow crashing by 7 per cent, its biggest one-day fall in two decades, to close at 10,365. Asian stock markets slumped. The TED spread shot up to 3.5 per cent, pushing interest rates on inter-bank lending above ten times the normal rate.

This was the first big signal that 'policymakers' — that loosely defined but tightly knit network of politicians, central bankers and regulators who were supposed to be in charge of global capitalism — might lose control of the crisis. Bernanke and Paulson had, up to now, improvised with great vigour and creativity. They had learned from the mistakes of 1929 and met the situation with alacrity, hubris and large amounts of takeaway lasagne — and it was the hubris that brought them down.

Letting Lehman collapse without a plan to stabilise the banking system was a big mistake. Relying on a 'blitzkrieg offence' to force Congress into a condition-free bailout of Wall Street was a much bigger one. The something-for-nothing principle on which the original TARP was based looked outrageous to small-town, fiscally conservative America; the determination to pay above-market prices looked like a scam. The insistence on leaving Wall Street free to continue paying extravagant bonuses — and on leaving Paulson himself all-powerful in the execution of the bailout – convinced millions of people that the US government had lost the plot.

In short, the TARP debacle severely damaged the credibility of Paulson and Bernanke. They had learned from the technical mistakes of Andrew Mellon in 1929, but ignored the political lessons. Mellon's policy in 1929 was not, as Bernanke thought, a 'blunder': it was the logical consequence of the ideology he was trapped in, an ideology that had shaped the reflexes of the whole financial system. The Federal Reserve in 1929 acted according to ideological principles built up during the greatest asset bubble in history, and it was blinded by its attachment to those principles. Now Paulson and Bernanke were similarly blinded: trapped by the belief that the market mechanism, not the state, must contain the best solution to any crisis.

'The cure was worse than the disease', Friedman had taught his disciples in respect of the state-imposed cure for the Depression of the 1930s. Now, nothing short of full-blown state intervention would be needed to save the global banking system; and such was the speed of the crisis that it would take four weeks – not, as in the 1930s, four years – for a radical break with the past to happen. And it would be much more drastic.

3. Financial Krakatoa

From the Banking Explosion
to a Volcanic Winter of Recession

THE METAPHORS WERE evolving fast. By the end of September, what had looked like a meltdown on Wall Street had now become a global banking crisis that was spilling over into the non-financial world – and crisis-management strategies were getting overwhelmed. Bernanke had warned of a financial cardiac arrest; now the word 'tsunami' started to be used. But even this did not capture the scale of the event.

The human brain searches for metaphors not just in order to illustrate but to understand and explain: above all in economics, where critical events often mean you have to rewrite long-cherished theories. During those days of panic-stricken analysts' emails, of life-changing admissions of error by major figures, it became clear that the most apposite metaphor was not tsunami or cardiac failure; rather, this was a financial Krakatoa.[1]

On 27 August 1883 the volcano Krakatoa erupted with a blast 13,000 times more powerful than the atom bomb at Hiroshima. An 800°C cloud of gas and rock shot across the ocean, vaporising everybody within a 40km radius. Next came the tsunamis, five in total. These wiped out villagers along every facing coastline within 150km. Even at that cataclysmic stage, Krakatoa seemed like a regional, not a global event. But then the sulphur dioxide spewed into the atmosphere caused the temperature of the entire planet to drop by 1.2 degrees. The night sky turned red. Crops failed. Weather patterns did not return to normal for five years. Scientists now believe the event delayed the onset of global warming by several decades.[2]

In the Krakatoa metaphor, the collapse of Lehman Brothers is the explosion. The cloud of burning gas is the collapse of the global banking system. The tsunamis are wave after wave of stock market panic. Then comes the volcanic winter: the immediate chilling of the real-world economy, felt from the floors of Chinese export factories to the bars of British pubs. This accelerates and deepens the recession that had already begun in the second half of 2008.

Fortunately, a cooling sky has no direct ability to feed back and make volcanoes erupt again. It is not the same with a cooling economy: the 2009 recession has the ability to cause further bank collapses, country-level debt defaults, stock market crashes and intensified recession. This is the difference between the Krakatoa eruption and the collapse of Lehman Brothers: the latter took the world to the brink of a systemic collapse. And it is what forced policymakers in October 2008 to abandon the strategy of buying up toxic debts, and move instead to partly nationalise the banks.

The silent run goes global

If the world should ever again go through a crisis like that of October 2008, one of the surest ways to predict the countries at risk will be to follow the trail of rhetoric laid by their political leaders. Ireland had declared itself the 'Celtic Tiger'; Gordon Brown had hailed the result of deregulation as a 'golden age' of UK banking; and Iceland's prime minister, Geir Haarde, had spelled out the secret of his country's success:

> The interference of the public sector in the economy has been greatly reduced and the powers of private enterprise have been allowed to flourish. Government enterprises have been sold . . . most areas of economic activity have been liberalized . . . The list could go on and on. The result of these measures can clearly be seen in our flourishing economy.[3]

Now every country in Europe that had embraced marketisation, deregulation and securitised finance would get burned.

On Tuesday 30 September, the day after Iceland nationalised Glitnir, savers from all over Europe began to pull their money out of two internet banks set up by Glitnir's Icelandic rivals: Icesave and Kaupthing Edge. Hundreds of thousands of British savers had moved money into Iceland's banking system because it was offering high interest rates — and now they began to panic. Meanwhile, in Russia, the stock exchange, reeling from heavy losses in the wake of the failure of the TARP, closed for two hours that morning.

In Ireland, where shares in Allied Irish Bank collapsed by 45 per cent in a single day, a run on the banking system was in progress. Despite raising the insurance limit on the deposits of ordinary savers, the government had been unable to stop people pulling money out and then going on radio phone-in programmes to urge others to do likewise. By mid-morning on 30 September the Irish government was forced to step in and guarantee all deposits in six major banks to an unlimited amount. It had, in effect, promised to back up €400 billion of deposits with an economy whose annual output is worth €200 billion.

The rest of Europe reacted furiously. Ireland could only take such unilateral action because it was a member of the eurozone: any country with an independent currency that did this would see the value of its money collapse. Now Ireland's move would start a 'beggar thy neighbour' stampede that, for seven days, completely disrupted any attempt at a coordinated EU response to the crisis. This was because Ireland's guarantee had worked too well: instead of a run on Irish banks, there now began a silent run on British banks, with high-value investors rushing to move their money across the Irish Sea. Unpopular though it was, Ireland's immediate stabilisation was in marked contrast to the situation in the US, where banks and government alike were still flailing.

In the UK that morning there was an urgent private meeting between Gordon Brown and the governor of the Bank of

England, Mervyn King. The next day the *Daily Mail* scooped the
world with the story that Brown would launch an Irish-style
bailout valued at £2 trillion. This, as it turned out, was wrong:
Brown was in fact planning something even bigger. That
evening a government official let slip to me in a phone conversation that the British government was looking at ways of
involving 'public and private sector bodies' in the re-capitalisation of the UK banks.

'What kind of public sector bodies can invest in a bank?' I
asked, incredulously. 'That's nationalisation!' The official hurriedly backtracked, withdrawing the comment and promising to
deny saying it if I reported it. As I pursued Treasury officials over
the phone that night I could not stand the story up with a second
source: but the seniority of the first one convinced me it was true.

As I swapped notes with newspaper journalists on the case, it
became clear that Brown was preparing to take a decisive
government stake in the troubled banks – a move no government had yet publicly contemplated during the weeks of crisis.
But it was still a bank-by-bank solution – and as with the TARP,
the original design favoured the banks at the expense of the
taxpayer.

The move was bold but fraught with danger: at a summit
planned for the weekend it was now being touted that the EU
should launch a continent-wide bailout. But if the EU was able to
come up with a coherent re-capitalisation plan for its own banks,
then suddenly the UK would be trapped between two very strong
currencies (dollar and euro), and two competing financial centres
(New York and Frankfurt), each with massive resources to
bolster the banking system. The UK banks, and sterling, would
face a precarious future unless the government acted fast.

In fact these pressures were already unfolding in the system.
Foreign capital had poured out of the UK banking system in the
second quarter of 2008: it was no longer a case of 'banks won't
lend to banks', one hedge fund economist told me, but rather

that 'Asia and Saudi will not lend to the UK banks'. By now, for reasons explored in Chapter 4, Asia and the Middle East were the only store of spare capital; investors there could pick and choose where they put their money. Any economy that looked precarious would be passed over. Thus, despite the intentions of the politicians, the risk of competitive bailouts was high. The TED spread, which had hit 3.5 per cent on Monday, finished at 3.83 per cent on Friday – this, remember, represents an economic Geiger counter, now showing an astonishing twelve times the 'safe dose' of risk within the system.

On 3 October George Bush signed the TARP into law, now with many bells and whistles to satisfy Congress, including the right of the government to take a stake in any bank whose debts it bought. The US bank Wells Fargo made a surprise lunge to acquire Wachovia, which was in the process of being bailed out by Citigroup. The only upside to this, it seemed at the time, was that if the banks still had energy to fight like crows over a dead rat, there was evidently some life left in the system.

All that week, bank shares across Europe continued to slide. Dexia, a Belgian bank specialising in lending to governments, was heavily exposed to the collapse of Hypo and Depfa, and was bailed out by the French and Belgian governments to the tune of $6.4 billion. Increasingly, though, the problem was not the lack of government willingness to launch bailouts, it was lack of financial power. Some of the biggest troubled banks (UBS, Fortis and the Dutch group ING) were headquartered in Europe's smallest countries (Switzerland, Belgium and the Netherlands) which didn't have the financial resources to support their own banks in full.

So the mood brightened when Italy, Germany, France and the UK met in Paris on Saturday 4 October to promise a united, Europe-wide response to the crisis. But this united front lasted about as long as it took for the leaders to fly home from the meeting. On Sunday morning, 5 October, German chancellor Angela Merkel went on TV to stumble through the announcement that Germany would launch its own, unilateral savings guarantee, worth €568 billion. So much for unity.

The situation worsened as it became clear the bailouts of both Hypo and Fortis had failed. Having poured €4 billion into the Belgian holding company of Fortis, the Dutch government was alarmed to find that none of the money had in fact reached the Dutch subsidiary. So it seized the Dutch half of Fortis on the night of Friday 3 October. In response, the governments of Belgium and Luxembourg had to plead with the French bank BNP Paribas to take over their share of Fortis, which it did.

The whole Fortis affair had been messy: there was no pan-European system for dealing with the kind of cross-border banks the eurozone had created. Only a giant bank backed by a big country could rescue Fortis. And the problem was that, once BNP Paribas had done its bit, it was not in a position to repeat the gesture. In the back channels, European Central Bank chief Jean-Claude Trichet had been pressuring the Belgian government to take decisive action, but he was beyond his remit: the ECB has no role in regulating European banks.

Finally, the banks that had agreed to back the German government's bailout of Hypo also pulled the plug. They had discovered that the black hole in Hypo's finances was about four times bigger than they'd been told. The figure had been 'correct at the time' said Hypo, sheepishly.

A very British bailout

As the stock markets opened on Monday 6 October, so did the floodgates of panic. That day, all major European stock exchanges lost more than 8 per cent of their value. The Danish government, trapped like Britain on the outside of the eurozone, launched its own Irish-style deposit bailout.

British bank shares slid dramatically, HBOS and RBS each losing 20 per cent of their value. British chancellor Alistair Darling made an anodyne statement to parliament, declaring that the government was 'ready to take any action necessary'. This simply accelerated the rout. Investors now had numerous press reports and half-hints from ministers that some form of part-nationalisation was on the cards. And if the value of your shares is about to be diluted, why hold onto them?

By now the crisis had bored through to the core problem with the British banks. They were not in general heavily exposed to subprime lending, but their business models left them heavily exposed to short-term global borrowing. Now, the sources of that borrowing had all but dried up, and what finance the banks could get was costing them seven or eight times the normal price. Both the beleaguered Scottish banks were politically close to the Labour government. RBS chairman Tom McKillop was widely referred to as 'Gordon's favourite banker'; HBOS stood at the centre of the Scottish business establishment with which Labour politicians seemed congenitally joined. As HBOS's share price collapsed, Lloyds TSB, which was supposed to be organising a private-sector rescue, would now have to be rescued itself.

The next forty-eight hours were a blur, during which I found myself repeatedly standing on the pavement outside 10 Downing Street, shouting questions at the whey-faced mandarins of British finance. It is clear now that there was a total mismatch between the timescale the British government envisaged for the bailout and the timescale of the crisis. Likewise, the severity of the action needed was miscalculated.

A bank's capital works differently from that of other companies. It acts as a cushion against the risks it is taking. Banking regulations require the value of a bank's capital to be at least 4 per cent of the value of the risks on its books. This is called its 'Tier I' capital ratio. However, by October the banks were facing a double whammy: the value of their shares was falling, while the size of their risks was being re-calculated upwards. Re-capitalisation means either taking the risks off their books, or adding to their capital.

Advisers from the banking sector had secretly been at work for a week on a plan to inject, I had been told, a 'mixture of public and private capital'. But as the share prices of the three stricken banks collapsed that day, any chance of private capital flowing into them evaporated. Darling's failure to stem the market panic on Monday set the advisers working frantically overnight on a state bailout.

Tuesday 7 October dawned with the news that Iceland had nationalised Landsbanki, and was now appealing to Russia for a €4 billion loan to bail the entire country out. Spain pumped €50 billion and Russia €37 billion into their own versions of the TARP. But stock markets across Europe had continued to slide. In Britain, they would slide big time.

Reports that the banks had been to Downing Street to discuss the details of a bailout sent their shares into freefall. RBS lost 40 per cent of its value and HBOS close to that. I stood outside the London headquarters of RBS for a while that morning trying to take in the scale of it all: instead, all that happened were surreal encounters.

A man in a woolly hat selling the *Big Issue* came up to me and, with a nod at the RBS building, said: 'They have been pissed off inside there for days; nobody is giving any money and they are all in a terrible mood.' I took refuge in a Starbucks across the road, where a very chic-looking American woman was doing some City wheeler-dealing on her laptop. 'This is a classic Goldman Sachs play, huh?' she said enigmatically – referring perhaps to the uncanny ability of Hank Paulson's former bank to ride out the crisis – and then left. I opened up my own laptop and watched RBS shares flash red to the tune of 41 per cent on the day.

Then news broke that there would be an emergency meeting of the government, the banks, the regulator, and the Bank of England. This was it. I joined the press pack again in Downing Street to shout questions at those arriving. A government press officer came out and explained, nervously, that there was about to be an entirely coincidental social event for City of London grandees, and would we mind not photographing as they and their bejewelled consorts tottered up the street in evening dress.

Not very likely. The last hours of the old banking system were illustrated with footage of some of the biggest fish in finance gawping blankly from our TV screens, their wives' diamonds glittering in the camera flash.

At 7PM came a terse announcement. The government would take a stake in the UK's banking system. If there were no details forthcoming, that was because at this point none existed. Fuelled by takeaway curry, officials worked through the night, calling us to a press conference at 7.45AM on 8 October.

We trooped through the warren of shabby offices, iron doors and dim corridors beneath Downing Street, scribbling our names on Post-it notes stuck to our mobile phones, which we were ordered to leave behind. It felt like a wartime bunker: there was no tea and no biscuits, only an austere double lectern, which Brown and Darling approached looking dazed. They announced that £25 billion would be made available to take a government stake in up to seven major banks, with another £25 billion if needed. But this vast sum was itself dwarfed by a semi-permanent guarantee, totalling £400 billion, to underwrite the banks' long-, short- and medium-term loans.

The scale of it was stunning. I asked Brown if he would apologise for the chaos and panic caused by his failure to act until now; we all knew the UK banking system was within twenty-four hours of total collapse. Brown told me that I had 'not understood' the 'long-term and comprehensive' nature of the deal, and that when I did I would 'rephrase the question'. In coded language, he was trying to signal that this was a far more strategic deal than we imagined, and that the delay had been worth it to achieve something more coherent. I trooped over to the Treasury, where a technical briefing in progress was being chaired by Paul Myners, Brown's financial services minister. 'Just outline for me, as it's a technical briefing, the long-term aspects of the deal?' I asked. He replied that they had not been discussed.

The deal's vagueness was not just a product of the speed at which it had been done. As with the TARP, free-market ideology had kicked in to blur its effectiveness. By nightfall I was getting my ear bent by Barclays, who were insisting they would not take any money at all from the governments and that they were determined to do this using the stock markets, not government cash. Meanwhile the finance director at Lloyds TSB, which would clearly need to take the government cash, was briefing analysts that there would be no conditions attached that might limit future profits or force any extension of credit to small businesses.

As the FTSE bounced back, I began to realise that the UK government had pulled off not a coup but a gesture. The banks were getting £400 billion of guarantees, but had very little intention of letting the government take its £25 billion stake. I don't think that this was a misunderstanding, either. Even as they scrambled to save the system from collapse, Brown and Darling hoped that the markets would revive, the crisis abate, and that, come Christmas, when the re-capitalisation deal was to be finalised, there would be little or no need for it. The private sector would re-capitalise the giant HSBC and the mid-sized Barclays, the HBOS disaster would get buried within the Lloyds merger. Maybe only RBS would have to take a sizeable govern-ment handout, and then only temporarily.

Weeks later it became clear that the UK government would have to fork out the full amount − £37 billion − and end up owning 60 per cent of RBS and 40 per cent of the combined Lloyds/HBOS. And then, as we will see, the whole thing had to be reworked anyway.

In addition to the bailouts, Wednesday 8 October also saw the first coordinated interest rate cut by central banks across the world. It was an attempt to signal that they were acting in concert, but it left the concept of 'independent' central banking looking a bit sick. Ben Bernanke had suggested the move to his counterparts at the ECB and Bank of England. These banks jealously guarded their interest-rate decisions from interference by politicians − but now it was OK for Bernanke to interfere. Though hailed as a triumph of coordinated monetary policy, it was the first signal that states were beginning to seize back control of monetary policy from the central bankers.

(By the end of 2008 traditional central banking had run out of tools. On 16 December the US Federal Reserve took interest rates to zero, and signalled that it would begin buying up debt, from both companies and the US Treasury. This strategy, known as quantitative easing, amounts to the central bank fabricating new money in its own computer system and flooding it into the finance system. By early 2009 this last, desperate monetary tactic looked like it had begun to free up lending between those US banks still left standing. But, like the other technical measures described in this chapter, it cannot provide a permanent basis for recovery: Japan, which pioneered the measure in 2002, avoided collapse but remained stagnant. As we will see in Chapter 8, this combination of huge government debts and printing new money – though it alleviated the symptoms of crisis – has the potential to make the disease afflicting capitalism chronic for a lifetime.)

Despite the bailouts and the rate cuts, the financial volcano continued to erupt. The Icelandic government announced that it could not compensate 300,000 British savers who had signed up to Landsbanki's Icesave accounts. The British government launched legal action to recover the debts. Meanwhile, in Japan, a bank called Yamato Life went bust owing $3 billion. And all across the world the stock markets slid. Every single day the slide went on there was more money being wiped out on the markets than the value of all the bailouts put together. By Friday, the Dow Jones had lost 22 per cent of its value in a single week.

At this point the eminent NYU professor Nouriel Roubini went public with his warning of a 'system-wide global melt-down'. He had been right about the onset of the credit crunch, but few had listened. Now they did, as Roubini spelled out the scale of the crisis:

The US and advanced economies' financial system is now headed towards a near-term systemic financial meltdown as

day after day stock markets are in free fall, money markets
have shut down ... There is now the beginning of a
generalized run on the banking system of these economies;
a collapse of the shadow banking system.[4]

On 9 October the Icelandic government took control of a
third big bank, Kaupthing Singer and Friedlander (KSF). The
British government used anti-terror legislation to freeze its assets;
Finland and Switzerland also prevented Kaupthing branches
from repatriating funds. It was revealed that large parts of the
UK's local government system had deposits with KSF, as did a
number of minor celebrities. As I listened to the news breaking
on the radio of a London taxi, the micro-level impact of it came
home: 'Stone me!' the driver shouted, 'Kaupthing? That's the
bank that lends you the money to buy the effing cab!'

What had happened in that crucial week was more than just
panic and contagion. It was the realisation that the political elites
had no idea what to do; that they had fired their bullets to little
effect; that the prolonged shutdown of the inter-bank markets
now threatened a rapid acceleration of the recession; and that this
would spread even to countries whose financial systems were not
heavily exposed to subprime lending – even those that had
despised the Anglo-Saxon model.

Stock markets were falling not just on the tremulous words
and shattered ideologies of the finance ministers in Britain and
Iceland, but on the private intelligence of corporate analysts.
Banks would fail for certain; this was already factored in. It was
non-financial companies that were flashing red on the warning
screens and, in the case of Iceland, the spectre of country-level
bankruptcy now came onto the radar.

Above all there was a lack of conviction and coordination at
government level in nearly every country. However boldly and
creatively governments managed to act, it had always been done
late, and without conviction. It was as if the politicians and
central bankers could never quite believe the crisis was bad

enough to junk their old ideology. Even as they pioneered new forms of state intervention they clung to leisurely timetables, opt-outs, gentlemen's agreements.

The most pressing need was for coordination. Every Western politician is trained to remember how the flight to trade protectionism after 1929 pushed the world into the Depression. But even as they disavowed protectionism at the level of trade, their actions – the seizure of Icelandic banks, the rival deposit bailouts of that week – were themselves a form of financial protectionism.

Finally, with the TED spread at a seismic 4.64 per cent and a G7 meeting looming on the weekend of 11 October, governments were faced with a choice: the collapse of the global finance system or the abandonment of their old system of ideas. They chose the latter. Britain's model – part-nationalisation of the banks – would be adopted worldwide. And now, while the finance ministers met in Washington, the British crisis would have to be solved all over again, this time – as they say in *Apocalypse Now* – 'with extreme prejudice'.

The circuit-breaker

The G7 communiqué itself was full of tough adjectives, but said very little.[5] It was the actions that spoke loudest. On Monday 13 October, France created a €40 billion fund to take a government stake in its major banks, and announced a €320 billion credit guarantee, along the lines of the British deal. The Netherlands did likewise, with a €200 billion guarantee and a €20 billion capital fund. Germany allocated €500 billion to its stricken banks.

In the US, Paulson drew $250 billion of the money allocated under the TARP and offered it to nine major US banks, on condition that the government could exercise its right to take a stake in those that used the money. Meanwhile Australia, Japan, Norway, Russia and the UAE launched smaller bailouts on similar lines. The central banks of the US, Britain, the eurozone and Switzerland launched a coordinated scheme to offer rolling,

unlimited loans direct to the banks. The TED spread fell back –
only slightly. It would still end the week above 4 per cent.

In London, shocked banking chiefs were confronted, bank by
bank, and ordered to accept massive government stakes: 40 per
cent in the case of the combined Lloyds TSB and HBOS, 56 per
cent in the case of RBS. Then the bosses of HBOS and RBS were
sacked. One insider told reporters:

> The numbers were doled out as though to school children.
> The bankers argued back saying they couldn't conceive, even
> in these extraordinary times, of any scenario where the banks
> would need so much capital. But they were told: those are the
> numbers, end of story.[6]

A crucial difference between this version of the bailout and the
botched one, a few days earlier, was that the UK government
would take controlling shares, not the symbolic preference shares
it had favoured. This was real part-nationalisation.

Barclays, which insisted it could raise capital privately, was
given a swingeing target. In the end, having rejected British
government cash, the only source of capital turned out to be
the governments of other countries: in the process of raising
it, Barclays would wipe out much of the property of its
existing shareholders and hand one-third of the bank to Qatar
and Abu Dhabi. By the end of the week, Credit Suisse had
sold a large chunk of itself to the Middle East, while its
counterpart, UBS, had been part-nationalised by the Swiss
government; ING, the giant Netherlands bank, had also been
part-nationalised; the EU announced a €2.7 trillion continental bailout fund.

It was not pretty but, as a circuit-breaker, it worked. Part-
nationalisation, combined with multi-trillion-dollar state guarantees, had stemmed the banking crisis. The gas-cloud phase of the
eruption was over: now the tsunami of stock market losses was
building, and the volcanic winter of recession was drawing in.

It would take Hank Paulson another month to summon the will to implement a decisive part-nationalisation. In that time, Citigroup, whose shares had been worth $250 billion, saw them slump to $21 billion. The world's largest bank, which had written off $50 billion in bad debts, owned up to another $350 billion. It was effectively part-nationalised on 21 November, with the US government assuming most of the losses.

The cost

We will only know later, when the memoirs are written, just how close the world came to system-wide financial bankruptcy in 2008. It certainly stood on the brink twice: on Thursday 18 September, and on Friday 10 October. It is not impossible that it will do so again before the crisis is over. What we can begin to calculate is the cost: in terms of share-price collapse, amounts committed by national treasuries, and therefore hung around the necks of future generations of taxpayers as debt, plus the capital written off and thus destroyed.

It was credible – just – for Ireland to declare that its government stood behind €400 billion of savings. It was credible, likewise, for the US to incur a $10 trillion national debt to stop the panic. By contrast, the phrase 'The Icelandic government stands behind the banking system' was by this point a sick joke, and the world was about to find out how many other countries would be bankrupted by the meltdown. Pakistan was first in line, on Monday 17 October, requesting and receiving a $15 billion bailout from the International Monetary Fund. Iceland requested $6 billion from the IMF, in addition to £3 billion it was forced to borrow from Britain to repay the victims of Icesave. Within a week, Hungary had received $25 billion and Ukraine $16 billion, while Serbia was in negotiations, with Latvia soon to follow. The IMF allocated $200 billion for emerging market bailouts, about a quarter of which had been used up at the time of writing.

Then came the fiscal stimulus packages. Fiscal stimulus means a combination of higher government borrowing to fund a mixture of tax cuts and spending increases. The aim is to pump demand into the economy to make up for the collapse in spending by the private sector. In the run-up to the G20 Summit in Washington on 15 November, China declared a two-year stimulus worth $800 billion, or 15 per cent of its GDP. In the US, the incoming Obama administration secured agreement on a $1 trillion fiscal stimulus designed to create three to four million jobs; even before that the US government's annual budget deficit had been set to double in 2009, to $1.2 trillion. In Germany, after initially labelling fiscal stimulus 'crass Keynesianism', the government signed up to a €50 billion stimulus.

The IMF called for a global stimulus equivalent to 2 per cent of world GDP; if the sums announced are delivered, the world is already well on track to achieve that. This will have to be paid for by higher borrowing by already cash-strapped governments, massively raising the size of national debts around the world.

In the UK the fiscal stimulus, despite a huge political build-up, was weak. There would be a VAT cut, releasing about 1 per cent of GDP into the economy if effective. There would be short-term tax cuts for poorer people, but a swift turn to tax raising on the upper middle class. The reason? The UK Treasury had a massive hole in its finances: heavily dependent on the finance sector for taxation, the UK's tax revenues rapidly collapsed. Brown's administration would have to raise the national debt – kept symbolically below 40 per cent for a decade – to 60 per cent at least. Black humour in London's Canary Wharf financial district described the place as 'Iceland-on-Thames': Britain, like other big countries, would not default on its debts – but the cost of raising them would rise, rapidly. Within a month of the stimulus package, the cost of insuring loans to the UK government had risen to double the cost of insuring a loan to McDonald's.

The total value of national-level banking bailouts is hard to quantify. The estimate for the US is $8.5 trillion; the eurozone allocated €2.7 trillion. A conservative estimate for the world may be something between $12 trillion and $15 trillion – but of course much of this is in the form of credit guarantees, rather than actual capital. As for the debt write-offs in the banking system, at the time of writing the total value is just short of $1 trillion worldwide: about half the losses estimated to be lurking within the system by Nouriel Roubini. We can safely assume that $2 trillion will have been destroyed by the end of the process.

And with what result? The October bailouts functioned as a circuit-breaker, but they did not, as advertised, kick-start inter-bank lending again. That is why, as 2009 opened, governments were forced to move again. On Monday 19 January I found myself once more in the passageways of Downing Street for a 'comprehensive bailout' announcement. The banks would be forced to sign legally binding agreements to lend more; in return, their losses on bad debts would be capped by a government insurance scheme. Northern Rock, for months forced to wind down its lending, would now be turned into a proactive state-owned lender; RBS would hand over a further 10 per cent of its shares to the government; £50 billion would be lent direct to major companies by the central bank, circumventing the banks.

As I write, it is too early to know whether these last-ditch measures will revive the UK banking system. If they do not, the alternative is clear, as it was throughout the crisis: full-scale nationalisation.

What can be measured is the massive cost to the value of companies quoted on the world's stock markets. In October 2007, when the market was at a peak, the 54 stock exchanges monitored by the World Federation of Exchanges had a combined market capitalisation of $63 trillion.[7] By the end of November 2008 this had fallen to $31 trillion. In under a year, half the entire value of publicly tradable shares on earth had been wiped out. Of those losing more than 60 per cent of their value, some were tin pot indexes, some were not: Spain, South Korea, Greece, Ireland and Austria all lost well above 60 per cent. The timing of the losses is uniform throughout the world: a slide from late 2007 followed by a slump in October 2008.

Global GDP is estimated to be $64 trillion, so the total amount of wealth destroyed to date is somewhere between six months' and one year's worth of toil by the whole human race. Another way of measuring the scale of the loss is against the total financial assets in the world. These, as measured by McKinsey, totalled $196 trillion in 2007. If more than $50 trillion has been wiped out, then a quarter of the world's financial wealth has been destroyed.[8]

The effects on the non-financial world will only be properly measured once we know the scale of the global recession. The IMF, groping in the dark as its figures are revised downwards, estimated in January 2009 that global GDP growth would fall from an average of 5 per cent a year in the middle of the decade to 0.5 per cent in 2009. It is calculated that, because of demographic pressures, anything less than 3 per cent growth worldwide constitutes a global recession, and this is considerably worse than that. How this will pan out, who it will hit hardest, where it will interact with political and social tension, are the stuff of real-time journalism, not prediction.

It is safe to say that Asia has already been drawn into the crisis: China's inflation is falling so fast that it, too, could face deflation in 2009; speculative capital is flowing out of the Asian superpower, and its growth is faltering. Meanwhile the alarm signals on country bankruptcy are flashing at the eastern periphery of Europe and for much of Central Asia.

On top of the financial costs are the moral costs. On 12 November, Henry Paulson finally abandoned the TARP. The $700 billion already allocated would be augmented by a further $800 billion to take direct government stakes in the failing banks. The US government would begin to lend direct to troubled companies; and it would shoulder hundreds of billions of credit card debt, in addition to the mainly housing debts already swallowed. America, said Paulson, had 'humiliated itself as a nation'. Many Americans found this hard to understand: they did not feel humiliated. But, then again, they had not staked their reputations on the free-market philosophy that had created this mess. Paulson had; so had Bernanke; so had the financial elites of America, Britain and many smaller countries.

The moral destruction goes deeper than reputations. The bailouts have promoted moral hazard to the guiding principle of finance for a generation. Having bailed the banks out once, it will be logical for consumers and banks to assume in future that they will be bailed out again. So the moral claim by the finance system to the high returns it has enjoyed for decades is no longer valid: the high risks it seems to take are not really high at all; the safety net extended in October 2008 will be there forever. This was why the bankers resisted so long the state-imposed solutions, whether TARP-style or re-capitalisation. They knew that, even if they could be reversed within a couple of years, with capital from Asia and the Middle East, the bailouts should logically and morally permanently depress banking profits. In other words, the bankers knew for a fact what the politicians could not admit: that the whole neoliberal party was over.

That is the provisional audit of the greatest man-made economic catastrophe in human history. To understand why it happened we need to retrace the course of what, to use Auden's words, now looks like a 'low, dishonest decade'.[9]

4. White Shoes

*How Deregulation Made
the Investment Banks All-Powerful*

I F YOU WANT to trace the 2008 financial meltdown to a
single moment, it was this: a cold afternoon towards the end
of the twentieth century. It was 11 November 1999, the NASDAQ
was up 44 per cent on the year, on *Friends* Rachel and Ross had
just got a divorce, and in Washington a piece of Depression-era
legislative junk was about to be scrapped. The man leading the
celebrations was Republican senator Phil Gramm:

> We are here today to repeal Glass–Steagall because we have
> learned that government is not the answer. We have learned
> that freedom and competition are the answers. We have
> learned that we promote economic growth and we promote
> stability by having competition and freedom.[1]

At his side, Bill Clinton, already a lame-duck president, drawled his
assent: 'This legislation is truly historic. It is true the Glass–Steagall
law is no longer appropriate to the economy in which we live.'[2]

Clinton had just signed the Gramm–Leach–Bliley Act (GLBA)
into law. There had been a bitter horse-trading session behind
closed doors, but now there was a deal. 'With this bill,' Clinton's
Treasury Secretary Larry Summers promised, 'the American
financial system takes a major step forward toward the
twenty-first century.'[3] At the time the rhetoric seemed a little
over the top. After all, the new law only made official what the
banking industry had been doing for a decade: merging, mod-
ernising, becoming complex, bending and twisting to get around
outmoded rules.

Gramm's law was designed, first and foremost, to remove the law that separated investment banks from ordinary people's savings. This had been the main clause in the 1933 Glass–Steagall Act. Gramm also repealed a 1950s law that forbade banks to operate as insurance companies. During the post-war boom these prohibitions had been highly effective in structuring the US finance system so that it fuelled industry and commerce rather than speculation.

Up to the last minute, Clinton had threatened to veto Gramm's law over an issue that seemed entirely unrelated: a 1977 provision that required banks to lend in poor, black and Hispanic neighbourhoods. Gramm's original idea was to repeal this together with the rest of the old-style banking regulations, but to get the bill past Clinton, he relented. The GLBA had cost the banking sector $300 million in lobbying fees, so its passage led to a mini-slump in the Washington lobbying industry. Gramm himself had received more than $4.6 million in campaign donations from the finance industry in the previous decade.[4] But he was not done yet.

A year later, in the final days of the Clinton administration, Gramm introduced the 250-page Commodity Futures Modernisation Act (CFMA). There was no debate on the measure, and it was nodded through the Senate unanimously on the day before the Christmas break. The Act was designed to exempt futures and derivatives from existing laws that could have classified them as gambling: indeed, it declared all attempts to regulate the derivatives market illegal. For good measure, Gramm introduced a clause specifically exempting energy futures from financial regulation. This had been drafted by lawyers from a company called Enron. Gramm had received $97,000 in campaign donations from Enron, and his wife sat on its board. In other words, it was all done according to the official standards of probity in Bill Clinton's America.

In the space of twelve months, Gramm's legislation laid the basis for four crucial developments in US finance that would, within a decade, sink the system: deregulated investment banking, expanded subprime mortgage lending to the poor and ethnic minorities, a planet-sized derivatives market, and the fusion of banking and insurance. For good measure, it had unleashed Enron on an unwitting world. But all this had been building up for twenty years. To understand why, you need to understand where investment banks fit into the capitalist system. This is harder than you think, because while their brand names are ancient they have shape-shifted rapidly in the past ten years.

Behind the nameplates

If you take out your mobile phone and look at the logo there is a 40 per cent chance it will be a Nokia.[5] Nokia started life in 1865 as a paper mill; in 1898 it became a rubber company; in 1967 it merged with a cable company; and in 1981 it built a telephone network. This makes Nokia's history about as long and complicated as that of most Wall Street banks. The difference between Nokia and Wall Street is that with Nokia it's easy to see the radical changes in the company's form and function over the centuries. With investment banks it's harder. On the surface they look like they have been doing the same basic thing for 150 years, but this is illusory.

Investment banks first moved to centre stage after the 1870s, as the business world rapidly abandoned two principles that had seemed fundamental to capitalism: free competition and private ownership. The classic company of the mid nineteenth century was medium-sized, privately owned by a single family, and it competed in a relatively free market with lots of similar firms. But in 1873 capitalism hit the first of its two long depressions: small firms were going under, and new technical innovations could not be deployed for the lack of large-scale investment.

The solution was the expansion of the joint-stock company – a company that could raise new capital by issuing shares to the public (often referred to as a public company). As well as being bought when they were first issued, the shares could be sold, traded and generally speculated upon. The result of the switch to joint-stock companies was to create massive firms, often through the amalgamation of smaller ones. In turn, this reduced the number of players in the big, new technologies of steel, railways and electrical engineering. Markets became a lot less free: in many sectors competition was actively stifled by cartels and syndicates. This new system has been called monopoly capitalism or finance capitalism, and by the 1880s it was becoming a reality across the globe.

The banks assumed a dominant position within this new capitalist ecosystem – though this took different forms in different countries. In Europe banks would hold large amounts of industrial shares and control the boards of non-financial companies: six German banks had directors on the boards of 740 companies.[6] In Japan the first wave of industrialisation was driven by state-owned firms, which were then handed over to family-owned industrial empires known as *zaibatsu*, usually with a powerful bank near the apex of power.[7] But in America it was an arm's-length process: John Pierpont Morgan financed the creation of US Steel and General Electric; Philip Lehman floated household names like Macy's, Woolworths and Sears on the stock market, in partnership with Mr Goldman and his son-in-law Mr Sachs. This has been called the Anglo-Saxon model of capitalism: banks and industry formally separate, joint-stock companies as the norm, stock-market values driving management to innovate and compete, and the whole system functioning transparently compared to the closed-door relationships of Europe and Asia.

The beauty of US investment banking in the run-up to the First World War was that its power derived from several perfectly ordinary and benign activities: issuing shares for companies that wanted to raise new capital; organising mergers and acquisitions; raising loans in the form of bonds, both for companies and governments; managing the money of rich people and companies, generally by investing it in the stock market or in bonds. But the sum total of these activities gave Wall Street incredible power over individual corporations. Lehman, Goldman, Morgan and their ilk looked like intermediaries, but their power within corporate America was just as great as that of German or Japanese finance in the rival systems. Indeed, Morgan stepped in to coordinate the bailout of the finance system during a stock market panic in 1907, proving himself massively more powerful than the government.

In the history of finance capital the First World War looks like just a blip – but it was an important one. It re-ordered economic power in the world, confirming America's status as the most dynamic economy. By the mid 1920s the US investment banks were at the centre of a huge speculative bubble in stocks and shares. It was fuelled in part by reality: output and profits were rising. It was also fuelled by America's new global position. The Federal Reserve cut interest rates at the request of Britain, Germany and France to ease the pressure on their currencies, the result being a lot of cheap money for American investors. But above all, as J. K. Galbraith wrote, it was fuelled by the 'inordinate desire to get rich quickly with a minimum of physical effort'.[8]

Every speculative bubble produces a unique new investment product, which mesmerises investors with its seeming power to generate money from out of nowhere. In the late 1920s it was the investment trust that played this role (in the seventeenth century it had been tulip bulbs). Investment trusts were companies whose only function was to own the shares of other companies. The money invested in them grew from $400 million to $3 billion in eighteen months, yet the end result was simply to dilute the value of all the shares in the system.

Likewise, every speculative bubble generates demand not just for more stocks but for 'leverage': the ability to buy $100 worth of shares with just $50 of cash, borrowing the rest. This is called 'trading on margin', and you need a stockbroker to do it. The

investment banks put themselves at the centre of this frenzy of
stockbroking, investment trusts and leverage. But they were not
big enough to cope with the demand. Ordinary deposit-taking
banks piled into the speculation as well, buying up whole
tranches of new shares, setting up new trusts, organising
share-dealing accounts for small investors, and lending them
money to trade with.

The rest, as they say, is history. The stock market crashed in
October 1929. Over the next three years 40 per cent of all
American banks went bust. People lost their savings, their homes
and farms; they stopped spending and the economy tipped into a
decade-long Depression. Coming to power in 1933, Franklin
Delano Roosevelt declared:

> The money changers have fled from their high seats in the
> temple of our civilization. We may now restore that temple to
> the ancient truths . . . There must be a strict supervision of all
> banking and credits and investments; there must be an end to
> speculation with other people's money.[9]

Congressmen Glass and Steagall wrote the law that put
investment banking back in its box: the Glass–Steagall Act of
1933 made it illegal for a bank that holds people's savings to
engage in speculative activity; it also introduced the first federal
scheme to insure bank deposits: the Federal Deposit Insurance
Scheme. As a result, the investment banks' access to capital was
reduced. Meanwhile, laws preventing the consolidation of banks
across different states ensured that the banks that did have access
to ordinary people's savings could not become huge. When the
post-1945 boom took off, the investment banks went back to
being rich people's banks and intermediaries. In the 1950s they
became known as 'white-shoe banks' after the white buckskin
loafers favoured by the Ivy League graduates recruited to work in
them. As this was the decade when most clever people wanted to
work for General Electric, Rand and IBM, you can take it that the

term 'white-shoe' was pejorative. Meanwhile the commercial banks went back to their core function: taking the savings of ordinary people and turning them into loans to finance business investment.

Only with the victory of neoliberal politicians – above all Ronald Reagan and Margaret Thatcher – did the opportunity arise to rip up these arrangements. Commercial banks would merge and consolidate, while investment banks would claw their way back to the top of the hierarchy. But because capitalism was now going global, instead of just being on top in America they would be on top of the world.

In 1987 the Federal Reserve changed the Glass–Steagall rules, allowing commercial banks to undertake financial wheeler-dealing to the tune of 5 per cent of their turnover. The Fed's then-boss, Alan Greenspan, progressively increased this exemption until in 1996 it reached 25 per cent, rendering the statute meaningless. At the same time, laws preventing the merger of banks in different states were repealed, as was the insurance/banking split. The banks then restructured themselves to get around the remainder of the existing rules.

Meanwhile as free-market capitalism took off in Europe and Asia, American banks stormed into the financial centres – Tokyo, Hong Kong, Frankfurt, and above all London – taking over Ye Olde pinstriped family-banking houses and gearing them up for a new round in the great game of speculative finance. Even the old Swiss giants got pulled into the US network: both Credit Suisse and UBS acquired large-scale investment banking operations in New York. Likewise Frankfurt-based Deutsche Bank, which scooped up ailing investment banks in London and New York before listing itself on the New York Stock Exchange in 2001.

This process has been summed up in the memorable title of Philip Augar's book, *The Death of Gentlemanly Capitalism*. Many of the old names got merged out of existence. But Wall Street never bought the craze for re-branding with new, vapid, brand names: they stuck with the grand old names – Lehman, Morgan, Merrill, Goldman, Bear Stearns – because they sounded traditional and reliable.

Merger mania pushed the Glass–Steagall Act to its very limits, most notably the $85 billion merger of Travelers (a giant insurance company which owned Salomon Brothers, an investment bank) with Citicorp in 1998. This created Citigroup, the biggest financial conglomerate in the world. Its boss, Sandy Weill, had to persuade Bill Clinton's then Treasury secretary, Robert Rubin, to waive the rules until Glass–Steagall could be repealed. Rubin was persuaded. Then, in October 1999, Rubin became co–chief executive of Citigroup. As the *New York Times* reported, in its inimitable deadpan style: 'Mr. Rubin acknowledged that even while negotiating his own job with Citigroup, he had helped broker the compromise agreement repealing Glass–Steagall.'[10]

Hot money conquers the world

Deregulation was only one factor in the creation of modern investment banking: the second, equally important, was information technology. At the start of the free-market era the foreign subsidiaries of US banks essentially operated independently. By the 1990s they had constructed huge, proprietary computer systems which allowed each bank to act as a global information network; meanwhile, the exchanges they operated on were going digital. The flow of money around the system was now quicker – some of it real, some of it unreal. The overall effect of new technology in banking was to increase the so-called information asymmetry at the heart of investment banking: firms which had always known more than the average steel mill owner or politician now had vastly greater knowledge than anybody else except rival investment banks.

As banks and exchanges became computerised, they also tended to move away from face-to-face relationships. Deci-

sion-making was automated according to 'models', and design-
ing and refining the model was seen as crucial to maintaining
your competitive edge against rivals. As the models improved, so
regulators came to accept that the amount of risk on a bank's
balance sheet could be calculated not according to some crude
total of loans but by the more abstract concept of 'value at risk'
(vaR). Though this concept is now treated like a biblical golden
calf within banking, it did not exist until the late 1980s. Its critics
believe it is worse than useless: if you include financial crisis in the
risk model it induces self-defeating timidity, so the 'once in a
lifetime' crisis is not included in the maths. But if you do not
include such crises in the maths it induces suicidal risk-taking.
One senior banking figure told me, in the aftermath of September 2008: 'Those that automated the most lost the most.'

A third factor that increased the power of the investment
banks was the massive wave of privatisations unleashed across the
Western world in the 1980s, and in the former communist
countries in the 1990s. Each privatisation was supervised by a
team of investment banks; it then added massively to the
amount of capital held in the form of shares, rather than by
the state. From near zero in 1981, the privatisation market
topped $160 billion a year in the late 1990s. Globally, by the
end of the decade 675 privatisations had generated $700 billion;
the eighteen biggest initial public offerings in history had all
been state-owned companies privatised through flotation.[11] The
process transformed most stock markets outside the us: they
became more liquid (with more shares in play, there could be
more buying and selling) and much bigger. And investment
bankers got rich. When Friends Reunited became a craze in the
early 2000s, I was surprised to discover that, out of all the film
directors, cops, journalists and priests that my Catholic grammar
school had produced, there was one guy who was different. He
had already retired, aged forty, to the south of France. 'I
privatised most of Europe's telecoms industry for Merrill Lynch',
he told us.

A fourth factor fuelling the banks was the rise of foreign-exchange markets. As countries abolished exchange controls and computer technology took off, so did the scale of foreign-exchange dealing: from around $70 billion a day in the early 1980s, to $500 billion a day in 1988, to $3.2 trillion a day in 2007. At least half of this daily business involves derivatives: the foreign exchange is not bought for the purposes of spending the currency in the country where it is legal tender, but for reselling it, swapping it, or taking a bet on its future price.[12] This is not all speculation. There is a perfectly functional reason for this massive volume of money changing hands in a highly globalised world. But much of it is speculation – and here, again, the investment banks are at the heart of it.

Finally, the same combination of deregulation and new technology made possible the emergence of the wider global derivatives market. Derivatives are forms of investment that have been around a long time: the most basic form is a future, where you agree to buy something – say, a barrel of oil – in the future at a price fixed now, usually with the intention of selling it again at an advantageous price. An option is the same thing, only you are agreeing the option to buy rather than buying the thing itself; a swap is where you agree to swap a commodity, share, bond, contract or currency at a set price for a set time, again with the expectation that you will make money. Some derivatives are traded on exchanges, such as NYMEX, where you can buy oil several months into the future; most are traded 'over the counter' – that is, point-to-point between buyer and seller.

The rate of growth in derivatives trading has been astonishing people since the mid 1990s, so it's easy to become blasé about it. But the real wow factor is to be found in what happened in the two years prior to 2008. The global derivatives market stood at $370 trillion in June 2006; by December 2007 it had reached $596 trillion. Foreign-exchange futures almost doubled in this period. Meanwhile, a little-known investment device called 'credit default swaps' had spiralled from under a trillion in

2000 to $58 trillion in 2007.[13] There was a massive rush of money into derivatives and currency trading in the run-up to the crash: for future reference, it will be safe to treat any similar event as a warning of catastrophe.

To put the derivatives and currency markets into context, in 2007 the gross domestic product of the world was around $65 trillion; the total value of the companies quoted on the world's stock markets, which peaked that year, was $63 trillion. But the total value of derivative investments stood at $596 trillion – eight times the size of the real economy. The total amount of currency traded stood at $1,168 trillion, or seventeen times world GDP.[14]

Two things are striking. First, the value of the financial economy is much bigger than the value of the real world on which it is based – and this is something that has happened only in the last twenty years. Secondly, the two main theories regarding derivatives during this time were alarmingly divergent. Alan Greenspan, the former Federal Reserve boss, believes derivatives make the finance system safer; we will explore the logic behind this in Chapter 7. Meanwhile Warren Buffet, the world's most successful investor, told his shareholders in 2002 that derivatives were a 'time bomb':

> These instruments will almost certainly multiply in variety and number until some event makes their toxicity clear. Central banks and governments have so far found no effective way to control, or even monitor, the risks posed by these contracts. In my view derivatives are financial weapons of mass destruction, carrying dangers that, while now latent, are potentially lethal.[15]

It is now clear that, since the 1990s, this new global finance system has injected gross instability into the world economy. But before we can properly get our heads around the changed nature of investment banks, there is one more outcome of the free-market revolution to understand, and it is geographic.

The global imbalances

During the 1990s, globalisation unleashed market forces into Asia with unforeseen consequences. From Mumbai to Shenzhen to Seoul, the rapidly developing industrial cities of Asia became the workshops of the world. As a result of this, Asia as a whole experienced a rising income level; China in addition pursued a conscious and sustained policy of urbanisation and an attack on absolute poverty.

Asia achieved its spectacular growth by doing the opposite of what the Anglo-Saxon model prescribes. The so-called Asian Tigers used state intervention, trade protectionism and exchange-rate manipulation to rapidly develop their economies, reduce poverty, and educate their populations. China's path was different, being marked by the mass destruction of state-owned heavy industry and the welfare state, but no less spectacular. Both China and the Asian Tigers adopted fixed exchange rates: the central bank would intervene to keep the Thai baht, the Korean won and the Chinese renminbi (RMB) pegged to the dollar come what may.

In 1997 the Asian Tigers were hit by the first big financial crisis of the globalised economy. Their pegged currencies were attacked by speculators and had to be devalued, as a result of which their stock markets suffered massive wipe-outs, many people lost part of their savings, and entire economies were plunged into recession.

Before 1997 the Asian economies were simply on a different development path to that of the West. After the crisis their governments, companies and savers would adopt behaviour that created a structural imbalance at the heart of global capitalism – so much so that, while we talk blithely about 'globalisation' as if it were a process of harmonisation, it has been in fact a process based on structural disharmony in four key areas: saving, investment, trade and government debt. On each of these measures Asia as a whole, and China in particular, stands as a mirror-image of Western capitalism. These global imbalances are products of each other, and they are worth considering one by one.

The most obvious imbalance is in trade: Asia produces, the West consumes. The balance of trade is measured by so-called current-account deficits – the difference in value between a country's imports and exports. From 1980 onwards the US ran a current-account deficit of about $100 billion, until 1997, when the curve took a sharp downward direction, reaching $856 billion by the end of 2006.

The next imbalance relates to saving. Here the pattern between East and West is strikingly different. Instead of simply spending their rising wages on TVs, cars and houses, and then rapidly borrowing more in the form of credit cards and mortgages, the population of Asia has saved its money. Meanwhile, the amount saved by the population of the US fell from about 10 per cent of income during the 1970s to zero in 2005.[16] Over the same period, China's savings rate grew from 20 per cent to 40 per cent: four out of every ten yuan earned by the Chinese workforce goes into the banking system. But this is not just a phenomenon of rich versus poor countries, or of East versus West: both Japan and Germany have high savings rates. It is above all the US that is the world's big spender and zero-saver, closely followed by the UK.

The third big imbalance, one that is not very well understood, is in investment patterns. During the 1950s and 1960s, Western companies ploughed most of their profits back into the economy directly as investments in plant, machinery, and R&D – above all, after the dotcom crash – but they have since been wary of investing, and have become used to keeping their profits in the financial system instead. This is especially true among small and medium-sized businesses. Asian companies generally do the same, but the imbalance lies in where the money ends up.

Asian company savings – together with individual savings – have tended to flow into the West, above all into the US, in the form of loans to finance consumer spending. Even if you factor in

the $250 billion annual flow of foreign direct investment from
the West to the East – to set up factories for the big Western
companies in places like Shanghai and New Delhi – the overall
flow is massively from East to West. The *Financial Times* com-
mentator, Martin Wolf, who has consistently rung alarm bells
about the scale of the imbalances, sums up the result: 'Capital
now flows upstream, from the world's poor to the richest
country of all.'[17]

Economists at the Bank of France have called this a 'global
investment strike'.[18] Wolf points out that this downturn in
investment is a product of the imbalance not just between
countries, but between classes. Both in the West and in China
the working class was stripped of benefits and bargaining power,
with the result that company profits rose. But Chinese companies
kept hold of their profits and invested them abroad, while US
companies simply kept them in the American financial system.
So another way of describing it would be that money flows
upstream from the working class of Asia to finance the credit-
fuelled lifestyles of the working class of America.

The final imbalance concerns the mismatch between Western
government debt and government surpluses accumulated in Asia
and the oil-rich countries. All the G7 countries have run up huge
national debts. Many Asian countries, and in addition oil-rich
countries in the Middle East and Russia, have done the opposite,
and hold large quantities of US government bonds. Again, this
phenomenon took off after the 1997 crisis. In the year 2000 the
total foreign-exchange reserves of the so-called emerging markets amounted to $500 billion; by 2004 it had reached $1.3
trillion. It skyrocketed to $3.5 trillion by 2008, and is set to reach
$4 trillion in 2009.[19] More than half of all foreign-exchange
reserves are held by China, with Russia a clear second and the
oil-rich countries third.

Very few people in the world think this situation is either
healthy or sustainable, and for several years the major topic of
conversation at the big-business brainstorm sessions was 'How

will the global imbalances unwind?' and 'Will it be orderly?' The meltdown of 2008 has begun the process of unwinding, and it will not be orderly. Indeed, it is not only the economics, but the geopolitics and patterns of social unrest of the next decade that will be shaped by the unwinding process. We will return to how the imbalances will shape the crisis in Chapter 8; for now, it is important to understand how they fuelled the dominance of the banking system, and laid the basis for its collapse.

If we step away from the statistics and ask what the imbalances tell us, it is this: that a huge proportion of capital in the world cannot be invested profitably in production. This may seem an odd conclusion, given that most individual companies report high profits – but not when you look at what they do with those profits. Rather than being fed back into production, profits go into the financial system. This is a new feature of the economic recovery in the 2000s, and did not happen in the recoveries following 1982 and 1991.

But in the finance system, long-term interest rates are low: they are below average and below what economic theory says they should be. If you think of interest rates as the 'price' of capital, then the price is depressed because there is an excess of capital compared to what can profitably be invested: an excess of capital supply over demand.

In turn, this low interest rate has fuelled repeated bubbles in the price of assets: stock markets, houses, and latterly commodities like oil and grain. What we have seen since the year 2000, as investment dipped and interest rates fell, is the tendency for capital to flow frantically into one asset bubble after another, with the finance system as the conduit. So the global imbalances and the repeated financial bubbles are two sides of the same coin. In the years leading up to 2008 there was too much capital chasing too little return on investment. But the chasing was important, and in itself generated huge profits for the banking industry.

The flow of capital from East to West was mediated by Wall Street; the flow of lending from the Chinese factory worker to the Detroit house-buyer was mediated by Wall Street; ditto the flow of US government debt into the vaults of the Chinese, Russian and Abu Dhabi governments. Wall Street sold high-interest opportunities in a low-interest world. And in the process it produced its own global imbalance – between what was declared in the glossy reports issued by the banks each year, and what was not.

The off–balance sheet decade

We can now go back to Washington on that cold November afternoon in 1999. Financial regulation in the US is toast. America is in the grip of the dotcom boom. On *Friends*, Joey is about to take possession of a new Porsche. In real life, Robert Rubin is about to take possession of his new office at Citigroup's Park Avenue HQ.

Investment bank profits are soaring on the back of a wave of internet company flotations. There are even signs that, at last, the famous Solow Paradox has been disproved. Solow argued that 'you can see the computer age everywhere but in the productivity statistics'.[20] But now, for the first time in decades, productivity is rising; even average male wages have climbed up above their 1979 level. What could go wrong?

We now know the answer to that: almost everything did. First came the dotcom crash. On 10 March 2000 the NASDAQ peaked at 5048; by October 2002 it had lost 78 per cent of its value. Many internet firms went bust without ever turning a profit; huge numbers of small investors who had been suckered into the financial mania lost their money.

But some companies still seemed a good bet: the big telecoms operators who had moved into fibre-optic cabling looked like the railway companies of the new information age. Then came the second shock: Enron, the telecoms giant, went bankrupt as it was revealed that its accounts had been systematically doctored, with the collusion of its auditors Arthur Andersen. Over the next twelve months the whole story was then repeated with World-Com, Tyco, and Global Crossing.

Central to the scams operated by the chief executives of these multi-billion-dollar technology companies had been off–balance sheet accounting. Investment bankers, lawyers and accountants had combined to invent new ways of hiding the debts run up by client companies in subsidiaries registered in various tax havens. In 2003 the SEC fined JP Morgan Chase and Citigroup a total of $255 million for their role in the Enron scandal. They had designed transactions whose complexity

> had no business purpose aside from masking the fact that, in substance, they were loans . . . Both financial institutions knew that Enron engaged in these transactions specifically to allay investor, analyst, and rating agency concerns about its cash flow from operating activities and outstanding debt.'[21]

The third shock was the investment banking analyst scandals. Essentially a product of the dotcom boom, these were uncovered by a wave of lawsuits after the crash. One of the rules of investment banking, where the same giant company can be acting both for the buyer of shares and the seller of shares, is the so-called Chinese Wall. The buy-side and the sell-side are supposed to be walled off to mitigate the obvious conflict of interest. This, as it turned out, had simply been ignored.

Merrill Lynch analyst Henry Blodget became a short-lived celebrity when it was discovered that, despite advising clients to buy the stock of a company called 24/7, he was privately telling Merrill's banking division it was a 'piece of shit'.[22] At Citigroup subsidiary Salomon Smith Barney, analyst Jack Grubman had put a target price of $30 on shares of a company called Focal, then trading at $15. Focal's bosses thought this was an under-estimate and complained. Grubman's email response, unearthed in a later lawsuit, was terse: 'If I so much as hear one more f——g peep out of them we will put the proper rating on this stock which every single smart buy-sider feels is going to zero.'[23]

Focal filed for bankruptcy in 2001 without ever making a profit. It turned out that Grubman and Blodget were not bad apples: much of the barrel was rotten. In 2003 the SEC issued fines and compensation orders totalling $1.4 billion on ten Wall Street banks for the systematic misleading of investors by analysts, stating:

> From approximately mid-1999 through mid-2001 or later, all of the firms engaged in acts and practices that created or maintained inappropriate influence by investment banking over research analysts, thereby imposing conflicts of interest on research analysts that the firms failed to manage in an adequate or appropriate manner. In addition, the regulators found supervisory deficiencies at every firm.[24]

Confidence in the Anglo-Saxon model of capitalism palpably drained away: the S&P 500 fell from 1500 in mid 2000 to 800 in the autumn of 2002; the Dow fell from 11,722 to 7500 in the same period. For one horrible month, September 2002, the markets just did not believe any figures they were presented with.

Capitalism had taken a reputational hit in two ways. First, widespread share ownership was seen to be an uneven bargain. The Wall Street bankers would always know more than you did; they would lie to you to boost the share price of a company even while they were selling the stock themselves. Second, the Anglo-Saxon model of public companies – their creditworthiness measured by rating agencies, their accounts probed by auditors – looked flawed. The West had lectured Asia about 'crony capitalism' after the 1997 crisis. Now the fawning personal correspondence between George W. Bush and Enron chairman Kenneth Lay was posted on the internet for all to read: in one letter Dubya joshes with Lay about his 'good looking' wife; in the next, Lay strongly urges the deregulation of the telecoms industry.

I remember, in the aftermath of the Enron debacle, a discussion with a senior financial regulator of a G7 country. We are, he said, in the middle of a 'systemic crisis of legitimacy for capitalism'; if we find one more company like Enron, he added, 'even I will stop believing it's legitimate'.

And then, suddenly, everything went right again. The British government published its dossier on Iraqi WMD in September 2002, moving the global news agenda away from corporate corruption towards the coming war. The Iraq war was 'won' by April 2003. The bosses of WorldCom, Tyco and Enron went to jail; the Wall Street analysts were disgraced and the banks fined – albeit pitifully small amounts compared to their profits. And capitalism had not collapsed.

A new bull market took off on practically the very day American tanks went into Iraq. And this time the broadband internet and proliferating financial news channels would make the stock-market boom into a global party. There would be buzz, noise and glamour from Shenzhen to San Francisco: a wiser world would learn the lessons of the dotcom mania and invest in real companies this time, not fakes. Analysts would stick to the rules. US company bosses would be forced to swear on oath that their accounts were accurate. Hardened bubble-watchers eyed the stock markets, searching for new scams, new hype. But we were looking in the wrong place.

The shadow banking system

If you prise the cover off a high-spec mobile phone you will find a lot more than a telephone in there: there's a radio antenna for receiving calls, another for connecting to wi-fi, a third for the global positioning system. There'd be a processor for data, a processor for images, and even the screen – once a dead piece of glass – probably now responds to the touch of your fingertip. But go back ten years and none of this was possible. A mobile phone was just a phone with text messaging.

Now consider your phone as part of a network. It's connected to the mobile network by three different signals – one for voice, two for data. It may also connect to your company email system; it can also jump to the wi-fi network, read information from satellites, talk to other devices using Bluetooth. When I was a computer journalist in the late 1990s we covered these innovations as distant promises: it was hard to imagine how even a single one of these networks would take off, let alone how this network-of-networks could link people invisibly across continents, as it does today.

In the same time frame, banking underwent the same kind of revolution as mobile telephony. It wasn't just what banks did that changed; what the banking network did changed dramatically. An investment bank or a major commercial bank might have the same logo as it did ten years ago, but it does different things. And the network itself has changed out of all recognition.

But there is one big difference between telephony and banking: strict global regulations and standards apply to every mast, every handset, every chip and wire in the telephone system. But in the ten years since the repeal of Glass–Steagall, a vast unregulated network has grown up in banking. Until that network crashed, not even regulators or politicians fully understood that it existed. It has become known as the shadow banking system: the term was only coined in 2007, but the thing itself had taken about seven years to put together.

To understand the 'shadow' part, you first need a proper understanding of the official system. At the centre of it were the big diversified global banks: Citigroup, JP Morgan Chase, Bank of America, UBS, Credit Suisse, HSBC, BNP, Deutsche, Fortis, ING. They were generally conglomerates, doing everything from high-street banking to investment banking and insurance. They worked under the scrutiny of national regulators guided by the Basel II treaty.

Next to them, until September 2008, stood the 'pure' investment banks: stockbroking and dealing, increasingly involved in the subprime finance system,[25] resting on their reassuringly familiar nineteenth-century brand names while occupying a role totally transformed during the process of deregulation. Philip Augar calls them Leviathans, and describes how they looked to the chief financial officer of an unnamed major firm on the eve of the crisis: 'You cannot move without the blessing of the Leviathans. They are extraordinarily powerful organisations. They bestride the planet. In less than twenty years they have established themselves at the crossroads of capitalism.'[26]

The third layer of the network is the hedge fund industry. In theory a hedge fund is a private vehicle for rich people to make high-risk investments with their own money: most hedge funds have a minimum investment rule of a million dollars. What they do is combine maths-driven investment strategies with hunches, inside information and political analysis to take bets, which they make using derivatives.

When I meet hedge fund people they never ask me about economics – they know far more about that than I do. What they ask about is politics. They know journalists and political analysts can be a source of inside knowledge and, for them, this is the edge that produces 'alpha' – profit beyond what an investment should, all things being equal, produce.

Hedge funds are usually highly profitable (until they go bust). In the neoliberal era they have grown massively – but again, never so massively as in the eight years leading to the meltdown. In 1990, the amount of capital invested in the world's hedge funds was $39 billion. By 2001 this had grown to $537 billion, and by 2007 it stood at $2 trillion.[27] But this is only half the story.

Hedge fund strategy is to borrow massively to multiply the profits of investors. This is called leverage. When Long Term Capital Management famously collapsed in 1998, almost crashing the financial system, it had borrowed $120 billion against capital of just $4.5 billion. It lost 90 per cent of this money in just two days, threatening to destroy the institutions that had lent it. The institutions that lend hedge funds money are mainly the investment banks or the investment arms of the global banks. Other institutions, such as pension funds, systematically lend shares to hedge funds so they can carry out short-selling operations, gaining a small fee in the process.

In this way hedge funds, though seeming like a niche activity for the rich, inject massive risk and instability into the entire system – but monopolise the rewards for their investors. In addition, for every clever bet or trade or maths formula that delivers a mega-profit to the hedge fund, there has to be somebody on the other side of the deal who has lost money.

Andrew Lahde, a highly successful hedge fund manager who made an 870 per cent profit in a single year, retired in the midst of the 2008 meltdown, penning an immortal letter to the *Financial Times*:

> I was in this game for the money. The low hanging fruit, i.e. idiots whose parents paid for prep school, Yale, and then the Harvard MBA, was there for the taking. These people who were (often) truly not worthy of the education they received (or supposedly received) rose to the top of companies such as AIG, Bear Stearns and Lehman Brothers and all levels of our government. All of this behavior supporting the Aristocracy only ended up making it easier for me to find people stupid enough to take the other side of my trades. God bless America.[28]

Lahde, at thirty-seven, had made enough money to live like James Bond for the rest of his life. He'd made it out of the idiocy of major institutions who were supposed to be looking after ordinary people's money and the capital of shareholders. He'd made most of it by betting, simply, that the subprime bubble would burst.

His missive revealed a truth few want to acknowledge: the hedge fund sector is effectively the creation of the investment banking system. However brave the rich individuals are being in taking leveraged bets with their own money (and they are), however useful derivatives trading might be for helping to find the true price of shares (and it is), the end result is that profits are funnelled from ordinary savers into the pockets of the rich. The hedge fund industry originated inside investment banking; most of its bosses learn their skills on the so-called proprietary trading desks of investment banks; and, latterly, investment banks took to setting up their own off-balance sheet hedge funds to reap the rewards themselves.

But hedge funds, investment banks, commercial banks and pension funds are only the visible part of the system. In the years after the dotcom crash, they combined to create a parallel, invisible system, mainly designed to get around the financial regulations outlined in Basel II.

The confidence trick at the heart of all banking, for all time, has been to borrow short-term and lend long-term. If we all drew our money out of the bank at once we would find it was not actually 'there', and had been lent to somebody else on terms that meant neither we nor the bank itself could get it back immediately. This is why banks are required to keep a 'cushion' of capital to fall back on in a crisis. This is the concept at the heart of Basel II – indeed, of all banking regulation: the 'cushion' consists of either cash or pieces of paper that can be quickly converted into cash. Since you don't earn any profits by holding money in this way, you want – if you are a bank – to hold as little as possible.

The essence of the shadow banking system is that it is designed to get around the need for any capital cushion at all. Almost everybody in the shadow system was 'borrowing short' by buying a piece of paper on the vast international money market, and then 'lending long' by selling a different piece of paper into that same money market. So it was basically just traditional banking: but they were doing it with no depositors, no shareholders and no capital cushion to fall back on. They were pure intermediaries.

They did it by exploiting a loophole in the regulations to create two kinds of off–balance sheet companies, known as 'conduits' and 'structured investment vehicles' (SIVs). I have seen MPs slumped with their heads in their hands trying to understand these entities, so bear with me if you are having trouble.

The conduits were set up by banks in offshore tax havens. The bank would, theoretically, be liable for any losses, but unless it deemed the conduit 'significant' it did not have to show this on its annual accounts. And guess what? Most conduits were deemed so insignificant that many professional investors did not know they existed until they blew up. Yet out of the $3 billion worth of paper flowing round the system by 2007, half had been issued by conduits.

The trick was for banks to insure themselves for a part of their exposure to the conduits. Companies like AIG were willing takers of these insurance contracts; in addition, a class of insurance companies known as monoline insurers grew up to specialise in taking on the exposure. The credit rating agencies said that such insurance contracts were 100 per cent safe, and thus the process of sharing out the risk apparently made it disappear.

SIVs were even riskier, since they had no backup from the banks at all: they were often joint ventures between banks and hedge funds. Both conduits and SIVs existed in a regulatory black hole. When they blew up it became clear that, far from being some kind of niche activity, a large part of international banking had been transferred into this unofficial system.

But there is more, and worse. Not only were they unregulated; the SIVs and conduits were actually kept secret from investors. Citigroup, for example, turned out to be responsible for 25 per cent of the entire market in SIVs. Its biggest SIV, called Centauri, had lent out $21 billion by the time of the crunch. Yet there was no mention of Centauri in Citigroup's 2006 annual report.[29] Time and again, once the bubble bursts, you find not only journalists and shareholders but even senior bankers scratching their heads and asking, 'What the hell are conduits?' One senior figure at a now-defunct bank told me, in September 2007: 'Who would have thought that those little gnomes sitting in the corner of the room issuing paper would be the cause of it all!'

This, then, is the secret structure: a huge, unannounced and unregulated banking network operating with almost no press coverage and little visibility in annual reports. It was as central to the official banking system as Enron's secret companies had been. Yet even some senior people in banking saw it as peripheral. It could only work as long as every piece of paper on sale could find a buyer. It collapsed because certain pieces of paper that had become central to the profitability of the system suddenly became unsellable.

And that brings us to the story of the subprime mortgage bubble: it blossomed and burst in the space of just six years, creating a crisis that made the Asian crisis, the dotcom crash and Enron look just like what they were: tremors and warning signs before the 'extinction level event' of 2008.

5. Subprime

How the Low-Wage Economy
Fuelled High-Risk Finance

I T IS 14 SEPTEMBER 2008, and I am standing in the rain on a derelict street in Black Bottom, Detroit. All around me are abandoned clapperboard homes, anti-war slogans daubed on their doors, and piles of junk made into sculptures. This is the Heidelberg Project, a surreal art installation that is now Detroit's second-most-visited attraction. It's a DIY monument to hope amid economic catastrophe.

On Heidelberg Street the housing pattern is the same as in much of America: box-shaped bungalows, porches, lawns. But the pattern is disrupted: 'snaggletooth' is what the estate agents call it. There are whole patches of land where the homes have been knocked out, like a tramp's teeth, and nature has taken over the spaces. A block away in this African-American neighbourhood there are stick-thin junkies doing the addict's jerky limp from one porch to another, like hurried ghosts.

On the street corner there is a sign stapled to the lamppost: 'We Buy Homes for Cash'. You can buy a house with a garden here for as little as $1,200, but you probably would not want to. Many of the homes are empty, with faded repossession notices taped to the cracking paint. A fair number have been torched: one recently trashed house has a pile of charred mattresses and people-junk outside it, and a lot of yellow tape and police stickers across the doors. Though Black Bottom has had the worst of it, the blight on housing goes way beyond this leafy slum. Across Detroit, one in four properties stands empty.[1]

'It looks', says Hollis P. Wood, a music promoter who has appointed himself my guide, 'like a nuclear strike'. Yeah, I think, but one where the government forgot to send in rescue teams. To me this neighbourhood testifies to the collapse of two economic-growth models: the first based on making cars; the second, newer one based on deregulation and debt. Economists like to call the old model 'Fordism', after the man who invented mass production and made this city famous. Whatever post-Fordism is, it has promised little and delivered less to places like Black Bottom.

We have to be careful of nostalgia. In the 1950s and 1960s, inner-city Detroit was no paradise. Housing was segregated; black people were poorer than white. But there was full employment and the city was the capital of the industrial world – not just economically but, it seemed to people here, culturally. On these porches and doorsteps soul music was born. The Motown sound seemed to sum up the deal Henry Ford's system offered the working class: hard work, frenetic leisure and a counter culture that made everything else look uncool. Above all, it was a world of rising real income. If you work eight hours a day on a production line that does not stop, these three words – 'rising real income' – represent the most important single fact in economics.

During the post-war boom you could escape from a place like Black Bottom through sheer talent: Motown legends Martha Reeves, Smokey Robinson and Diana Ross were all raised within a mile of Heidelberg Street. But you could also work your way to a kind of rough prosperity without leaving here. In 1960 there were 114,000 automotive workers in the city, about 50 per cent of them African American, and they were paid well enough that newspapers at the time referred to them as a 'black middle class'. It was this high-wage economy that supported sixty recording studios and 400 record labels in Detroit.

With the crisis of the mid 1970s the city, its workforce and its traditional neighbourhoods began their long decline. There are only 36,000 car workers in Detroit now, many of them under pressure to take lump-sum severance payments and leave. The big three car manufacturers – Ford, Chrysler and GM – will not survive without a state bailout totalling tens of billions of dollars. The city itself looks shattered: art deco palaces tower, smashed, above the half-deserted thoroughfares. I am not exaggerating: since the mid 1970s the population of Detroit has halved.

In the intervening decades, high-wage manufacturing jobs were replaced by lower-paying service jobs. The most popular job in Michigan now is to work in a restaurant or fast-food joint: 155,000 people across the state earn their living this way. Second in the jobs league table are 150,000 shop assistants, and third are 108,000 cashiers. Not one of these occupations pays above $10 an hour. As in the rest of America, the average male worker in this city is in 2008 earning less in real terms than in 1979. As a result, according to the Michigan League for Human Services: 'For at least twenty-five years more than one-fifth of all Michigan workers have been earning a wage that would not lift a family of four out of poverty.'[2] An army of working poor has replaced the Motown generation. Forget Martha Reeves and the Vandellas: this is the world of Eminem's hip-hop movie *8 Mile*, named after the road that severs black Detroit from its mixed and middle-class suburbs.

An economist from the Motown era time-travelling to present-day Detroit would be faced with a puzzle. If wages have fallen, then who's buying all the burgers, training shoes, six-packs, televisions and hair extensions that keep this army of low-paid people at work on six to nine dollars an hour? Henry Ford said you can't have mass consumption without high wages, so where is the money coming from? The answer is credit: credit cards, short-term 'payday' loans, zero per cent car finance, low interest rates and self-certified mortgages.

Next question from Puzzled Sixties Guy: who would be mad enough to lend serious money to people here? A population on a downward income spiral, living in an urban wasteland and in a city in distress? The answer is, not everybody. And that is why, when the subprime lending boom hit Detroit, we should have known it had reached the height of craziness.

Because of the law requiring banks to demonstrate lending to minority communities, there had been subprime lending in Detroit throughout the 1990s. But it only took off properly after 9/11. Many observers, including myself, expected 9/11 to tip the fragile US economy into recession, with much of the Western world following on behind it. This is because, by the time of 9/11, 70 per cent of GDP in America was driven by consumer spending – and consumers were feeling fragile even on the eve of the attack.

But consumer spending did not slump; indeed, it was revived by the availability of cheap credit. The Federal Reserve slashed interest rates from 6.5 per cent to 3.5 per cent in the first eight months of 2001, and then, in the aftermath of 9/11, took them down to 1 per cent. For thirty-one months interest rates were below inflation: money, if you could borrow it, was effectively free.

This was the first of the conditions that created the debt bubble: free money looking for places to invest, at a time when the stock market was falling and had further to fall. The second contributing factor was the global savings imbalance described above,[3] with huge amounts of Asian savings poured into the US finance system, creating a glut of capital. By 2002 the banks were awash with cheap money; now they had to think of a way to turn it into high-profit investments. Fortunately, in the coffee queue of a Chicago bank, that way had just been invented.

What Sherman did next

In Tom Wolfe's novel *Bonfire of the Vanities*, investment banker Sherman McCoy gets lost in the Bronx, kills a black teenager in a hit-and-run accident, and sparks a race war. Wolfe cast McCoy as a bond trader – buying and selling IOUs issued by governments and big companies. And the novel captured the real-life moment of transition of the bond-trading floors of investment banks from Dweebsville to Master-of-the-Universe status:

There was no more talk of Bond Bores these days . . . The
bond market had caught fire, and experienced salesmen such
as himself were all at once much in demand. All off a sudden,
in investment houses all over Wall Street, the erstwhile Bond
Bores were making so much money they took to congregat-
ing after work in a bar . . . to tell war stories and assure one
another this wasn't dumb luck but rather a surge of collective
talent.[4]

What Sherman made his money out of, back in the 1980s, was
selling chunks of the bonds to financial institutions which needed
the reliable income generated by the interest on the debt. In the
book, his wife disparagingly calls this 'collecting golden crumbs
every time somebody cuts a cake'. Lucrative though this was, it
was not until the mid 1990s that financial whiz-kids worked out
a way of creating a derivative on the top of it. Derivatives,
remember, are where you separate off the risk involved in a deal
– be it oil, shares or currencies – and create a financial product
that is just the risk, not the deal itself.

   In 1997, JP Morgan launched a product called BISTRO: it was
such a big event that there were press releases and long feature
articles explaining how it worked. It took a bundle of loans
worth $10 billion, set up an arm's-length company, and then
swapped the risk on these loans, valued at $700 million, with that
company. This is called a 'credit default swap'. Then it sold off
the arm's-length company chunk by chunk to investors. The
official name for such a product is a 'collateralised debt obligation', or CDO.

   There were two innovative features to this deal: first, the $10
billion was not actual debt. Some of it was debt that might be
incurred in the future, making this effectively a derivative, not a
straight Sherman McCoy–era bond. Second, the swap contract
itself was complex: nobody was quite sure what the risk of default
was. Moody's, the credit rating agency, estimated it at 0.82 per
cent, but one sceptical investor said it could be as high as 2 per

cent. That left massive scope for one side of the deal to make money. In racing terms, it's like one bookmaker giving odds of 50/1 while another gives you 100/1: somebody on the course is going to make a lot of money.[5]

There was an added bonus for JP Morgan: remember that banks have to hold a certain amount of capital compared to the risks present on their books. By creating the arm's-length company, they could get $10 billion worth of risk off their books at a cost of only $700 million. Confused? So was everybody else. It took months of studying this deal before anybody else felt confident about making it work.

Then they all wanted a piece of the action: Deutsche Bank, Bank of America and Citigroup all became players in the early credit derivatives market. But throughout the 1990s there were false starts, because the swap contracts were tricky and hard to enforce. So in 1999 the contracts were standardised. Then, in 2001, Argentina defaulted on its debts and Enron – the only player in the swap market that was not a bank – collapsed.

It was now noted that the credit default swaps had assumed an interesting and unanticipated role: movements in their price had begun to predict disasters where no other data signalled it. Loud mutterings in the press wondered whether inside information was flowing within the banks that were selling the swaps. Regulators had a look, but could find nothing.

For all these reasons, by 2001 the market was still struggling to get above $1 trillion a year. Then David Li, a Chinese maths genius working for JP Morgan, published a calculation designed to wipe out the uncertainties about the risk.[6] Though he warned traders it was dangerous if treated as foolproof, they were enthralled. 'The beauty of it is, it's so simple', one fund manager enthused. Now, apparently, this complex trading could be done by anybody.[7]

But it wasn't Li's formula that finally ignited the market for CDOs. It was the discovery that Wall Street's existing business model was in trouble. The dotcom and Enron crises had left the investment banks bearing heavy risks that required high reserves of capital. Mergers and acquisitions were drying up. Suddenly they were staring at a low-profit future. As the *London Financial News* put it in 2000:

> Unable to establish the credit derivatives market as an effective hedge against default, bankers have been quietly reinventing the market . . . It exploits the pressing need among commercial banks to reduce the regulatory capital they are required to set aside and rides a growing eagerness among investors to trade credit as an asset class in itself.[8]

It is worth unpacking this statement, for clarity's sake. Simply put, it states that (i) credit default swaps had never really worked as an insurance policy against default; (ii) they did work as a new way of moving liabilities off–balance sheet; (iii) to speculators who had just seen one bubble burst, it was like a guy turning up at a rave with a bag of Ecstasy pills right after the drug squad has just left.

No matter that Enron had collapsed because of the debts hidden within arm's-length companies; no matter that the last two speculative bubbles had burst; no matter that the author of the maths formula warned them it was not totally reliable: the banks were already recruiting new teams to start playing in this market for CDOs. This, says Janet Tavakoli, who has written the textbook on CDOs,

> opened the door to the rise of inexperienced CDO managers, new and unknown offshore entities, hedge fund investors . . . CDO managers of all types – from the savvy to the naive – waded into the global securitisation market. Even former stints at SEC-alleged Ponzi schemes or fines paid after SEC-alleged accounting fraud were not deterrents for investment banks doing business with re-invented CDO managers.[9]

But there was one thing missing. For this new business model to take off you needed a ready supply of high-risk loans. Low-risk loans are no good, since they don't take you into the 50/1 betting bracket. The problem was, where to find so many high-risk borrowers? Answer: places like Black Bottom.

Gillian Tett, the *Financial Times* journalist who spotted the crisis building, takes up the story: 'As the new century dawned, the teams that had traditionally handled subprime mortgage finance . . . started talking to the derivatives groups.' A top executive at Bank of America told her: 'The bingo moment was in the coffee queue of our Chicago office when the two groups met by chance and realised they needed to talk to each other.'[10]

This was the ultimate irony. In *Bonfire of the Vanities*, tough black neighbourhoods were represented as a nightmare landscape for bond traders like the fictional Sherman McCoy. By 2002 they had become business opportunities for his all-too-real buddies. That year the *Economist* ran a front cover hailing 'The Houses That Saved the World'. A more accurate headline would have been 'The Poor People Who Rescued Wall Street'.

The subprime pushers

In Detroit, 2004 was the year subprime lending took off. In the next two years there would be 38,000 new mortgages issued, three-quarters of them subprime. A whole new breed of mortgage companies sprang up to push debt into the hands of people who could never pay it back.

What is subprime? It means you agree to pay higher interest than normal on the grounds that your debt is riskier than that of the average Joe – that is, there is a greater probability that you may not be able to pay it back. Millions of Americans – and later people across the developed world – agreed to do this because it gave them a foot on the property ladder, and property prices were rising. On top of high interest rates, subprime mortgages always include small-print penalties: an upfront fee; a termination

fee; variable instead of fixed interest rates; an obligation to renew
the loan in two years' time, with another fee; and usually a higher
interest rate.

You might say 'fair enough' if the high-interest loans were
only given to needy and chaotic people. But subprime was never
confined to the riskiest borrowers: millions of Americans who
could have got ordinary mortgages were pushed into taking
subprime loans. They did it because the loans were structured to
look more attractive, or because they were pleasantly surprised at
being offered such easy credit. In a 2007 study, 55 per cent of all
subprime loans had been sold to people with credit scores high
enough to get a better deal.[11] A disproportionately large number
of such mis-sold loans went to black and Hispanic people: 55 per
cent of loans to African Americans were subprime, but only 21
per cent of those to whites.[12]

The biggest subprime mortgage lender in Detroit was
Countrywide Financial: about a third of all its loans in the
city were subprime. Because of lawsuits and investigative
journalism, we now know how Countrywide operated. It
would aggressively search for new borrowers using junk mail
and cold-calling. The company's computer system was rigged
to steer borrowers towards taking out a subprime mortgage,
even if their finances could support an ordinary one. Countrywide would lend you hundreds of thousands of dollars
even if you were 90 days late on an existing mortgage. It
would lend you money even if you couldn't get a credit card.
It would lend you money without a deposit. It would lend
you 95 per cent of the value of a home without seeing any
proof of your income. Its sales reps got higher bonuses for
selling people the riskiest loans:

> Such loans were made, former employees say, because they
> were so lucrative – to Countrywide. The company harvested
> a steady stream of fees or payments on such loans and busily
> repackaged them as securities to sell to investors. As long as

housing prices kept rising, everyone – borrowers, lenders and
investors – appeared to be winners.[13]

As the subprime mortgage brokers flooded into black Detroit,
it was obvious to some that this was predatory lending. As early as
2002, Detroit's city council had tried to ban aspects of subprime
lending, attempting to impose a cap on interest rates and ban
loans where it was compulsory to refinance at a higher rate. One
councillor told the press: 'In a city like Detroit, it is a crucial issue,
I don't think there is any doubt that predatory lenders do target
the city and its residents.'[14]
But the ban was opposed by mortgage lenders, nixed at state
level, and finally declared illegal by the Federal government.

By 2004, 8 per cent of all Detroit homes bought with subprime
loans had been seized; but, ignoring the warning signs, lenders
were undeterred. The real boom – in Detroit and all across
America – was between 2004 and 2006. You may ask why, even
as the high-risk loans turned into deserted shacks overgrown by
weeds, the finance industry kept pumping out the easy money?
First, because it was profitable to the middlemen like Countrywide, which was making $4 billion profits on an $11 billion
turnover, half of it fuelled by subprime. But above all it was
because of the insatiable demand for high-risk loans coming from
Wall Street.
It has become fashionable to blame the poor, misinformed and
struggling families that took the loans. 'We're all to blame for the
credit crunch', runs the argument in a thousand tabloid television
programmes. They have a point. But who is *mainly* to blame?
Was it demand from the streets of Black Bottom or demand from
the trading floors of Manhattan that created the disaster? New
York's banking superintendent put it like this:

I believe the origins of the problem in large measure stem
from increased institutional demand for higher yielding sub-

prime investments. As stock values fell earlier in the decade,
real estate became an appealing investment alternative and
property values increased in response to renewed investor
appetite. As a result there was a significant increase in institutional investor demand for higher risk subprime mortgage
securities that generate a higher yield.[15]

In non-financial English that means: Yeah, it was Wall Street.

Structured by cows

It is time to look in detail at how the system worked – and how it
became so unstable that it crashed the world economy. There are
five stages to structured finance, and one way of getting your
head around them is to think of a vaudeville magician at work.

The first stage is to find the object to work the magic on: the
top hat from which a rabbit is going to be pulled. In this case it is
bonds. A bond is an IOU that is supposed to generate regular
interest payments, and thus a predictable return for a known risk.
This could be bundles of similar mortgages, credit card debts,
student loans, car loans – it doesn't matter.

Stage two is to mix different bonds together into a bigger
package. You don't care what the mix of actual loans is; you do
care what the mix of risk is. So you 'structure' it into layers – for
mortgages, the layers represent different risks of default. The
package is the 'collateralised debt obligation' (CDO) that we met
earlier.

Stage three needs to be split up into two parts. Stage three (a) is
where, using the magic analogy, the wand is waved. You now go
to the derivatives market and, effectively, buy insurance on the
package of loans. The net result is that the risks bundled up in it
are averaged out, reduced, and moved off your balance sheet.
This is the 'credit default swap'. Stage three (b) follows the
standard magician's routine: you get a trustworthy and entirely
unbiased member of the audience to come up and watch you do

the whole trick. They step up, observe the magic and say: 'Yes, it's genuine, there was no cheating!' In banking, this role is played by credit rating agencies.

In stage four, you break your CDO into little chunks and sell it. But even here there is scope for complexity. When a theatre sells tickets, those with the best seats have to pay the highest price. With debt, the person with first claim on the collateral if things go wrong is the one who pays the highest price. This breaking up into tranches turns out to be very important when things go wrong.

Stage five concerns the buyers of the CDO: what they get is a guaranteed return. Who buys them? In addition to other investment banks, it is mainly people and institutions that need a regular income: pension funds, mutual funds, local governments and building societies. Or, at the other end of the scale, hedge funds who want to speculate with them to make money – even sometimes betting they will fail.

Now let's look at the motivation, stage by stage. Why create bonds at stage one? Answer: so that a lot of smaller investors can get together and make one big loan. At stage two, why pick and mix? Because it allows you to put high- and low-risk bonds into the same bundle, average out the risk, and generate a higher return. It's theoretically safer than putting all your money into exclusively high-risk investments. Why take out insurance? Because, above all, it allows you to move the risk off your balance sheet. Why get a credit rating agency to validate it? Obviously, to check that it's genuine, stupid! There are a lot of scam-artists out there – and a lot of chumps.

Finally, why would you buy such a thing? Because throughout the decade the interest rates received by the buyers were between 2 and 3 per cent higher than if the products had not been bundled up. And we are talking like-for-like. That was the magic. And at every stage, the norms and legalities of capitalism were seemingly observed.

Structured finance sucked in vast amounts of wealth. The value of asset-backed securities issued each year ballooned from a few billion in the late 1990s to $2 trillion when the bubble burst. The value of the credit default swaps grew much faster: from zero to $58 trillion in 2008. And the profits of investment banks boomed: in 2002 the combined pre-tax profits of the five broker–dealers was $9.5 billion. In 2006 it was $30 billion.[16]

But the whole process went catastrophically wrong. First, the actual calculation of the risk was wrong at stages one and two: house prices fell by 25 per cent; more people defaulted on their mortgages than expected; unemployment rose, and people couldn't pay their credit card debts. Remember the maths guy's warning that it was dangerous to believe the formula was infallible? People didn't listen. They just piled into the markets, in some cases with just a letterhead.

Janet Tavakoli recounts a conversation with one CDO trader:

He told me he'd been an unsuccessful emerging markets trader, but now he felt he'd found his niche. Lack of experience was no impediment. He informed me he was a native Italian and the language skill was more important. He cloned mandate letters of his more experienced colleagues and sent them to banks.[17]

Second, the process of taking out insurance massively amplified the damage that would be caused by getting the initial risk assessment wrong. Fifty-eight trillion dollars' worth of credit default swaps is not far off the size of global GDP. Even if you calculate the potential losses as much lower – the $3.1 trillion conservatively estimated by the Bank for International Settlements – that is a still a massive amplification of risk.[18]

Third, and crucially, the 'trustworthy audience member' proved totally incapable of spotting whether the magic was fake. In some cases, you will be shocked to hear, the audience member was simply a 'plant' for the magician, who after all was paying them. Payments to the credit rating agencies – Moody's, Standard & Poor's and Fitch – doubled in the five years of the subprime boom, totalling $6 billion by 2007. Unfortunately the efficiency of those agencies did not keep pace with their earnings.

In July 2007, the US financial watchdog published a damning account of the role of ratings agencies. Not one of them could provide adequate documentation for their method of calculating the risk on CDOs. After 2002 they had become overwhelmed by the scale of new business they were doing. The conflict of interest – bond issuers paying for their own products to be rated – was never properly managed.[19] Emails seized by a 2008 Congressional inquiry show the depth of collusion.

One instant message exchange sums it up. Analysts Rahul Shah and Shannon Mooney of Standard & Poor's are exchanging views on a CDO the company has just rated. 'By the way,' says Rahul, 'that deal is ridiculous.' 'I know, right,' Shannon replies, '[the] model def[initely] does not capture half of the risk.' 'We should not be rating it,' Rahul chips in, prompting Shannon to type – on a system that is flashing constant reminders that they are being recorded – the immortal line: 'We rate every deal. It could be structured by cows and we would rate it.'[20]

Another analyst email exchange at S&P concluded: 'Rating agencies continue to create an even bigger monster – the CDO market. Let's hope we are all wealthy and retired by the time this house of cards falters :o)' This last set of characters is what they call an emoticon: an email symbol, indicating a grin.[21]

At the top level of the three main rating agencies, alarm bells were ringing by 2006, but there was no decisive action until it was too late. Getting the ratings right was seen as a threat to the whole business – if they did, they risked annoying the investment banks issuing the CDOs and losing market share. As a result, one senior manager at Moody's admitted to his colleagues in an email: 'Analysts and MDs are continually "pitched" by bankers, issuers, investors – all with reasonable arguments – whose views can color credit judgment, sometimes improving it, other times degrading it (we "drink the Kool-Aid").'[22]

When, belatedly, credit analysts did begin to stick the right labels on the mis-priced investments, downgrading them, it was too late. By mid 2007, many of their customers had stopped believing them. 'If the ratings are bullshit,' the head of investment at Fortis told Moody's, privately, 'the only use in ratings is comparing bullshit relative to more bullshit.'[23] Fortis would go bust a year later.

There was one final piece of the catastrophe. If a magician takes your watch and smashes it with a hammer, and then you realise he was not joking, and it's really smashed, that is one watch destroyed. But because securitisation breaks up the product into little chunks to be traded throughout the system, if it turns out that one watch is smashed, hundreds of watches are also smashed.

The whole problem was memorably foreshadowed in a 1991 episode of *The Simpsons*. Krusty the Clown, whose burger empire has lost $44 million dollars, appears in a TV commercial in a state of nervous breakdown: 'You people are pigs! I, personally, am going to spit in every fiftieth burger!' Homer Simpson, watching on TV, responds: 'Mmm, I like those odds!'[24]

Initially, that was how the banking system responded. There was still only a 50/1 chance of getting spit in your burger. It was only later that they realised, because of the way structured finance worked, that the spit was not in the individual burgers: it was in the mince vat. And it was lethal. Suddenly nobody wanted to eat burgers anymore.

'Likely to be contained . . .'

By late 2005 the US housing market had peaked. Four out of ten homes being bought were either buy-to-let or holiday homes. A building boom in the suburbs had produced a glut of housing, some of it unappealing: the term McMansion entered the lexicon. By this time, 20 per cent of all mortgages were subprime. And house prices were unsustainably high. The average price of a US home, which for two decades had hovered around three times the average wage, was now 4.6 times the average wage.[25]

The US economy looked to be booming, but it was riding on a wave of debt. Some of it was money borrowed against the rising value of homes. Much of it was credit card debt, car loans and student loans. In the twenty years before 2000, America's consumer debt had risen from 80 per cent of disposable income to 96 per cent; by 2005 it had shot up to 127 per cent.[26] There were nine credit cards in circulation for every American citizen, averaging $5,000 of debt per card.

Yet, despite these dizzying numbers, there was one statistic that made things tolerable: the average cost of servicing these debts had only crept upwards slowly. That was because interest rates had remained low. In addition, with other household costs there was actually deflation, so even if your wages were being eaten by your mortgage, there was a ready supply of unbelievably cheap Chinese stuff to buy at Wal-Mart.

But by 2004 the deflationary impact of China ran out, and oil prices had begun to rise. From 2003 until the end of 2005, the price of oil doubled from $30 a barrel to around $60. This too was mainly driven from China, whose economic growth had begun to gridlock the streets of Beijing with cars, and fill villages with the smell of overheated diesel generators.

As inflation picked up, central banks in the US, the UK and the eurozone began to raise interest rates; the Fed jacked up its rates from 2.5 per cent to 4.5 per cent in the space of twelve months. As interest rates rose, the US housing market began to cool down. But Wall Street's ardour for structured finance did not. The global market for CDOs had been $271 billion in 2005, growing to $551 billion in 2006. Even as subprime mortgage brokers began to go bust in the first half of 2007, the CDO market soared. At $362 billion in the first six months of 2007, the market was on course for $700 billion for the year.[27] And why not? The man in charge of the Fed was saying, as late as March 2007, that it would be OK: 'At this juncture . . . the impact on the broader economy and financial markets of the problems in the subprime markets seems likely to be contained.'[28] Even as late as May 2007, Ben Bernanke was confident that the housing market too would be alright: 'Given the fundamental factors in place that should support the demand for housing, we believe the effect of the troubles in the subprime sector on the broader housing market will likely be limited.'[29]

By then eight of the top ten mortgage brokers operating in Detroit had gone out of business. Sixty-seven thousand homes had been seized by mortgage companies across the city, 65 per cent of which remain unoccupied at the time of writing. In just two years, one in every five mortgage-payers in Detroit had lost their home. Detroit had been hit harder than any other city in America.[30] But the rest of America had also been hit hard. Building projects ground to a halt; half-finished estates stood empty from Florida to California.

In late spring 2007, a rising level of defaults in the US subprime mortgage market began to show up in the shadow banking system. The SIVs and conduits that had been set up to handle the CDOs began to call on their parent banks to make good their losses. In May, UBS shut down its hedge fund, Dillon Read, which had lost $125 million on subprime CDOs. Next, the credit rating agencies, realising that many of the CDOs they had rated as safe were looking distinctly dodgy, unleashed a spate of downgrades.

In June 2007 two hedge funds run by Bear Stearns, worth $1.6 billion on paper, announced that they were losing money fast. Merrill Lynch, which had $850 million in the funds, seized its money back. As Bear's management struggled to keep the funds afloat, pouring in $1.2 billion of the bank's good money after bad, this was the point at which CEO Jimmy Cayne stayed in Nashville to play bridge. By the time he returned, in mid July, the funds were toast.

Now the $58 trillion worth of credit default swaps that had been issued during the boom began to play the role of economic

Geiger counter. The cost of buying them shot up, making short-term credit harder to get. By now the big five Wall Street banks had become so enmeshed in playing the game of short-term finance that a quarter of the money on their books was held in the form of loans that had to be repaid the next day. In addition, they were exposed to about $1.2 trillion of short-term debts issued by conduits and sivs.

Remember how the shadow banking system works: you issue a long-term loan and you fund it by short-term borrowing. Now that the short-term borrowing had dried up, the graph fell off a cliff, from $1.2 trillion to $800 million. This is the key mechanism that transmitted the crisis from housing to banking: it began to dawn on the banks that, as the short-term credit market evaporated, it was becoming impossible to put an accurate value on any of the money in the shadow banking system.

In mid July 2007, a small German bank called IKB declared big, subprime-related losses in its conduit. It had to be bailed out by the government. The moment of truth came on 9 August 2007. The French bank BNP Paribas suspended subprime investment funds theoretically worth $2.2 billion, saying: 'The complete evaporation of liquidity in certain market segments of the US securitisation market has made it impossible to value certain assets fairly regardless of their quality or credit rating.'[31]

By mid afternoon that day, the upmarket beaches of the world were disrupted by the crackle and burp of Blackberry phones calling bankers and their lawyers to urgent conference calls. Inter-bank lending had frozen all over the world. The credit crunch had begun.

6. The Big Freeze

The Credit Crunch and the Inflation Spike of 2007–8

F ROM 9 AUGUST 2007 the financial system was in a state of deep-freeze. At the time we called it the credit crunch; but the totality of what happened is not encompassed by the term 'credit crunch', and it certainly did not feel like that to me as a reporter trying to make sense of it. There have been many detailed timelines of the thirteen months leading up to the meltdown of 2008 – but it is easier to describe in terms of processes rather than dates.

There were in fact three processes shaping economic reality during this period: the credit freeze, a rapidly expanding commodities bubble, and the increasing disorientation of policy-makers. The financier George Soros has described the whole process as the bursting of a 'superbubble' built up over a thirty-year period and driven by credit expansion, globalisation and deregulation. 'It is', writes Soros, 'not business as usual but the end of an era'.[1]

The process at work during the credit freeze can be characterised as destruction and denial: destruction of capital that had been badly invested; systematic denial of the scale of the problem by executives desperate to maintain a façade of profitability and competence. The denial was aided not only by the normal financial engineering that precedes all quarterly results, but also by the very existence of the shadow banking system. That system, being point-to-point and largely private, made it impossible for bankers to know their own losses and for the regulators to see what was happening within the system.

The second process shaping events was the commodities boom. After 2005, about $250 billion of speculative money was moved out of other assets and into recently invented commodity indexes. This, plus a mismatch between supply and demand of the physical commodities themselves, produced a dramatic spike in the price of nearly every raw material on earth. To the extent that you can attribute psychology to any market, there is an element of denial here too. The property boom was clearly over by 2007, and it became common to hear commodities described as the 'next big thing': a one-way bet on upward-moving prices.

In human terms, the commodities craze was the shortest, steepest and most disastrous of the bubbles. If subprime ruined the credit scores of millions of Americans, the commodity inflation took food out of the mouths of children from Haiti to Bangladesh, and made many middle-income people in the developed world feel instantly poor.

In politics, too, there was denial. G7 politicians generally tried to address the combined credit freeze and commodity inflation with the old tools and the old obsessions. The inflation hawks fought inflation; the monetarists flooded the system with money; fiscal conservatives attacked government profligacy. And economists, consulting their graphs, saw the end of a cycle instead of the end of an era.

With hindsight, the dominant story of this period is the credit freeze. As of early 2009 the oil price is back below $50 a barrel, but the banking system is still on life-support. But it is important to remember that, in the run-up to the meltdown, it was the financial crisis that seemed to be contained while the inflation problem seemed uncontained. This in turn shaped the policies of the central bankers and politicians, which were often worse than ineffective.

Whether the meltdown of September 2008 could have been prevented by different policies and swifter action is an academic question. I would provisionally answer no. The super-bubble was always going to end at some point, and the economists' graphs were right: by mid 2008 a recession had already begun. At some point, as the downturn began, the finance system was going to take a big hit.

The credit freeze

The credit freeze began on 9 August 2007. A few days later, when everybody was still trying to make sense of it, a Lehman Brothers executive told me: 'Lehman has enough cash so that even if nobody lent us a cent we could survive for over a year. But we want to make sure: it's the same for everybody. That's why nobody's lending.'

I should have paid more attention to that 'over a year' bit, but the statement sums up what had happened. Lending costs between banks had rocketed because lending itself had dried up; this was because banks looked at their own pile of toxic debts and said, like BNP Paribas, 'They're impossible to value.' Then they looked across the road – sometimes literally, as in the case of Bear Stearns and JP Morgan Chase on Park Avenue – and thought: 'If our trading partner has the same problem then there is no longer any guarantee of getting back the money we lent them.'

The striking fact is how quickly the freeze went global. IKB in Germany was followed by the bailout of SachsenLB; in the US Countrywide Financial collapsed within days and had to be bailed out to the tune of $11 billion (which, if you remember, is a sum equivalent to a year's turnover).

Though the virus was in the US housing market, structured finance had spread exposure to it like a giant sneeze across the world's banking system. Those who went down first were not the closest, but those with the weakest immune system. Some of the earliest losses declared were not on mortgage debt but on loans advanced to private equity groups during the last months of a takeover boom, which now collapsed.

And once the crisis hit, it also spread rapidly down to micro-level: a mortgage broker in San Francisco described how, day by day, potential lenders on a high-risk mortgage for a well-heeled client dwindled from two, to one, to none. 'He can't buy even though he had superlative credit [scores], money in the bank and a whopping down payment,' she complained.[2] Most big banks were having the same problem: it was impossible to take out new loans, and rolling over the old ones was becoming difficult. Those banks with cash reserves began using them to fill the gaps.

These were mindblowing days for the 'quants', the PhD mathematicians who had built the risk models at investment banks. 'Events that models only predicted would happen once in 10,000 years happened every day for three days', said Lehman's risk boffin. Goldman's chief finance officer declared that '−25 sigma events' were happening 'for days in a row'. A −25 sigma event is one that should not happen ever, even if the history of the universe is relived fourteen times over.[3]

But the scale of the crisis was not obvious to some policy-makers. Mervyn King, the UK's central bank chief, said: 'So far, what we have seen is not a threat to the financial system, either in the United States or Germany, let alone in the United Kingdom. It is not an international financial crisis.'[4] King was the only major central banker who failed to pump money into the system on the first day of the freeze-up. Meanwhile, George W. Bush called journalists together and told them: 'The conditions for a, you know, for the marketplace working through these issues are good, and that's how I look at it . . . I happen to believe the war has clouded people's sense of optimism.'[5]

Though it spread across borders, credit types and even down to individuals, this was not a total freeze. Those banks that looked safest were still able to create new bonds and sell them on the global markets. In the fourth quarter (Q4) of 2006 the European banks had issued €187 billion worth of CDOs and other secur-itized loans; in Q4 of 2007 this more than halved, to €75 billion. But if you slice the data up by country, you see the one massive drop that made this happen: the collapse of new mortgage lending in the UK. This fell from €62 billion in the second quarter of 2007 to €18 billion in Q4, and just €8 billion in the

first three months of 2008.[6] In most other European countries
the credit market fluctuated but did not collapse. Even in the US,
about half the market was still open to the highest-quality
borrowers at the end of 2007.

The story the politicians tell is that the UK was 'caught up' in
the American subprime crisis. The official data tell a different
story: the UK was the weakest link in the shadow banking system,
and suffered the greatest drop in securitised lending before the
Wall Street meltdown one year later.[7]

For these two reasons – the reluctance of the Bank of England
to inject liquidity and the extreme exposure of the UK to the
short-term money markets – the first big casualty was the British
mortgage bank, Northern Rock. The news of Northern Rock's
collapse broke late on Thursday 13 September 2007. I remember
looking Newsnight's presenter in the eye as we scrambled to cover
it, and saying: 'Whatever you do you must make clear that
people's deposits are safe: there's an insurance scheme for
deposits. There is no need to start queuing outside the bank.'
The next day depositors began to queue outside the bank. It was
the first run on a British bank for more than 100 years.

I spent the following Monday talking to troubled savers in
long queues outside Northern Rock branches. Whatever I
thought UK finance minister Alistair Darling would say, he had
not been prepared to say it: that despite the deposit guarantee
being limited to £35,000, in reality all deposits were safe. In a
way, George W. Bush was right: the war had clouded something
– but it was not optimism, it was trust. Many savers I talked to
raised the issue of Tony Blair and Iraqi weapons of mass
destruction. This was five years after the start of the Iraq war,
but as one middle-aged saver memorably put it to me: 'In the
past, if the Chancellor said your money was safe then your
money was safe. Now, nobody believes the Chancellor.'

I went straight from the queue at Northern Rock to Downing
Street for a press conference with Darling and Henry Paulson,
who was on a routine visit to London. Paulson looked bemused

and jangled the change in his pockets, as Darling attempted yet
again to reassure savers. I told Darling: 'I've been with Northern
Rock savers all day and the problem is nobody believes you.
That may not be rational but it is real. What are you going to do
about it?'

It was at this point that Darling spelled out clearly that he was
indeed standing behind every penny in Northern Rock's bank
accounts. 'There's no need for legislation,' his special adviser
hurriedly told us afterwards, 'this is the word of the Chancellor.'
The Rock would be bailed out with a loan from the Bank of
England. I could see, from the body language of Darling's aides,
that they were in completely uncharted territory, for which there
was no protocol or playbook.

Darling would spend the next five months grappling with
what to do with the failed bank: first assuring the markets that
Northern Rock would pay 'penalty rates' for its bailout money,
then not; then trying to sell it to various private equity groups;
then finally nationalising it at a cost of around £100 billion. Both
the savings bailout and the nationalisation were done late,
reluctantly, and with an absence of conviction.

The big milestones of the period between Northern Rock and
the collapse of Bear Stearns in March 2008 were the debt write-
downs by the investment banks and the sacking of their chief
executives. It started with a trickle: Bear Stearns said it would lose
$200 million on its hedge funds; Goldman Sachs said it had lost
$1 billion on loans advanced for corporate takeovers. Then, in
October 2007, UBS wrote off $3 billion and Citigroup wrote off
$6 billion.

The processes of writing off dud loans and taking a hit to your
profits are linked, but not straightforwardly: there is a lot you can
do to delay the one affecting the other. So it was not until early
2008 that the massive losses began to rack up. By April 2008, UBS
had written off $19 billion, Merrill Lynch $17 billion, and
Citigroup £19 billion. In the same month the financial data
company Bloomberg announced a new league table of banking

write-downs: its total then was around $300 billion. One by one, the chief executives who had overseen these losses were sacked: Stan O'Neal at Merrill Lynch; Jimmy Cayne, the bridge-playing boss of Bear Stearns; Charles Prince of Citigroup; Adam Applegarth at Northern Rock.

But as the process of destruction, discovery and denial limped on, it became clear that writing off bad loans might not be the worst that could happen. Could a major bank go bust? Attention turned to the most likely victims, the five Wall Street broker–dealers. They had the thinnest cushion of capital to draw on in the event of major losses: indeed, many of them had set up or bought subprime mortgage broking businesses and were directly exposed. Unlike Citigroup or UBS, which were diversified commercial banks, the pure Wall Street banks had no other forms of business to fall back on, and no savers.

But, yet again, there was denial. On 11 March the chairman of the SEC, Christopher Cox, who regulated the big five under a voluntary agreement, told the press: 'We have a good deal of comfort about the capital cushions at these firms at the moment.'[8]

On Friday 17 March Bear Stearns' shares collapsed by 50 per cent, prompting the Fed to engineer its bailout and takeover by JP Morgan, and creating the 'moral hazard' problem that haunted policymakers during the summer of 2008.

At the time of writing, Bloomberg's index of write-downs stood at $965 billion.[9] It lists fifty banks that have lost more than £1 billion in the crisis. The top ten losers include not just the Wall Street bankers Merrill Lynch and Morgan Stanley, but also the big, diversified banks. Citigroup, Wachovia and Washington Mutual all declared losses in excess of $45 billion, with more to come, and together with Merrill and UBS they form an elite 'top five'. Of the next five, only Morgan Stanley was a pure invest-ment bank: JP Morgan, Bank of America, the British-listed HSBC and the German IKB make up the numbers. Lehman and Bear Stearns declared much smaller losses, but then again, they lost everything and disappeared. Goldman Sachs, whose fund managers had bet that subprime would collapse and pulled their money out in time, survived with relatively minor losses.

But economists believe there is much destroyed capital still to be worked through the intestines of the system and deposited as junk. Nouriel Roubini of the Stern Business School believes that, out of an estimated $10 trillion worth of troubled, toxic or otherwise tainted loans on the planet, $2 trillion will have to be written off. Thus, by early 2009, we were about halfway through.[10]

By March 2008 only the two big, state-backed mortgage lenders in the US, Fannie Mae and Freddie Mac, were issuing serious amounts of credit. They had tightened their loan criteria and were now responsible for nearly all the securitised debt issued in the first half of 2008.

It was the Bear Stearns collapse and bailout the same month that began the slide towards the meltdown. Bear Stearns caused a new, mini credit crunch to ripple through the markets in spring and summer 2008. In June 2008 retail banks all over the world began summarily withdrawing credit to small businesses and drawing in their credit card offers. But to understand the final sequence of events that triggered the meltdown we have to factor in the last of the big financial manias.

The commodities bubble

Between August 2007 and September 2008 the price of every tradable commodity on earth went crazy. Oil had already doubled in the years since the Iraq war. Now it would double again, hitting a headline figure of $147 a barrel on 11 July 2008. And it was not only oil. Rice had doubled in price in the year to March 2008.[11] In the same period gold went from $650 an ounce to more than $1,000. The Dow Jones AIG Commodity Index – which includes everything from aluminium to zinc via 'lean hogs' and sugar – grew from 165 in the summer of 2007 to 240 in March 2008.

The commodities spike of 2007–8 was driven partly by the previous round of oil price rises: oil contributes to the price of food, transport and lots of other stuff as well. It was also the result of rising Chinese demand: when I visited China in March 2008, I found there was an under-reported shortage of soya and cooking oil, and above all pork (lean or not), which had sent wholesale prices up 60 per cent. In a market outside Shanghai I found myself surrounded by angry butchers. 'Tell us why', one shouted, 'our profits are being wiped out by the rising price of pork?' 'You journalists should launch an investigation!' another demanded. Their total lack of restraint in front of a Western news crew told the whole story.

But as well as these real-world factors, there was also speculation on a huge and sudden scale. The total value of commodity futures contracts rocketed from under $2 trillion in 2004 to $9 trillion in 2007.[12] The number of commodity futures transactions rose from 150 million a year in 2005 to 450 million in 2007. Zinc, coffee, sugar, aluminium, cattle – you name it: it was all traded with global gusto from the summer of 2007 until the crash of 2008.

What had caused this sudden rush of speculative capital into commodities? Hedge funds were certainly responsible for some of it. As the housing market crash gathered pace, those who could move their money out of structured finance did so. In 2003 there were just twenty-eight hedge funds in the world making money out of commodity speculation. By 2007 this number had swelled to 310, and to 450 by 2008.[13] But that was only half the story.

An American hedge fund manager called Michael Masters spilled the beans about what was happening: in May 2008 he testified that the price of oil could be halved if speculation were banned. He produced graphs to show that the spike in commodity prices was being driven by a new kind of speculator: pension funds, governments and other big institutions. They had seen the commodities market rise and were advised – by who else but the investment banks? – to pile in. But instead of traditional speculation – buying to sell again quickly – they simply bought into the commodity indexes and then held onto them. That is what pension funds do: invest for the long term. But if you buy and hold onto wheat, rice and soya, somebody else is going to starve. To give a sense of the scale of this big-investor speculative rush, the money invested into the commodity indexes grew by a staggering 2,500 per cent, from around $10 billion in 2002 to $250 billion by March 2008.

Masters showed that, as with almost everything else, it was the deregulation of investment banking that was the problem. A 1936 law had limited the size of banks' speculative positions in commodities, but in 1991 Wall Street had been granted an exemption. 'Think about it this way', Masters railed:

> If Wall Street concocted a scheme whereby investors bought large amounts of pharmaceutical drugs and medical devices in order to profit from the resulting increase in prices, making these essential items unaffordable to sick and dying people, society would be justly outraged. Why is there not outrage over the fact that Americans must pay drastically more to feed their families, fuel their cars, and heat their homes?[14]

But there was outrage – and not only in America. Food riots swept West Africa, then Haiti, Morocco, Bangladesh and Egypt, where a mass strike closed the industrial city of Mahalla over the price of bread. In April 2008 the *Economist* summed up the effect of what the UN was calling a 'silent tsunami':

> The middle classes in poor countries are giving up health care and cutting out meat so they can eat three meals a day. The middling poor, those on $2 a day, are pulling children from school and cutting back on vegetables so they can still afford rice. Those on $1 a day are cutting back on meat, vegetables

and one or two meals, so they can afford one bowl. The desperate − those on 50 cents a day − face disaster.[15]

Yet the us commodity futures regulator was unconvinced that the price rises were caused by speculation: 'There is little economic evidence to demonstrate that prices are being systematically driven by speculators in these markets. Price levels . . . are being driven by powerful fundamental economic forces and the laws of supply and demand.'[16]

Strange, then, that from a peak of 238 in July 2008, the Dow Jones AIG Commodity Index would plummet to 122 by October; that the value of Dow's food index would halve in the same period; that the price of aluminium would fall from $93 to $51; that sugar would halve in price; that wheat and crude oil would both lose two-thirds of their market price − all in the space of the few months after commodities peaked. Had 'powerful fundamental economic forces' really changed so much in such a short space of time?

Certainly, by the autumn of 2008 the futures market for commodities was reflecting the expected onset of recession. But it is also clear that billions of dollars were pulled out of the commodities markets as the meltdown of September–October forced both hedge funds and large institutions to 'deleverage' − that is, to call in and pay back the loans that had been fuelling one speculative bubble after another.

The bursting of the commodities bubble was met with a deafening silence from regulators, politicians and journalists, who claimed it was all down to supply and demand. They had blamed everything, from the growth of China, to the virulence of wheat field pests and the intransigence of OPEC. They were wrong on all counts.

The legacy of the commodities mania was acute starvation in villages across the developing world, and acute disorientation among Western policymakers. The rise in commodity prices fed through into global inflation, which by the spring of 2008 had begun to take off, as factories, farms and petrol stations passed on increased raw material prices. Meanwhile the rise in petrol and home energy prices had depressed spending power, helping push the world towards recession. Faced with a worsening recession and tighter credit, the textbook advises cutting interest rates; but if you are faced with rampant inflation, the same textbook advises raising interest rates. For six months policymakers on both sides of the Atlantic split the difference. They did nothing.

The central banks flounder

At the point the credit freeze began in August 2007, central banks had been raising interest rates or holding them high to restrain inflation. In the US the cost of borrowing money was officially 5.25 per cent; in the UK it had been raised to 5.75 per cent in July; the European Central Bank had raised rates to 4 per cent the previous April. In Japan, where rates stood at 0.5 per cent on account of the country's scant growth since the 1990s, the central bank was also on the verge of a rate increase.

Once the freeze happened the central banks responded with rapid and repeated attempts to pump money into the banking system: in excess of $200 billion on the first day, followed by – in the case of the Fed and the ECB – rapid changes in the quality of collateral they would accept in return for short-term loans. These multi-billion-dollar liquidity injections, it should be stressed, were not bailouts: they are the central bank's equivalent of filling the ATM when it's empty.

However, both the ECB and the Bank of England were reluctant to cut interest rates. As the commodities bubble reached its peak in July 2008, the ECB actually hiked rates to 4.25 per cent. The Bank of England cut interest rates only once between September 2007 and September 2008, and only agreed to give UK banks systematic access to short-term loans in April 2008.

Globally there was a total lack of coordination. In each case the central banks' decisions were driven by their pre-existing policy stance. Bernanke at the Fed had made his career out of criticising the 'tight money' policy of 1929, so he threw money at the banking system and interest-rate cuts at the general public. Faced with the tricky task of managing fifteen eurozone economies, some highly inflationary, the European Central Bank kept rates high. But the ECB compensated by injecting short-term money into the banks – repeatedly and to the tune of tens of billions. The Bank of England simply put its head down and fought inflation, even as UK economic growth ground to a halt in spring 2008.

Denial was built into the politicians' response because so many of them had reputations to lose. The European Commission had championed financial deregulation as part of the creation of the eurozone; just six weeks before the freeze-up, Gordon Brown had hailed the deregulation of British banking as 'an era that history will record as the beginning of a new golden age'.[17]

Henry Paulson was, as we now know, 'shocked' at the state of US banking regulation. But, while chief executive of Goldman Sachs, he had led a delegation of the big five banking bosses to the SEC on 28 August 2004 to request a change in the law regarding the ratio of debt to capital they were required to hold. This ratio had been 12/1; now it was relaxed to 40/1. This major change in banking regulation was agreed at a fifty-five-minute public hearing that was neither attended nor reported by any major news outlet at the time. Had the old capital restrictions been in place, it is unlikely that any of the Wall Street banks could have built up toxic debts on the scale that eventually sank them.[18]

Under the August 2004 agreement the SEC assigned just seven people to monitor Wall Street's combined assets of $4 trillion. After March 2007 there was no director in charge of the monitoring office, which had not completed a single inspection at an investment bank in the eighteen months prior to the meltdown.[19]

Of all the governments, America's was the most proactive during the thirteen months of the credit freeze. Interest rates were slashed to 2 per cent; tens of billions of dollars were injected overnight into the credit system; and there was rapid bipartisan agreement on a $140 billion tax cut to stimulate the US economy. But the US government seemed blind to the need for active regulation. Once you understand its guiding ideology, this is not a contradiction. Cheap money was a free-market solution to save the free market. What the policymakers could not contemplate, right until the end, was any solution that encroached on the sovereignty of market forces.

The failure of market-led solutions

The thirteen-month credit freeze had been, on any measure, the biggest financial accident in the lifetime of those who lived through it. The astonishing surge in commodity prices – with oil at $150 a barrel and the bottom billion of the world's population missing regular meals – may go down in history as the first truly global economic disaster. Yet both these events originated in parts of the financial system that were impenetrable to public scrutiny.

Consider the amount of so-called 'disclosure' in the equities market: there are two US-based financial news channels; many rolling news channels fill airtime with stock-market updates; there is Yahoo! Finance, Bloomberg.com and ADVFN.com. On top of this there are analysts who have the right to demand meetings with company finance directors; there are laws forbidding the use of inside information on the markets; there are quarterly results. All this to track the shares of 46,000 publicly listed companies worth, before the slump, about $63 trillion.

Yet for the $58 trillion market in credit default swaps there is no regulator, no public information, no exchange. Two-and-a-quarter trillion dollars is invested in hedge funds, over half of which is based in barely regulated and impenetrable offshore tax havens, the Cayman Islands being the bolt-hole of choice. Four trillion dollars of Wall Street bank assets were overseen by a voluntary agreement policed by seven people, with no manager in charge.

Transparency is supposed to be at the heart of the Anglo-Saxon model, and the source of its strength. Transparency is what was preached by the investment bankers in the 1980s as they fanned out from Manhattan to London, Geneva, Hong Kong and Shanghai. Yet in the shadow banking system, which they built in less than seven years, there was no transparency whatsoever.

And in the crucial thirteen months after August 2007 this lack of transparency would make it impossible for the usual anti-crisis mechanisms to work. All the billions of central banking dollars pumped into the system overnight were as effective as blood transfusions on a patient with unstaunched arterial bleeding. And as fast as new capital was poured in from Asia and the Middle East, it would shrink in value, taking the crisis global.

For banks, once bad debts are written off on such a massive scale, there is an urgent need for capital. Hence, those facing the biggest losses began to go in search of new money from cash-rich investors. This is called 'recapitalisation', and as we now know it was the only circuit-breaker that stood a chance of ending the crisis. The traditional way of doing this was to go to the stock markets, dilute the value of existing shares, and issue new ones. This is called a rights issue.

In April 2008, a slew of British banks made massive debt write-downs and went to the markets to raise more capital. The first in the queue, Royal Bank of Scotland, raised £12 billion; HBOS, another giant in trouble, tried to raise £4 billion but failed; Barclays dithered and eventually had to place a rights issue not with its existing shareholders but with the government of Qatar and a major Japanese bank. Bradford & Bingley, a smaller mortgage bank that had fuelled a buy-to-let boom using securitised debt, tried to raise just £400 million – but this flopped. The problem was, while they were trying to convince new share-holders to pump money in, the existing shares were rapidly losing value. By the time RBS was bailed out by the British government, it was only worth £12 billion: those who had put money in just six months before had seen its value shrink by half.

In the US, the big banks went down a different route: they sold huge stakes direct to foreign investors, governments and pension funds. In January 2008 Merrill Lynch sold chunks of itself to Singapore, Kuwait and a Japanese bank; Citigroup sold stakes to Kuwait, Saudi Arabia and the State of New Jersey; Morgan Stanley sold a chunk of itself to the Chinese government. These were, in retrospect, bum deals for the new investors. Citigroup's shares were valued at $130 billion in January 2007; ten months later they were worth just $20 billion. Merrill's new investors saw much of their money wiped out when the bank was sold to Bank of America on the weekend of the meltdown. Lehman's attempt to sell itself to the Korean Development Bank famously failed because that country's regulator demanded too much scrutiny, and because Dick Fuld demanded too high a price. By September 2008, putting new money into most American banks looked like financial suicide: the opaque nature of the system they were embroiled in made them impossible to value at all. And there was another problem created by the shadow banking system: it meant the repeated short-term cash injections by central banks did not work, and that interest rate cuts had only a limited impact. The normal transmission mechanisms for central bank intervention were not working.

On the eve of the credit freeze, investment banks were holding 25 per cent of their assets as overnight loans.[20] When lending froze, this money evaporated. But when central banks pumped money into the system overnight, all this did was replace that 25 per cent; it did not persuade banks to start lending to each other again. Likewise, cutting the interest rate on short-term loans to banks and extending the repayment period failed to thaw the lending freeze.

Only on 12 December 2007, when the Federal Reserve allowed banks to borrow up to $100 billion from it anonymously, did a thaw begin. This prompted the Fed to ignore its own rule-book and begin swapping near-worthless bank debts for crisp, new dollars. By March the Fed had committed about half of its own reserves to the banking system on these terms, but still the crisis would not abate. Eventually, against every rule in the book, it was forced to lend direct to Bear Stearns to facilitate the takeover by JP Morgan.

The Fed's action has been hailed as 'creative': certainly the crisis would have worsened quicker if it had not acted. But in the process it proved three things. First, the traditional concept of the central bank as 'lender of last resort' was outmoded: it had become lender of first resort. Second, the sheer complexity and shadiness of the off–balance sheet banking system had weakened the central banks' ability to stabilise the markets. Third — and quietly, because almost nobody outside banking understood what was going on — the US banking system had moved a stage closer to state capitalism.

From freeze to meltdown

As summer turned to autumn in 2008 there was rising inflation, not just in the developed world but in the emerging markets. There was exhaustion after repeated injections of cash into the banking system: Mervyn King told UK banks to start preparing for the end of the emergency liquidity scheme he had introduced. There were recriminations over the moral hazard injected by the Bear Stearns bailout, and a growing frustration at Wall Street's failure to put itself in order. There was growing anecdotal evidence that recession had started.

Growth statistics take between three and six months to solidify, giving the world's finance ministers a whole half-year to avoid using the word recession. It is now clear that the UK fell into recession in July 2008. The eurozone had actually entered recession in April 2008.[21] In the US, where consumption was boosted by a massive emergency tax rebate, the onset of recession was delayed until the fourth quarter. Japan's economy had begun contracting in March.

The stock markets, which had made a final and irrational surge in October 2007, had begun to factor in the possibility of recession early in 2008. A global risk index invented by analysts at Dresdner Kleinwort began to capture the takeoff of the crisis after Bear Stearns: it measures the level of risk in stock markets, foreign exchange markets, commodities, and interest rates, as well as credit. After the Bear Stearns rescue this volatility refused to fall back, driven by stock-market losses and foreign-exchange volatility.

In July Fannie Mae and Freddie Mac, two US government-backed mortgage lenders that had become heavily exposed to the US subprime collapse, were given emergency funding by the Fed. Since a financial crisis wiped out many mortgage lenders in the 1980s, Fannie and Freddie had become the main originators of mortgage lending. In addition, during the credit freeze they had become the only institutions able to carry on issuing structured finance loans. Their collapse would have wiped out the mortgage industry and many banks; but even now the full scale of the crisis was still not evident. Fannie and Freddie had always been part-nationalised: the government bailout simply ended a necessary fiction of independence.

Meanwhile, rumours began to circulate about Lehman Brothers. The bank had sacked its chief financial officer and chief operating officer, closed itself to new mortgage business and was trying to sell itself to the Koreans.

On 7 September, Fannie and Freddie were seized by the US government, their managements sacked and their shareholders effectively wiped out. They had run out of money. The Chinese government had dropped a heavy hint that, unless the US government bailed them out, there would be a run on the dollar: China's foreign exchange reserves were highly exposed to bonds issued by Fannie and Freddie.

The Fannie-and-Freddie bailout was shocking but decisive action. Yet it seemed to increase moral hazard. Now Paulson had intervened to save not just Bear Stearns but two giant institutions whose management had been repeatedly criticised for their accounting practices. The impression was developing that Paulson would, basically, save anybody.

Two days later, the Lehman crisis began. After a day covering Alistair Darling's fractious appearance at the Trades Union Congress, I came into the TV studio to discover that Lehman's shares had fallen by 45 per cent in the last few hours of trading. I frantically got ready to break into the programme live, which involved interrupting a tetchy discussion about a nineteenth-century Catholic theologian and his gay lover. 'From God to Mammon,' I ventured, as a confused clergyman was cut off in mid-sentence, 'and Mammon is in trouble.'

7. Helping Is Futile

The Life and Death of Neoliberal Ideology

'I HAVE FOUND A FLAW. I don't know how significant or permanent it is. But I have been very distressed by that fact.' The scene was a House Committee session in Washington, 23 October 2008. The speaker was Alan Greenspan: Bernanke's mentor, Gordon Brown's adviser, former chairman of the Federal Reserve and the prophet of deregulation. The admission electrified thousands of traders, economists and politicians watching on the internet: so much so that markets began to slide. The chairman pressed him: 'You found that your view of the world, your ideology, was not right – it was not working?' Greenspan answered: 'Absolutely, precisely. You know, that's precisely the reason I was shocked, because I have been going for forty years or more with very considerable evidence that it was working exceptionally well.'[1]

Greenspan had repeatedly claimed that self-regulation was the only basis for a modern financial system; that, far from being a danger, the aggressive pursuit of self-interest by bankers was the most effective self-defence mechanism of the market system. Regulators could never know more than the two participants in any deal, so they could never effectively police the system better than the bankers themselves. But now he had found 'a flaw in the model that I perceived is the critical functioning structure of how the world worked':

> Those of us who have looked to the self-interest of lending institutions to protect shareholders' equity, myself especially, are in a state of shocked disbelief . . . I made a mistake in presuming that the self-interest of banks and others was such

that they were best capable of protecting their own share-holders.[2]

If 15 September 2008 marked the end of the age of greed, Greenspan's frank admission was a signal moment for neo-liberalism, the ideology that has shaped the era.

To understand why, we need to use the word ideology in the sociological sense: a set of ideas that justifies the economic dom-inance of a ruling group; which describes experience accurately enough for the mass of people to accept it; which is propagated through the ruling group's control of the media and education; but which is, on examination, a collection of secrets, superstitions and non-sequiturs. Neoliberalism, like all ideologies, needs to be under-stood exactly as it wishes to *avoid* being understood: as the product of history. And that history starts with a train journey.

Lord of the Rings for capitalists

She is young, beautiful, gaunt, pissed off. Staring out of the window of a railway carriage sometime in the 1930s, 'collar raised to the slanting brim of her hat', she would, if portrayed on celluloid, have to be played by her idol Greta Garbo. She is Ayn Rand, an émigré Russian writer, and what she is pissed off with is Roosevelt's New Deal, which has put the state at the centre of American capitalism, making her novel about the evils of state intervention unpublishable.

The New Deal was about something more than economics: it was driven by mass dissatisfaction and a desire for social justice. Rand would have heard Roosevelt insist in March 1933: 'Americans must forswear that conception of the acquisition of wealth which, through excessive profits, creates undue private power over private affairs and, to our misfortune, over public affairs as well.'[3]

Now, fast-forward to 1947. Communism has replaced fascism as the greatest threat to American civilisation, and Rand's novel,

The Fountainhead, has not only found a publisher but has become a film starring Gary Cooper. And she is at work on another book, one that will become as popular with adolescent boys as Tolkien's *Lord of The Rings*, and is destined to become the *Das Kapital* of the American right.

Atlas Shrugged opens with its heroine, Dagny Taggart, on a train flashing through the mid-American night. The language and imagery shimmer with the same metallic futurism as the AIG building. The 'blond and young' brakeman is whistling Richard Halley's Fifth Concerto, filling the carriage with 'a symphony of triumph'. But Halley, like the whole creative cadre of US capitalism, has disappeared: he has skipped off to a valley in Colorado to join a strike by the rich 'against the creed of unearned rewards', led by a mysterious figure named John Galt.

One thousand pages later, following numerous sadomasochistic sex encounters with men resembling Gary Cooper, Dagny joins this uprising of America's downtrodden rich and becomes Galt's lover. At the climax of the novel, in a radio speech running to sixty pages, Galt promises to reconquer America 'with the sign of the dollar as our symbol − the sign of free trade and free minds'. He promises to build a world of 'smokestacks, pipelines, orchards, markets and inviolate homes'. And he concludes with what would become the Randroids' credo: 'I swear − by my life and my love of it − that I will never live for the sake of another man, nor ask another man to live for mine'.[4]

This is the main tenet of the ideology Alan Greenspan will admit to be 'flawed' fifty years after the novel's publication: self-interest, not just as the guiding principle of commerce, but as the replacement for the state and regulation. It's an idea as old as Adam Smith (as long as you ignore half of his writings). But in Rand's doctrine it is given a sharpened edge. Not only is greed good, but all attempts to be moral are bad: they hamper greed, which is the driving mechanism of order. If you believe self-interest not only makes for an effective market but is a better policeman than the state, then moralism makes the policeman soft. 'Since childhood, you have been hiding the guilty secret that you feel no desire to be moral', Galt harangues America's capitalists in *Atlas Shrugged*; 'Accept the fact that the achievement of your happiness is the only moral purpose of your life . . . As a basic step of self-esteem learn to treat as the mark of a cannibal any man's *demand* for your help.'[5]

How this celebration of selfishness went from the pages of a fantasy novel to become the guiding economic principle of the world is a story about class. The working class inhabit the pages of *Atlas Shrugged* as insolent, mindless drones. Occasionally you get an idealised worker like the whistling brakeman, his face 'tight and firm, it did not have that look of loose muscles evading the responsibility of a shape, which she had come to expect'.[6] For the rest, however, the workers are depicted as Tolkien depicts the dwarves: untrustworthy, often on the side of wrong, unattractive, dunderheaded, prone to collective acts of futility.

But they are not the worst monsters: the orcs of *Atlas Shrugged* are government bureaucrats, corrupt businessmen, journalists and the intellectuals who accommodate them.

Their collective crime is to squash entrepreneurship in the name of social justice for the workers, with the result that sloth, indolence and greed pervade the capitalism of Rand's dystopia.

But consider the world into which *Atlas Shrugged* was born. It was not a world dominated by strife, stagnation and graft: it was capitalist America approaching the zenith of its power. In 1940, 80,000 people were employed in industrial R&D departments; by 1960 there would be 800,000. Twenty years of Keynesian state intervention in the West produced the rocket, the helicopter, the television, penicillin, nylon, the ballpoint pen, and the mainframe computer.[7] Nor was the real America a world of rampant labour militancy. The Taft–Hartley Act, passed in 1947, placed shackles on union activism that galled militants for decades.

What had disappeared, for sure, was the world of the private inventor. The engineer-as-entrepreneur, tinkering off the side of the desk, was replaced by innovation as an industrial process, just as the one-off genius manager was replaced by the widespread roll-out of scientific management.

Also on the wane was inequality. Between 1947 and 1973 the income of the lowest-paid fifth of American families rose by 116 per cent – faster than any other group. Meanwhile the graph showing the proportion of income going to the top 1 per cent had cratered, from 20 per cent at the time of the Wall Street Crash to about 10 per cent at the time of Pearl Harbor, where it stayed until the Reagan era.[8]

The power of finance capital had declined, too. The Dow Jones Industrial Average, which had measured 352 in 1929, recovered to that price only in 1954, and had only achieved 441 on the day *Atlas Shrugged* came out, 10 October 1957. The proportion of US income generated from stocks and shares fell from 25 per cent on the eve of the Wall Street Crash to 19 per cent in the late 1950s.[9]

America, in other words, achieved the greatest economic boom in history – the most rapid spurt of innovation, the fastest rise in living standards for the majority – all within a heavily state-managed mixed economy. There was bipartisan commitment to managing demand in order to smooth out cycles and sustain growth. Though the rhetoric of social justice died with Roosevelt, the basic project survived the transition from wartime to peacetime. America not only planned its own reconstruction, but also that of Europe and Japan.

One fact about the post-war economic settlement is often forgotten: that it was the outcome of a conscious strategy among trade unions and working-class parties. All across the Allied countries, organised labour had demanded a commitment to the welfare state, union rights and full employment. In return they would ally with right-wing politicians who had in some cases appeased Hitler, and in many cases previously attacked labour rights. After the war, in the defeated Germany, Italy and Japan, strong welfare-state models were actually imposed by the Allies as an insurance policy against the revival of fascism.

To those who lived through the boom, its most obvious downsides were in the sphere of individual liberties: stultifying conservatism, family values, censorship, the McCarthy witch-hunts, institutionalised racism, the untrammelled projection of US military power, the abiding everyday stuffiness.

In that Doris Day era, a book advocating minimal state intervention, belittling organised labour and depicting multi-partner S&M as the route to personal liberation was only going to be popular with a minority, but it was to this minority that Alan Greenspan belonged.

Greenspan met Ayn Rand in 1952, and was one of a small circle allowed to hear her read from the draft of *Atlas Shrugged* at Saturday night séances. Outraged by the *New York Times* book review, which had accused the novel of being 'written out of hate', Greenspan bristled: 'Justice is unrelenting. Creative individuals and undeviating purpose and rationality achieve joy and fulfilment. Parasites who persistently avoid either purpose or reason perish as they should.'[10]

Until 1968 Greenspan remained closely associated with Rand's project. In the pages of her newsletter he railed against the welfare state, income tax and budget deficits, and called for America to return to a 'pure' gold standard, unhampered by the existence of a central bank that could print money:

> The financial policy of the welfare state requires that there be no way for the owners of wealth to protect themselves. This is the shabby secret of the welfare statists' tirades against gold. Deficit spending is simply a scheme for the confiscation of wealth.[11]

At the time he wrote this he was forty years old, and just about to go mainstream as chief domestic policy adviser to Richard Nixon. Though he would abandon much of the dogmatism

that surrounded Rand's 'Objectivist Movement', he would stick
with its central tenets: relentless pursuit of self-interest is the best
guarantee of social good; regulation and state intervention are, as
cures for market failure, 'worse than the disease'. Taking control
of the Federal Reserve in 1987, he would pursue the doctrine of
deregulation under Reagan, Clinton and both presidents Bush,
nominating Bernanke as his heir apparent at the height of the
subprime bubble in 2005.

But to get a man like Greenspan off the letters pages of the
New York Times and into the centre of power would take an
intellectual revolution – and others had driven that.

The monetarist shock

The lineage of neoliberal economics has been well documented.
Friedrich Von Hayek leaves the London School of Economics
for Chicago, where he promotes his free-market doctrines to a
small group including Milton Friedman. Friedman co-authors a
revisionist history of the Depression, identifying the Federal
Reserve as the cause. Running throughout their writings is
the idea that private property and the market are the essential
conditions for freedom. Friedman proclaims:

> Historical evidence speaks with a single voice on the relation
> between political freedom and a free market. I know of no
> example in time or place of a society that has been marked by
> a large measure of political freedom, and that has not also used
> something comparable to a free market to organize the bulk of
> economic activity.[12]

But these are, as yet, voices in the wilderness.

Then, in 1971, two events begin the process by which neoliberal economics comes in from the cold. First, beset by rising
inflation and slowing growth, President Nixon imposes wage
controls and abandons the dollar's convertibility to gold, ending

the fixed exchange rates agreed at Bretton Woods in 1944. Domestically, Nixon's move is the last hurrah of Keynesianism, and should appal gold-standard purists like Greenspan; but globally it signals the end of the currency framework that made Keynesianism possible. And it is sold as part of a coordinated attack on organised labour.

One week later, Supreme Court judge Lewis Powell sends a secret memorandum to the American Chamber of Commerce demanding an ideological offensive against the campus radicals who are decrying capitalism. Appalled at the puny leverage business holds within the political elite, he warns:

> Political power is necessary; that such power must be assidu-
> ously cultivated; and that when necessary, it must be used
> aggressively and with determination – without embarrassment
> and without the reluctance which has been so characteristic of
> American business.[13]

What worries Powell is the individual liberty and sexual freedom advocated by the New Left: he sees its anti-capitalism as secondary. What is striking is that the neoliberal coalition is born as an alliance of libertarian economists and strict moralist politicians: Rand had celebrated S&M, Friedman wanted to legalise marijuana, but no matter. Under the impetus of the Powell Memorandum, money is collected from right-wing businessmen to launch the neoliberal think tanks that will shape the coming policy change: the Heritage Foundation, the Hoover Institute, the Cato Institute.

But it is not the think tanks that clinch the ideological battle. Keynesianism is killed off by reality. The oil shock of 1973 brings both stagnation and inflation. The Keynesian levers are pulled, but have stopped working. Meanwhile, governments across the world begin to run up massive budget deficits, posing the dilemma: raise taxes or cut the welfare state?

In 1973 the elected socialist government of Salvatore Allende in Chile is overthrown by a CIA-backed military coup, bringing to power General Augusto Pinochet. Naturally, as lifelong fighters for political freedom, both Hayek and Friedman rush to Chile to congratulate the general. Friedman urges Pinochet to inflict a neoliberal economic 'shock' on the economy, even as the wires are sparking on the genitals of tortured political prisoners.[14] Chile becomes the laboratory for the Chicago School: public spending is slashed by 25 per cent, unemployment rockets, the majority of state-owned companies are privatised, together with the pension system.

Next, the economic crisis forces centre-left governments in Britain and the US to adopt the remedies tried out in Chile. The 1976 IMF bailout of Britain forces the Labour government to cut public spending and raise taxes. Then, in the death-throes of the Carter administration, with inflation at 18.5 per cent and the *New York Times* comparing America to the Weimar Republic, Paul Volcker is appointed to run the Federal Reserve.[15] Volcker unleashes the first comprehensive monetary shock on a developed economy, hiking interest rates and forcing banks to hold more money in an attempt to provoke a recession: which is the neoliberal remedy for inflation, high wages and the power of organised labour.

But the architects of neoliberalism have hardly started. In Britain, even before the Labour spending cuts take effect, Friedman disciple Sir Keith Joseph warns that 'monetarism is not enough': 'By itself, the strict and unflinching control of money supply though essential is not enough. We must also have substantial cuts in tax and public spending and bold incentives and encouragements to the wealth creators.'[16]

Thatcher came to power in 1979, Reagan in 1980, both committed to inflicting the monetarist shock as a prelude to wider neoliberal reforms. Both adopted policies that deepened the impact of the recession on industries where organised labour was strongest. Mass unemployment not only broke the resistance of trade unions in the US and Britain, it destroyed in working-class communities immeasurable reserves of what we've come to know as 'social capital'. Reagan and Thatcher each sought symbolic battles with the die-hard sections of the labour movement: Reagan sacked every single striking air-traffic controller and placed their union leaders in chains; Thatcher sent the police to occupy Britain's mining villages during a year-long strike, labelling the miners' union 'the enemy within'.

Neoliberalism in this first phase promised many freedoms: freedom for small businesses from tax and regulation; freedom for cross-border investment. But it was also strikingly allied to social conservatism. The first-phase neoliberal politicians saw the economics as a useful tool in a bigger game – the project to tame organised labour and create a flexible labour market, which by 1989 they had more or less achieved.

Above all they had shattered Keynesian ideology – not only in the universities and the media, but among the millions of ordinary people. Neoliberal politicians propagated individual share ownership, self-employment and mass home ownership even among the poor: you could buy your council flat for a tenth of its real value in Thatcher's Britain.

Then, in 1989, neoliberalism scored its historic triumph: communism collapsed in Eastern Europe. This not only sent Chicago-inspired economists breezing into finance ministries across the continent; it seemed to vindicate the wisdom of the founders of neoliberalism. Both Hayek and his fellow Austrian philosopher Ludwig Von Mises had predicted a chaotic finale for the Stalinist command economy, and now it had come to pass.[17]

Economic freedom and democracy had triumphed together as predicted, and a new era opened: the era of globalisation. Economist John Williamson coined the phrase 'the Washington Consensus', and boiled the policy down to nine bullet-points: balance budgets; end state subsidies; tax the poor more and the rich less; let the market set interest rates; tear down trade barriers; tear down barriers to foreign investment; privatise state-owned industries; abolish as many regulations as possible; and finally, legislate to guarantee property rights.[18]

But neoliberalism would now evolve. It had been a doctrine of class struggle, social conservatism and anti-communism. Now, even as the Washington Consensus was being imposed on the developing world and former communist states, it would be challenged in the centres of power. In response it would morph into a kind of secret religion for the super-rich.

A balance sheet of neoliberalism

We have now had twenty years to judge the impact of neo-liberal economic policies. I will list five obvious negative impacts. First, rising inequality in the developed world. From 1974 to 2004 the income of the poorest fifth of American families, which had doubled in the post-war boom, now grew by just 2.8 per cent.[19] In the UK the share of national income received by the bottom 10 per cent fell from 4.2 per cent in 1979 to 2.7 per cent in 2002.

Second, the replacement of high wages by high debt in the Anglo-Saxon economies. The real wages of the average male US worker are today below what they were in 1979 – and for the poorest 20 per cent, much lower.[20] In 1979 personal household debt was 46 per cent of America's GDP; now it is 98 per cent.[21]

Third came the redistribution of profits from non-financial companies to the finance sector. In 1960s America the pre-tax profits of financial firms made up 14 per cent of corporate profits; now they make up 39 per cent.[22] Most of this profit is not generated from financing productive business: the world's total stock of financial assets is three times as large as global GDP. In 1980, however, it was about equal to GDP.[23] The enhanced power of finance capital has fuelled asset bubbles such as the dotcom, housing and commodity manias of the past decade.

Fourth, the growth of personal and financial insecurity, the destruction of social capital and the resulting rise in crime. If you want data, then the four stark pages of membership graphs at the end of Robert Putnam's *Bowling Alone* show the decline of almost every voluntary association in America during the neo-liberal age.[24] If you prefer qualitative research, just walk the streets of any former industrial town at night. Though contested, it is now mainstream within modern criminology to link rising crime not to poverty directly, but to the two conditions created by neoliberalism: the celebration of material wealth and the breakdown of voluntary social controls associated with traditional working-class communities.[25]

Fifth is the relentless commoditisation of aspects of human life traditionally provided socially: from the privatisation of drinking water that provoked the people of Cochabamba, Bolivia to revolt in the year 2000 to the patent granted to the food giant Monsanto for ordinary Indian chapatti flour in 2003. Both these land grabs were overturned by mass popular campaigns – but they reveal an urge within neoliberalism towards the commercialisation of services and property that were formerly communal, or provided by the state, even where it conflicts with the stated desires of the majority, and the stability of civil society.

But there is also a plus-side to neoliberalism. Since 1992 there has been stability and growth across the OECD countries and beyond, albeit lower than the average growth achieved during the post-war boom years.[26] There has been a marked fall in absolute poverty, with sub-$2-a-day poverty falling by 52 per cent in Asia and 30 per cent in Latin America (albeit rising by 3 per cent in Africa) between 1982 and 2002.[27]

With developing-world inequality, the picture is less clear. Textbook economics states that inequality should fall as national income rises, but then rocket again as countries reach maturity, making a 'U' shape. But the data is inconclusive. Nevertheless, even neoliberalism's critics recognise that, if you measure inequality by pay alone, then inequality has declined as countries have developed.[28]

Though the birth of neoliberalism was accompanied by shocks, the world it produced looked, until now, to be less chaotic. The big fluctuations of GDP that gave rise to the term 'stop-go economy' were smoothed out after 1990. But, as we have seen, that instability did not disappear. It simply moved into the realm of high finance.

In addition there has been a huge movement of humanity from the farm to the factory, and in the last twenty years 200 million people have migrated from the poor world to the rich. As a result, the size of the world's workforce employed by capital has doubled since 1979, to about 3 billion people[29] – which is roughly equal to the number of urban dwellers, though obviously these are not always the same people.[30] It may stun you to realise that there are now also 3.3 billion mobile phone users in the world. This 3 billion is a significant figure: it represents half of the world's population.[31]

Women have been drawn into the workforce on a massive scale: in America women's hourly earnings rose over the same period that median male real wages fell. Access to the financial system has brought rising liquidity. Mortgages and overdrafts for low-paid families in Detroit and Dagenham were real, whatever the macroeconomic outcome. And above all, the musty cultural and institutional barriers that made life a misery for young people in the 1960s and 1970s are largely gone. The flipside of commoditisation has been the decline of dependency and paternalism in social life.

This positive side of the balance sheet has been the source of neoliberalism's strength as an ideology: borrow big-time, negotiate your own salary, duck and dive, migrate if you have to . . . but lock your door at night. And let your hair down. They can treat you like shit at work, but they can't tell you who to sleep with or what time the pubs close anymore. That is the new way of life for the world's workforce. My father's generation, which saw their whole tradition of social solidarity destroyed in the 1980s, could never really accept it, but hundreds of millions of people under the age of forty know nothing else. If you live in a Kenyan slum or a Shenzhen factory, you have seen your life chances rise spectacularly higher than those of your father's generation, even if the reverse is true for the huge new underclass in the slums of the developed world.

Once the destructive phase was over, free-market capitalism's promise to the world was of steady growth, low inflation, rising access to the ownership of capital and property, and, instead of social conservatism, a frenetic liberalism and individualism. The year that marks this turn is 1992. Bill Clinton is elected; Britain begins inflation-targeting; Boris Yeltsin unleashes a neoliberal shock; Deng Xiaoping tours southern China founding the Special Economic Zones and telling the masses that 'to get rich is glorious'. Meanwhile, in an implicit nod to the end of an era, an entire episode of *The Simpsons* is devoted to puncturing the status of Ayn Rand. Maggie is sent to a nursery called the Ayn Rand School for Tots, at which a wall poster proclaims 'Helping Is Futile'.[32]

To fulfil its promise and maintain its ideological grip in a world full of Bart Simpsons, neoliberalism would now have to deliver one thing above all: relentless growth. As we have seen, it was in pursuit of such growth that the bubble economy was created. But even as it delivered growth and easy money, the doctrine was under pressure and had begun to split apart.

The fragmentation of a doctrine

Two economists stand at the centre of the project to 'humanise' free-market capitalism: Jeffrey Sachs and Joseph Stiglitz. Both were insiders revolted by the results of neoliberalism, who turned their fire against the institutions that had promoted it, the International Monetary Fund (IMF) and World Bank.

Sachs worked as an economic hit-man in reform programmes stipulated by the IMF. He designed and implemented the Chilean-style shock that privatised Bolivia's economy after 1985. Then, in 1990, he typed out the plan for Poland's transition to capitalism in a single night. Then he went to Russia to urge Yeltsin to inflict the same shock therapy, hard and fast.

Stiglitz was already a distinguished academic before he joined Bill Clinton's Council of Economic Advisers in 1992. His research had convinced him that markets did not operate 'perfectly', as Adam Smith described, because some participants would always have more information than others. Since he accepted the neoliberal critique of state planning – that it could only end in chaos – Stiglitz outlined what came to be known as the 'third way': strong markets moderated where necessary by an interventionist state. He was also critical of the doctrinaire way in which economists like Sachs had pushed market reforms onto countries lacking the institutions to deal with them.

The event that first concentrated both men's fire on the same target was the Asian financial crisis of 1997. The crisis had been created by a financial bubble and deregulation. But when it waded in to bail out the economies facing meltdown, the IMF insisted on the full Washington Consensus remedy: public spending cuts and high interest rates. If followed, this would push the Asian economies into a deeper recession than the one they were already facing. Furthermore, those that the IMF seemed keenest to bail out were Western companies that were in danger of losing their shirts. Finally, the Fund did not seem very keen to talk about any of it publicly.

Sachs fired off urgent warnings to the press:

> These bailout operations, if handled incorrectly, could end up helping a few dozen international banks to escape losses for risky loans by forcing Asian governments to cover the losses on private transactions that have gone bad. Yet the IMF decisions have been taken without any public debate, comment, or scrutiny.[33]

Stiglitz had by now joined the World Bank as its chief economist. He had been arguing for a moderation of neo-liberalism: less dogma, more case-by-case solutions. Now he saw the dogma inflicted on the Asian economies:

> I saw how the IMF, in tandem with the US Treasury Department, responded. And I was appalled . . . Under such circumstances, I feared, austerity measures would not revive the economies of East Asia – [they] would plunge them into recession or even depression.[34]

Both Sachs and Stiglitz identified dogma and secrecy as the cause of the problem. As economists, they expected the masters of the financial universe simply to listen to their impeccable logic. They would soon discover otherwise. Stiglitz was forced to resign as chief economist, though he remained as a special adviser to the Bank. Exasperated, on the eve of the mass protests taking place at the IMF/World Bank meetings in Washington in April 2000, he warned:

> Next week's meeting of the International Monetary Fund will bring to Washington, DC many of the same demonstrators who trashed the World Trade Organization in Seattle last Fall. They'll say the IMF is arrogant. They'll say the IMF is secretive and insulated from democratic accountability. They'll say the IMF's economic "remedies" often make things worse – turning slowdowns into recessions and recessions into depressions. And they'll have a point.[35]

He was sacked and told to vacate the World Bank's premises. At the same time the Bank's annual *World Development Report*, which had been heavily critical of market fundamentalism, was re-edited on the insistence of the US Treasury, prompting the resignation of its author.[36]

What both Stiglitz and Sachs had run into was the fact – up to now concealed from them, but obvious to thousands of politicians, journalists and activists – that the World Bank and IMF were simply mechanisms that the US was using to impose neo-liberalism on the developing world, and that these mechanisms were part of a wider strategy to maintain its global dominance.

Both men's response was to engage with the alliance of non-governmental organisations that had become active in opposition to neoliberalism. Sachs became an adviser to the debt forgiveness campaign, Jubilee 2000, and led the design of the United Nations Millennium Development Goals. Stiglitz, whose book *Globalisation and Its Discontents* became a bible for the 'fluffy' wing of the anti-globalisation movement, delivered a keynote speech at the World Social Forum in Mumbai in 2004, at the height of the movement's influence.

The two men differ on many issues, but on one they agree: globalisation is good, and needs to be made better by the intervention of benign governments and the activism of civil-society groups. More aid and massive debt write-offs to the poorest countries, combined with capacity-building for demo-cratic government, can make free trade work to the advantage of developing countries. This in turn became the agenda of the 2005 G8 summit, held at Gleneagles in Scotland.

At that summit I observed – from a range so close I could feel the police batons swishing through the air – a Chinook military helicopter disgorge riot cops into a field full of protesters dressed as clowns. The event struck me then as a piece of theatre in which both sides were complicit performers: the state coming on heavy-handed even as it acceded to the key demands of the protest movement; the protesters going through the motions. The protesters attacked the iconic chain-link fence surrounding the summit and tore it down, only to find that it was a 'dummy', placed there for the purpose of being destroyed.

Looking back, the event was symbolic in a bigger way, for nobody within the anti-globalisation movement had much to say at all about the finance sector. Subprime and structured finance were the real time-bombs within the system, yet they were hardly on the agenda of capitalism's most vociferous critics. They were concerned primarily with climate change, third-world poverty and the iniquities of the IMF/World Bank. In this their agenda — if not their solutions — merely mirrored that of the mainstream politicians.

'Third way' politicians certainly wanted a major rethink of the neoliberal agenda on development and debt – but when it comes to the finance sector, they seem to have systematically bought the idea that it was best left undisturbed. The mid 2000s saw them don sackcloth and ashes for the developing world's debt and poverty, but cheering on the creation of a giant, unsustainable asset bubble – which, now it has burst, will bring massive debt and poverty to the developing world.

It was the Clinton and Blair administrations who designed the light-touch banking regulations that unleashed financial mania. It was as if they had a tacit deal with the finance sector: the market would be bent and regulated to achieve different, more 'progressive' social ends than those imagined by the Thatcher–Reagan generation. In return, all regulation would be as light as possible on principle, and the giants of the finance system would be left alone to generate spectacular wealth for themselves. And if the bankers were guided by what seemed to everybody else as a slightly crazy belief in selfishness and aggression, who cared? They had helped create this wonder-world of full employment, with a Starbucks on every corner and a credit-card offer in every letterbox.

The beauty of the mid-decade bubble economy was this cosy confluence of interest between mega-rich financiers, the working poor, and the middle class. The bankers could get richer, quicker: the rapid rise in pre-tax profits among the Wall Street banks in the mid 2000s was directly linked to the rise in subprime issuance. The middle class could get rich through equity withdrawal on their homes, or by joining the buy-to-let boom: by 2006, around 3 per cent of all American consumption was being financed just by re-mortgaging. The working poor, meanwhile, received hundreds of billions of dollars' worth of credit – which they could never pay back. All the historical graphs said the housing market was over-valued; experience told people that the graphs were wrong, and that the ideology was right.

The power elite

To understand the current crisis of neoliberalism, it is important to understand the power elite that has clustered around it. This is not the same as the elite that fought for it. During the Cold War, neoliberalism claimed to be a universal doctrine. The assumption was that market reform was good for everybody. But in the post–Cold War era neoliberalism became increasingly identified with the maintenance and consolidation of America's position as the world's sole hyperpower.

Anthony Lake, an adviser to George H. W. Bush, described this move from a strategy of containment to enlargement:

> During the Cold War, even children understood America's security mission: as they looked at those maps on their schoolroom walls, they knew we were trying to contain the creeping expansion of that big, red blob. Today . . . we might visualize our security mission as promoting the enlargement of the 'blue areas' of market democracies.[37]

The literature on power elites is vast, but as an academic discipline it is not universally respected. The most authoritative text, C. Wright Mills' *The Power Elite*, is indelibly marked by the peculiarities of the 1950s.[38] Meanwhile, in Europe, the study of elites gave way to the study of power itself, which led away from sociology towards psychiatry.

Fortunately, even if it is hard to theorise, the power elite of free-market global capitalism is remarkably easy to describe. Although it looks like a hierarchy, it is in fact a network. At the network's centre are the people who run banks, insurance companies, investment banks and hedge funds, including those who sit on the boards and those who have passed through them at the highest level. The men who met in the New York Federal Reserve on the 12 September 2008 meltdown would deserve a whole circle of their own in any Venn diagram of modern power.

Closely overlapping with this network is the military–diplomatic establishment. Hank Greenberg's AIG board provides probably the purest case study: it included former UN Ambassador Richard Holbrooke, former defence secretary William Cohen, and former trade representative Carla Hills, together with former secretary of state Henry Kissinger. 'They were there for Hank,' Greenberg's former aide recalls, 'no other reason. Just to add prestige to his board.'[39]

Another tight circle comprises those companies in the energy and civil engineering businesses that have benefited from marketisation at home and US foreign policy abroad. Dick Cheney chaired the controversial services corporation Halliburton; Halliburton built the Enron Field stadium in Houston; Enron money paid not only for the Bush/Cheney campaign in 2000, but also for the 'Florida Recount Fight Fund' when the election result was disputed; Enron boss Ken Lay met Cheney six times in the run-up to the publication of the administration's National Energy Policy, which included seventeen specific measures requested by Enron.[40]

If this power elite sounds close to the list of givers, beneficiaries and supporters of the Bush administration, that is because Bush happened to be in power at the time, and America is at the centre of the universe of the global economy. The transition to the Obama presidency shows that both individuals and institutions within the power elite provide continuity beyond electoral cycles and across borders. Alan Greenspan was a case in point, working for four presidents, while Greenberg's AIG board likewise spanned both Democrat and Republican inner circles.

In his exposé of the neoliberal power elite, David Rothkopf calls them a 'superclass', describing a permeable group of around 6,000 businessmen, politicians and officials.[41] Rothkopf contends that privatisation combined with globalisation and the weakening of the nation state has produced 'a marked shift from public to private power'. This makes the networked character of the modern elite more important than, say, for the elite that ruled Brezhnev's Russia, or Wilson's Britain, where formal hierarchies were prevalent. Rothkopf points out that subscribing to the neo-liberal idea-set has been one of the pass keys to entry into this group.

The point about this elite is that it exercises power through networks that are subtle and interconnected. The Council on Foreign Relations (CFR) is a case in point. For years this Democrat-leaning think tank was chaired by AIG's Hank Greenberg: both of Greenberg's AIG board members, Carla Hills and Richard Holbrooke, also sit on the board of the CFR. This has turned the CFR into something of a magnet for the rising stars of Wall Street. 'It's becoming a prestigious, hot-ticket kind of thing', analyst Lisa Greenberg told Bloomberg.com in 2005. She'd joined while working at Goldman Sachs. 'There is a patina related to it – it's almost like you are stamped "smart".'[42]

The Council's international advisory board includes two of the top twenty global billionaires: Indian industrialist Mukesh Ambani and Russian oligarch Mikhail Fridman. Of Ambani's company, Reliance Industries, one New Delhi lobbyist says: 'Everyone is trying to bend the rules: they just do it better, with a combination of understanding, relationships and a bit of cash.'[43] (Ambani rejects the cash part of the accusation.) Fridman, meanwhile, is the man who controversially seized control of British Petroleum's joint venture with TNK in 2008, with the help of the Russian government.

Clearly, the CFR does not exert power directly: it functions as a network rather than a hierarchy, making informal connections that advance neoliberal policies and American power in tandem. To take just one example, in 2003 Stephen Brock, a mid-ranking commander in the US Navy serving in the Pacific, 'connected with' a fellow CFR member who happened to be working for Goldman Sachs in Hong Kong. The two arranged lunch for their respective bosses: Robert Willard, commander of the US Seventh Fleet, and Richard Gnodde, Goldman's Asia boss. 'We compared our security concerns as a fleet and their views based on the security of their investments', Brock told reporters.[44]

Gnodde's fellow Goldman director, Stephen Friedman, is also a director of the CFR – and, of course, former Goldman CEO Hank Paulson is also a member. In fact, any rudimentary power analysis would show Goldman Sachs, the Council on Foreign Relations and the US Federal government to be highly interconnected, both in personnel and objectives.

With an up-to-date copy of *Who's Who* and some decent offline intelligence, you could map the whole network of the neoliberal elite, starting with the Washington think-tanks, before moving to the less transparent networks of the Group of Thirty and the Bilderberg Group.

None of these linkages are corrupt. They are seen as normal within the power elite. What neoliberalism as an ideology does is to mask their significance. It presents free-market capitalism as a system of transparency and accountability, with quarterly analyst reports, credit ratings, conference calls, and above all the digitally driven market to keep everything straight.

According to the ideology, just as every American has the opportunity to become president, so a meeting between the commander of the US Pacific Fleet and the boss of Goldman Sachs has no greater status than, say, a conversation between two horseracing aficionados in the Roxy Delicatessen, Times Square. In reality it is different: if it were not for the gushing feature article on Bloomberg.com about the CFR becoming the new hot ticket for stock analysts, the Pacific Fleet meeting would never have been public knowledge.

This is how closely neoliberalism became bound up with a tight, interlocking network of bankers, politicians and military-related companies. That is not to say these people and institutions never disagree. Indeed, as Robert Reich has pointed out, most of the lobbying money that swills through Washington is spent by one company or sector lobbying for its own interest against a rival company or sector.[45] Here again, the appearance of competition and rational self-interest masks the effective rule of corporate power over civil society, and an exclusive kind of corporate power at that.

By the final year of the Bush administration, neoliberalism was looking too closely aligned for comfort with specific people and policies. It had portrayed itself as a universal doctrine, guiding the hand of Jiang Zemin in China, John Howard in Austrialia, Mwai Kibaki in Kenya; but it increasingly looked like an offshoot of US foreign policy and a lever for Wall Street.

During the Asian financial crisis of 1997 it was only countries like Malaysia and South Korea that refused to take the medicine. Ten years on, following the meltdown and with the rapid emergence of India and China, the moral authority of the neoliberal business elite has been shattered by the events of 2008. Basically, whatever you think about it, the neoliberal experiment is over.

As Richard Wachman wrote during the first week of the meltdown: 'The crisis has underlined the fact that US power is ebbing away and that free market fundamentalism has become an ideology that is beginning to look as outdated as the Leninist doctrine of democratic centralism'.[46]

So what comes after? History tells us that ideologies representing the interests of serious segments of business, nations or classes do not simply die. They have to be replaced by something more coherent.

But this will be difficult for the current generation of Western political leaders. No mainstream G7 politician has yet outlined a plan that goes beyond tinkering with the broken mechanisms of neoliberal finance. Obama railed against 'trickledown economics' and promised to clear out the whole elite who had promoted it. Then he appointed Tim Geithner as his Treasury Secretary and Larry Summers as his chief economic adviser: Geithner had been Bernanke's right-hand man; Summers had proclaimed a new century of deregulation on the day Glass–Steagall was repealed.

Neoliberalism fought its way to dominance against the power of the Keynesian establishment: against Nixon, Carter, Callaghan; against the Marxist and Keynesian influence in academia. Above all it was a doctrine of conflict and vision. To suggest to the generation of steelworkers I met during the 1980 British steel strike that the Soviet Union would one day disappear, that effective trade unionism could be outlawed, that the Labour Party would abolish Clause 4 of its constitution, would quite simply have made them laugh. But such was the vision of the neoliberals.

The problem for neoliberalism's critics, for now, is that they have no coherent world view to take its place. There are elements of such a world view, scattered within the writings of neo-Keynesians, the anti-globalisation left and the Stiglitz critique of neoliberalism. But so far these forces have failed to coalesce around any concrete programme in the face of the crisis. Indeed, two decades of powerlessness have inculcated a profound lack of ambition upon capitalism's critics. They have become satisfied with small-scale, granular and horizontalist projects, like the 'utopian' socialists of the early nineteenth century. Their stated aim, for the best part of two decades, has been to live 'despite capitalism'. Organised labour, meanwhile, is in a state of weakness and fragmentation.

So we're at a point of hiatus in history. It's not unique. It took three years of economic collapse after 1929 for FDR to emerge with a coherent alternative to laissez faire, and another two after that for the New Deal to take on its radical, social dimension. By then, it is worth remembering, Keynesian strategies had been adopted by both the left and the far right.

Right now, with the world's politicians still in crisis mode, it would be foolish to predict events. What seems certain, however, is that the search for an alternative to neoliberalism is on.

8. The Disrupted Wave

On the Eve of Depression or a New Long Upswing?

R AINCLOUDS GLOWER OVER Pennsylvania Avenue. Groups of rival protesters assemble under the gaze of snipers. It's 15 November 2008, and I'm in Washington for the G20 Summit. Around me there are Tibetans with rainbow flags, Falun Gong supporters with photos of victims tortured by the Chinese state; facing them across the road is the usual claque of Chinese Communist students carrying neat red flags, protesting against the other protesters. Elbowing their way through it all are some women protesting against the ban on gay marriage. Wrapped in purple sashes saying 'Bride To Be', they push to the edge of the pavement to witness the birth of a new world order.

As the sky darkens and rain spatters across the tarmac, a siren screams. Motorcycle cops vroom out of the side streets. Behind them is the fifteen-vehicle convoy of the Russian president, Dmitry Medvedev. From the open door of a Humvee, one of the armed guards uses his mobile phone to film us all: the lesbians, Communists, Buddhists, and journalists. Next come EU president José Manuel Barroso, Indian premier Manmohan Singh, Nestor Kirchner of Argentina, Silvio Berlusconi of Italy. There is more raw political power on this street than ever assembled in one place. But the world's leaders are here because the economic crisis has rendered them powerless.

'What's going on?' a passing American tourist asks. 'It's the G20', I answer. His face goes as blank as George W. Bush's face reportedly went when somebody first said there was going to be a G20 summit. Normally the summits that matter are called by the G8: the seven powerful developed countries plus Russia. But the scale of this crisis is too great. China, India and Brazil, as well as Russia, will have to play a central part in the rescue mission, and they have come to Washington as equals, not spectators.

At the summit there was just time for each leader to read out a fifteen-minute statement. They issued a detailed communiqué, staged more press conferences than the media could handle – and decided nothing. The whole event was a lesson in the inefficacy of politics in the face of economics. But the global leaders in their bullet-proof bubble were not the only ones gripped by inertia.

One of the most startling features of that weekend was the absence of significant protests. At the 1999 G8 summit in Seattle, there had been tens of thousands of people; at Prague, Cancún and Gleneagles, there had been a vibrant movement of eco-warriors, trade unionists and aid activists. Washington 2008 was different. 'We can't figure out why there are no protests', one NGO leader told me. 'Maybe it's because everything's focused on the gay marriage ban, maybe time was just too short.'

I suggest a different explanation: at this point most politically active people in the world were in denial about the scale of the crisis. They stuck to their old obsessions. The Chinese and Tibetan protesters faced off over their usual issues. Likewise, the NGO movement. In the same month that half a million American workers would lose their jobs, the main focus of the NGO leaflets was 'Don't forget aid to Africa'.

One fact could not be missed. The summit showed the rising economic, diplomatic and ideological power of the countries that stand on the 'plus' side of the global imbalances. From now on countries with capital, growth, trade surpluses and sovereign wealth funds would have increased gravitational pull. And they had arrived in Washington with an implicit message: the irre-sistible march of the Anglo-Saxon model is over. Gravely wounded in its own heartland, neoliberalism would be in no position to lecture Asia about 'crony capitalism', Russia about pipelines, China about democracy, or anybody at all about the virtues of Ayn Rand's *Atlas Shrugged*.

We may look back on the Washington G20 summit as the beginning of an un-American century. To understand how it could pan out, we need to see the financial crisis of 2008 as just one signal of the fundamental change the world is going through.

An information-driven upswing

It is clear, from the sheer level of social and economic upheaval in the world during the last thirty years, that we have lived through the birth of something. Its founding ideology was neoliberalism; its most tangible results were the spread of free markets, globalisation and the dominance of the finance industry. It was achieved through a sharp and conscious break with the social partnership strategies of the post-war years.

But none of these facts can encompass the scale of the transition, because none of them allows for the most fundamental change: that information has become a primary factor of production. The computing power of a 1985 Sinclair Spectrum computer is surpassed by the computing power of my workplace identity tag. Between Nixon and Obama, the number of transistors on an integrated circuit board has grown from 2,300 to 1,000,000,000, doubling every twenty-four months come rain or shine. Half the world's population has a mobile phone. Together, the internet and mobile telephony have altered the pattern of human life, even patterns of human thought.

The impact of information technology has been inadequately theorised. This is unsurprising given that most operational business models are still in the process of adaptation to it. But the information technology revolution is the central fact of the twenty-first century. Its emergence has already disrupted everything from politics to pornography. And, I would argue, it is the driving force behind the arguments that have turned mainstream economics upside down.[1]

One of the problems faced by those trying to explain this new, information-driven economy is that it does not even fit with what their old conversations were about: comparing neoliberalism to the Keynesian era is like comparing a branch of Starbucks to the Apollo spaceship. Thus, early attempts to construct a theory of 'post-Fordism' based on changes in industrial production and mass consumption told only half the story: equally big changes were taking place in the finance system, in human geography, and in trade.

As a result, all attempts to 'define' the economy that is emerging have had to be revised fairly rapidly. Obviously, after September 2008 they will have to be revised again. I am not going to come up with any better theory in this book – but I do want to describe the sharpness of the change we've gone through since 1979.

Think of the various features of economic life that seemed permanent to our parents' generation: the mass production of standardised goods; the stable, predominantly male, manual workforce; graduates as a tiny elite within the workforce; industrial production centred on the G7 countries; the developed countries as front-runners for economic growth; the domestic market as the main sphere for economic decision-making; the state as a major economic player; half the world economy dominated by a system of state ownership and bureaucratic planning; the strong welfare state; land in the Third World mainly farmed by peasants; banks constrained by strict regulations and generally subordinate to industry; the decisive influence of industrial companies on US politics; banking based on face-to-face relationships; computing mainly located in the corporate infrastructure and in universities; expensive analogue telephone systems; fixed exchange rates; the industrialist as hero; hierarchical organisations.

What has replaced all this? The mass production of individualized goods, through a much more decentralised process; the insecure, temporary workforce, often with women as the majority; fewer manual workers and more 'service' and desk-based workers; the emergence of a mass graduate workforce; industrial production distributed across the rapidly developing countries instead of concentrated in the G7; high growth becoming typical in the developing world, not the rich countries; a relatively open, globalised market, with booming international trade; the weakening of the nation-state in the face of a globalised economy; the weakening of the welfare state, and in many countries its replacement by a rising market in social provision; the farming of most land by global agribusiness; the wielding of more power by banks than by industrial corporations; the development of banks into essentially global information networks, with many decisions automated and face-to-face relationships in decline; the ubiquity of standardised and ever cheaper computers; cheap, digital mobile telephony available to half the people on the planet; exchange rates between the main currency blocks that are no longer pegged; the replacement of the industrialist by the entrepreneur as hero; the flourishing of decentralised organisations and the collapse of hierarchical ones.

The most striking thing about this second list is that, without the revolution in information technology, none of it would have been possible. It is too crude to say the silicon chip 'causes' the rise of the free market, globalisation and finance capitalism. But the silicon chip and the internet protocol were surely key to their rapid rise to dominance.

There is consensus among economic historians about the long epochs that capitalism has moved through: the merchant capitalism of the seventeenth and eighteenth centuries; the free-market industrial system of the nineteenth; the monopoly and mass-production system of the twentieth century. If you want to reduce it all to technology, you could sum up the progression as sail, steam and then petroleum.

By the same crude technological measure, we are now in the information age. The challenge is to understand where the 2008 crisis fits into the history of this new, emergent form of capitalism; what the results might be; and what policy responses may emerge once the panic settles and a global recession takes its toll.

Conventional economics is not well suited to answering these questions. Instead, I draw on the works of two unconventional economists, both of whom have fanatical supporters in the hedge fund fraternity and among anti-capitalists: Nikolai Kondratiev and Hyman Minsky.

The Kondratiev wave

Nikolai Kondratiev was a Soviet economist executed in 1938, after eight years in the Gulag, for advocating market socialism. His single most important contribution to economics was an account of the way long periods of growth are followed by long periods of stagnation. He called these 'long cycles'; this got mistranslated as 'long waves', and then converted into the funky appellation 'K-waves' by American investment gurus. These gurus would construct share portfolios to survive the Kondratiev cycle, sold with the assurance that the big K himself was only the latest keeper of a deep, cyclical understanding of history first discovered by the Mayans (I kid you not).

If you skip the mumbo-jumbo and go back to Kondratiev himself, there is a lot of evidence that his basic idea was correct: capitalism moves through roughly fifty-year cycles, in which periods of economic growth are followed by periods of crisis and then depression. This does not invalidate the traditional theory of business cycles lasting between seven and eleven years, but it puts them into a historical context. Until the K-wave theory, there was no systematic attempt to measure patterns of economic growth longer than a business cycle or shorter than an entire epoch.

In Kondratiev's cycle, the upswing period always coincides with the widespread deployment of a key technology: the factory steam engine in the first half of the nineteenth century, railways in the second half, and the combined roll-out of industrial chemicals, the petrol engine and electricity in the early twentieth century. In the theory, each long wave reaches a peak about halfway through, plateaus, and then collapses. During the decline phase interest rates fall – because the supply of capital is bigger than demand for it – and agriculture suffers a prolonged fall in prices, while more power accrues to the banks.

Kondratiev's theory proved more influential with capitalists than with Marxists. Even Marxists like Trotsky, who did not want to shoot him, accused him of seeking economic causes for events that were essentially shaped by external factors, like war, new inventions, the conquest of new colonies, or the expansion of the gold supply. Kondratiev replied that these factors – above all the roll-out of new technology – were not external, but intrinsic to each wave. To use a technical term that economists love, they were endogenous. This is the word that turned Kondratiev's prison sentence into a death sentence. It implies that capitalism always finds new ways to reinvent itself, and that the route to a socially just society does not lie through some kind of 'final crisis'.

Tested against the reality of the past sixty years, Kondratiev's theory looks, at first, startlingly helpful. The upswing phase, the post-war boom, begins in 1949. In the theory, the up-phase always ends with a catastrophic war, born out of the tension and febrility of decades of relentless growth; it also produces an inflationary bubble. This describes pretty accurately the role of the Vietnam War in destabilizing the US economy through inflation, and therefore allows us to place the peak of the so-called 'fourth K-wave' at around 1973. In the theory, the top of the cycle generates a sharp recession: the world recession of 1973–75 was indeed sharp, and led to the adoption of neoliberal policies between this and the 1979–82 recession.

Once we are in the downswing, according to Kondratiev, technological innovation becomes a salient feature:

> During the recession of the long waves, an especially large number of important discoveries and inventions in the tech-

nique of production and communication are made, which, however, are usually applied on a large scale only at the beginning of the next long upswing.[2]

Anybody who lived through the agonising wait for personal computers to revolutionise economic life during the 1980s has experienced exactly this. In the end, however, it was not the computer that laid the basis for the new upswing, but the network. Kevin Kelly's famous 1997 article in *Wired* magazine, which captured the euphoria of the dotcom boom, was right about one thing:

> The grand irony of our times is that the era of computers is over. All the major consequences of stand-alone computers have already taken place. Computers have speeded up our lives a bit, and that's it. In contrast, all the most promising technologies making their debut now are chiefly due to communication between computers.[3]

In the years since that article was written, digital networks have grown dramatically. The number of internet users in the world has grown from 70 million in 1997 to 1.45 billion today.[4] There are now more internet users in Burkina Faso than there were on the globe ten years ago.[5] Mobile telephony is growing even faster. Of the 3.3 billion mobile phone subscribers on the planet in 2007 – double the number in 2002 – half a billion of them were in China, a quarter of a billion in India, and another quarter of a billion in Africa.[6] And these figures represent only the raw data for mass consumption. They say nothing of the scale of robotisation in factories, the digital control of supply chains, the move of entire retail sectors online, and the automation of back-office systems.

If the downswing of the 'fourth K-wave' is measured from the crisis of the mid 1970s through the recessions of the early 1980s and early 1990s, then the widespread global deployment of networked digital devices in the early years of the twenty-first century should signal the start of a fifth long wave of capitalism.

Got your head around Kondratiev's wave theory? Good. But now I am going to disappoint you. Because the most interesting thing about the K-wave is that, though it fits almost exactly what has happened in technology and what happens to the economy up to the mid 1980s, when faced with the reality of the 1990s it falls apart.

K-Wave theory predicts that the downswing ends with a massive financial crisis, a slump caused by overhanging debt, followed by a decade-long recession while that debt is paid off. The theory fits precisely the Long Depression of 1873–86 and the Great Depression of 1929–39. But it does not fit the 1990s. There was some bad stuff in the 1990s: they started with a recession and ended with the Asian crisis of 1997, the Long Term Capital Management scare, a Russian stock-market collapse, and then the dotcom crash of 2000. All this was bad, but there was no global depression. Even if you move the start of the downswing to the year 2000, you still get eight years of uninterrupted growth in the developed world and spectacular progress in Asia.

The second fly in the theoretical ointment is this: if we date the start of the fifth K-wave from the deployment of digital networks and the integration of China into the world market early in the twenty-first century, then the Wall Street meltdown of September 2008, followed by the rapid descent of all major economies into recession, seems to disrupt the pattern completely. The best that can be said – if we want to maintain the theory – is that, instead of a clean turning point, we have a pretty substantial overlap between two cycles.

This, I believe, is exactly what has happened. The explanation for it lies in the collapse of communism, in the rapid emergence of the global imbalances between capital-rich Asia and the debt-driven West, and in the effectiveness of policy tools developed in the early 1990s by central banks.

As a result, the outcome of the 2008 financial crisis remains highly unpredictable: we have an 'end of cycle' crash combined with a technological revolution and the rise of a new kind of capitalism in East Asia. The beauty of Kondratiev's theory lies not in its power to predict, still less in its continuity with Mayan civilisation, but in the fact that it allows us to see a disruption of the wave pattern. Kondratiev helps us understand that, probably for the first time in 200 years, we are – as Dorothy tells Toto in *The Wizard of Oz* – 'not in Kansas anymore'.

Here's why. When Richard Nixon ripped up the Bretton Woods currency agreement in 1971, forcing the world to switch to floating currencies, he created a global system of money with no relationship to precious metals, which was based instead simply on the paper promises of governments. This is called fiat money – money decreed to exist 'by fiat' rather than deriving its value from gold. This change could not prevent the decade of economic crisis that gripped the developed world between 1973 and 1982; indeed, by unleashing inflation, it helped cause crisis. But it could, for the first time, prevent the switch from growth to deflation that K-wave theory said should happen. In fact the ability to print money independent of the gold supply made growth intrinsically more inflationary.

Then a second one-off event came along: the Soviet Union collapsed and China went capitalist by decree, rapidly followed by the marketisation of India after 1991. Suddenly, the global relationship between capital and labour was massively tilted in favour of capital. Instead of 960 million workers in the developed world, plus a few industrial enclaves like South Africa and Brazil, there were an extra 1.5 billion workers for capital to employ, rapidly joined by an extra billion created by the industrialisation of the developing world and population growth. Harvard professor Richard Freeman has estimated that this doubled the ratio of labour to capital in the world, strategically weakening the bargaining power of workers in every country.[7]

Kondratiev, who had pored over the details of gold discoveries in the Yukon to explain the dawn of the second K-wave in 1849, would not have missed the significance of this. New workers, new markets, and a new unlimited supply of money: it was like discovering gold all over again, right at the point where the downturn should have started. This, in turn, allowed governments to develop the policy tools to put an end to economic volatility.

Since the early 1990s governments in the US, the UK and the eurozone pursued inflation-targeting policies designed to smooth out cyclical ups and downs. First they used higher interest rates to stifle inflation, at the cost of imposing lower-than-potential growth; then they used low interest rates to stimulate a debt-driven recovery after the dotcom crash. The flood of cheap goods into the developed world from China and the developing world also helped suppress inflation.

In the wake of the meltdown, policymakers like Gordon Brown and Ben Bernanke have been derided for their claims about this period. Brown hailed 'an end to boom and bust'; Bernanke dubbed it 'The Great Moderation'[8]. But the phenomenon was real. Between 1947 and 1982, the US suffered eight recessions, the last being the worst; between 1982 and 2007 there were just two recessions, both short and shallow. The volatility of GDP after 1990 dropped to about half what it was in the post-war boom.[9] The growth graph of the US over a fifty-year period looks like the temperature chart of a patient who suddenly gets better around about 1992; but if you superimpose a graph of consumer debt on top of it, it's clear what the medicine was.

The politicians' mistake was to believe they had achieved stability by policy alone. Bernanke theorised this explicitly: not structural change, not 'good luck' as represented by the collapse of the Soviet Union, but policy. It is now clear that they were wrong: stability was sustained by the altered power balance between bosses and workers, the deflationary impact of China, and the relentless rise of cheap credit.

Now that the cheap credit model has collapsed, and the deflationary impact of China turns out to be transitory, we are left with just the capital–labour mismatch, which Richard Freeman predicted would take thirty years to play out. All this makes the path of the current crisis highly unpredictable – but one economist did give us the tools both to predict it and resolve it.

The Minsky Moment

Hyman Minsky was an economics professor based at Washington University, St Louis, who died in 1996. He was not shot, or put in a Gulag; he was simply ignored by the policy establishment and treated as crazy. Once you understand his theory, you can see why. He warned: 'The normal functioning of our economy leads to financial trauma and crises, inflation, currency depreciations, unemployment and poverty in the midst of what could be virtually universal affluence – in short . . . financially complex capitalism is inherently flawed.'[10]

Minsky showed that speculative bubbles, and the financial collapses that follow them, are an integral part of modern capitalism. That is, they are not the result of accidents or poor decision-making, but a fundamental and recurrent feature of economic life once you deregulate the finance system. He is mentioned only once in Ben Bernanke's book on the 1930s, in a dismissive footnote. But he stands as a kind of 'anti-Bernanke' in US economics, sharing Bernanke's theory that the finance system can accelerate economic crisis, but not his belief that the era of crisis is over.

Minsky described three types of investment: hedge, speculative and Ponzi. The last is named after the infamous Carlo Ponzi, whose property scam defrauded thousands of people during the Wall Street Crash. The typology goes like this. A hedge borrower is a firm that can meet all of its commitments out of its income. A speculative borrower can meet the interest payments on its debt, but cannot pay off the actual loan, so has to keep rolling over the debt. Finally, there is Ponzi finance. With Ponzi finance you are in trouble already: you can't afford to pay the interest, let alone the loan, unless you continually borrow from somebody else. A bank that did this would have to find a constant supply of new investors (a.k.a. suckers) to put money in, just to pay off its creditors. In December 2008 New York hedge fund boss Bernie Madoff was charged with doing precisely this, to the tune of $50 billion. However, Minsky pointed out that, though illegal, this Ponzi phenomenon in its wider sense is not the result of deliberate law-breaking, but a natural outgrowth of credit booms.

Minsky pointed out that, given sustained economic growth, there was a tendency for the finance system to move from the hedge situation, where everything is under control, to the speculative and Ponzi situations, which are precarious. To complete the picture he wrote, prophetically:

> If an economy with a sizeable body of speculative financial units is in an inflationary state, and the authorities attempt to exorcise inflation by monetary constraint, then speculative units will become Ponzi units and the net worth of previously Ponzi units will quickly evaporate. Consequently, units with cash flow shortfalls will be forced to try to make position by selling out position. This is likely to lead to a collapse of asset values.

This, as it turns out, is a precise description of what happened between 2005 and 2007. The subprime lenders in the US – Countrywide and its ilk – were becoming Ponzi finance schemes: their losses were only being covered by new lenders coming in.[11] Most banks were in the speculative position. When oil prices took off, and central banks raised interest rates, everybody was pushed one notch further towards the scary end of the scale. First the mortgage brokers went bust, then the bank-linked hedge funds, then the banks.[12] It prompted veteran UBS economist George Magnus to ask, six months before the meltdown, 'Have we arrived at a Minsky Moment'?[13] The rapid sell-off of trillions of dollars' worth of shares, stocks, derivatives and bad debts into a falling market gave the answer.

Minsky's theory not only explains why credit bubbles emerge during periods of stability. He also explains how the easy-money strategies of central banks after the end of the post-war boom had actually stopped financial crisis turning into recession: instead of depression, he argued, you get inflation. In other words, though Minsky never to my knowledge wrote about Kondratiev, his theory provides the best explanation of why the K-wave pattern was disrupted.

Minsky's proposed solution to financial crisis was state intervention on two fronts: the government should run a big budget deficit and the central bank should pump money into the economy. It will be noted, despite Minsky's pariah status in economics, that his remedy is exactly what has been adopted – in the US, the UK, the eurozone and much of the developed world. The problem is, it has not so far worked. Trillions of dollars of ready money, tax cuts and state spending were shovelled into the world economy to stop the credit crunch producing another Great Depression. Yet all these trillions are up against a powerful backwash of collapse within the real economy.

Fortunately, Minsky had spent his time in academic exile musing on a more permanent solution, outlined in the chapters that the hedge fund managers skip and the Marxists dismiss: the socialisation of the banking system. This he conceived not as an anti-capitalist measure, but as the only possible form of a high-consumption, stable capitalism in the future. Minsky argued: 'As socialisation of the towering heights is fully compatible with a large, growing and prosperous private sector, this high-consumption synthesis might well be conducive to greater freedom for entrepreneurial ability and daring than is our present structure.'[14]

Minsky never bothered to spell out the details of how it might be done. But there is no need to do so now. Stumbling through the underground passageways of Downing Street on the morning of 8 October 2008, I saw it happen. Tetchy and bleary-eyed, fuelled by stale coffee and take-away food, British civil servants had designed and executed it in the space of forty-eight hours. Within ten days, much of the Western world's banking system had been stabilised by massive injections of state credit and state capital.

The problem is, although they were prepared to 'go there and do that', the leaders of the G20 had no intention of 'getting the T-shirt'. The state takeover of large parts of the banking sector was seen – like the tax cuts and liquidity injections – as a way of speeding the return to the 'normality' of the past decade. It is also clear, on the basis of conversations with senior UK policymakers, that the consensus by the time of the Washington G20 summit was that the recession would be a 'blur', a sharp V-shape, over by mid 2009.

In reality, the world is facing a much more strategic problem: its growth model is in crisis, and the banking business model is in crisis. Those who assume that either debt-fuelled consumption or Lehman-style banking will quickly return are missing the point.

A growth model in crisis

'A voracious appetite for economic growth lies at the heart of the boom that has now gone bust', wrote Morgan Stanley economist Stephen Roach, on the eve of the meltdown.[15] It is worth reiterating just how spectacular that growth has been, and how spectacularly uneven. In 2007 global GDP growth was 5 per cent – well above its historic trend for the fourth year in a row. Growth in the developing world averaged 8 per cent; and in Asia specifically it was 10 per cent. Across the G7 countries it was 2.6 per cent – slightly below the average for the 1990s. Roach summed up the problem:

An income-short US economy rejected a slower pace of domestic demand. It turned, instead, to an asset- and debt-financed growth binge . . . For the developing world, rapid growth was a powerful antidote to a legacy of wrenching poverty. And the hyper-growth that was realized in regions like Developing Asia became the end that justified all means – including . . . inflation, pollution, environmental degradation, widening income disparities, and periodic asset bubbles. The world's body politic wanted – and still wants – growth at all costs.[16]

He concluded: 'This crisis is a strong signal that these strategies are not sustainable'. But if the old growth model has reached a dead end, what can follow it?

There are three rational alternatives for the developed world. The first is to revive the high-debt/low-wage model under more controlled conditions; the second is to abandon high growth as an objective altogether; the third is to find a radically different basis for high growth, with a return to higher wages, redistribution and a highly regulated finance system.

The first course of action is implicit in the approach agreed at the Washington G20 summit. In the summit communiqué, globalised markets and free trade are treated as hallowed principles, as is the essentially national basis of regulation. Regulation would be more coordinated, there would be more information-sharing, governments would commit to do better next time – but the only concrete measures to re-regulate the system remained disputed in actual practice: hedge funds to be brought under regulation, intelligence on tax havens to be shared, and so on. Even within the EU there was strong resistance to a single banking regulator, as London, Dublin, Frankfurt and Milan vied with each other to become global banking centres on the basis of different regulatory systems.

The second solution embraces the end of a high-growth, high-consumption economy: if it can't be driven by wages, debt or public spending, then it can't exist. And if it can't exist in the West, then Asia's model of high exports and high savings does not work either. In previous eras, any proposal to revert to a low-growth economy would have been regarded simply as barbarism and regression. Yet there is a strong sentiment among the anti-globalisation and deep-green movements in favour of this solution. And it has found echoes in mass consciousness and micro-level behaviour as the world has come to understand the dangers of global warming. The problem is that it is only an option for the developed world: every slum-dweller and roadside migrant labourer I have ever met south of the equator had electricity and a flush toilet high on their wish list, which will need high growth for at least another couple of decades – possibly half a century.

A discussion of the climate change agenda is beyond the scope of this book. Suffice to say, any new growth model that emerges during the 2010s will be shaped by whatever kind of agreement is achieved on carbon emissions to replace Kyoto. If there is no global agreement, then carbon-emission targeting will become just another weapon in the emerging economic rivalry between Asia, the West and the global South.

As for the third option – a high-growth economy that transcends the limitations of both Keynesian and neoliberal models – it was Minsky who spelled out how it could be achieved: nationalise the banking and insurance system; place strict limits on speculative finance; change the tax structure to decrease inequality so that the bottom half of the income scale benefits from growth, and growth itself sustains consumer demand rather than debt. Finally, limit the power of large-scale enterprises so that you create permanently benign conditions for entrepreneurs. This, it should be stressed, was Minsky's prescription to rescue capitalism, not to destroy it, though the outcome would seem highly 'anti-capitalist' to anybody who defines capitalism as being essentially about free markets.

Surreally, as this book goes to press, large parts of the Western financial system are either semi-nationalised or on life-support with taxpayer money. New, tentative laws to limit speculation are being formulated. A blunt form of the Minsky solution has been improvised as a crisis measure – but it leaves many questions unanswered.

Senior UK ministers and officials told me in December 2008 that they had 'no intention' of owning any bank long-term. It was equally clear that they were still in crisis mode, and exploring the technicalities of a major nationalisation programme, should it become necessary. They had not actually begun to think about the long-term form that the banking system should take. But for the bankers themselves the issue was a highly urgent one.

Banking lurched into the securitisation boom because its old business model, driven by flotations, mergers and privatisations, had faltered. But the securitisation boom is surely over: even if you only make the rules of Basel II effective – as the G20 leaders have promised to do – much of the bloom goes off the finance sector. Further, if you close the offshore tax havens, as the Obama administration has threatened to do, the opportunity to speculate is massively diminished.

The paradox is, even if you stuck to the old regulations, the old banking business model would be difficult to revive. In fact the momentum lies in the direction of a more permanently socialised banking sector – a 'mixed economy' with large parts of the system run by the state. One senior banking analyst told me in December 2008 that we will probably 'end up with banks that are essentially financial utilities; investment banks that are more Lazard than Lehman; and with a public lending institution of some description.' Conversations with senior bankers, lawyers and hedge fund managers have pointed in the same direction.

At the heart of the Basel II treaty, as I have already discussed, is the concept of capital adequacy. Banks have to match the risks they take by holding a certain amount of capital in the form of cash or bonds that can be easily cashed in. The more of this stuff they hold, the less profitable their operations, because being risk-free it generates minimal returns. The original Basel II treaty set a Tier I capital ratio at 4 per cent.

As we have seen, the shadow banking system was designed to push risks off the balance sheet and allow banks to hold less capital. Now it has collapsed, and all the risks are shown on the books, that 4 per cent limit becomes important. But it's no longer 4 per cent. In response to the crisis, national regulators have imposed higher capital ratios.

During the 13 October 2008 bank bailout, the British government imposed a 9 per cent limit. The French government did likewise. Nobody in the banking world knows what the new, permanent replacement for 4 per cent will be, but if it is anything approaching 9 per cent, this means permanently lower profits for the banking sector.

But that's only one problem. The second problem is that banks will become more risk-averse. Modern regulation relies on the banks calculating the risk side of the balance sheet using computer models based on data. One senior banking figure told me:

> If you go back beyond ten years all you have are paper records. Helpfully, all the digital data the banks relied on was accumulated in the boom years. In the next twelve months we will have very accurate data about what a crisis looks like and that will have to be factored into the models. If a banker tells me there's a 99.9 per cent chance this will never happen again, I say to them: let's see in a thousand years' time – because 99.9 per cent certainty is like saying this will never happen again in a thousand years.

A combination of regulators shutting the stable door and the new availability of negative data will push banks into raising so much capital that they will seem overcapitalised. Their profits will look meagre.

On top of that, there will be new limits on their profitability imposed from outside traditional banking regulations. Traditionally, banks have been unfettered by competition law; now the huge banks created by the process of merger and collapse will face tighter legal safeguards for their customers. Bankers dealing directly with savers and borrowers expect to face a series of controls on their profits. Their products and service levels will be standardised, with enforced transparency replacing the opaque pricing models they relied on to maximise profits in the past.

It's uncharted territory for the bankers, but actually we have a long experience of what happens when companies cannot make money, form a natural monopoly, and are essential to the functioning of the rest of business. They are called utilities. Many believe banking is now about to become just like a utility: heavily regulated, low-profit, orientated by law to achieve a social aim rather than a financial one. This prospect has already got some in the banking industry so depressed that they are predicting the mass departure of the teams engaged in the high-risk parts of the banking business into the hedge fund and consultancy businesses.

With low-profit, utility-style commercial banking, the question then arises: If banks are being asked to meet social objectives, like avoiding foreclosures or continued lending to small businesses, and are already supported by vast quantities of state finance, would it not be more efficient for the state to own key parts of the banking sector? One senior figure in the industry told me: 'Once they become low-profit utilities, I don't really care whether they stay in the private sector or are nationalised – they're just doing the same thing.'

In short, reality is pushing the banking industry towards a utility-style solution. We have already had the Minsky Moment; now some governments may be forced towards a more permanent Minsky-style solution. The result would be some form of 'mixed economy' in banking, with a base layer provided by a state-owned lender, large utility banks on top, and then a big gap between this world and a slimmed-down speculative sector.

Many people in banking believe that, in future, the speculative end of finance will be carried out by niche organisations. Hedge funds will bifurcate: those that remain onshore will become the new investment banks, handling increasingly large amounts of institutional investment money. Over the 2000s, the amount of pension fund money in UK hedge funds grew from 5 per cent of the total to 30 per cent; one fund manager confidently told me it would grow to 75 per cent within a decade. It is likely that those who wish to handle such serious amounts of ordinary people's money will be required to come onshore, and that the offshore tax havens themselves will have to submit to more international regulation.

It is entirely possible to reconcile the utility-style banking, and even permanent nationalisation, with the survival of a more regulated high-risk private banking sector dealing in derivatives. It is unlikely, however, that the derivatives markets can remain in their current form. The creation of an exchange for credit default swaps is high on the G20 agenda already; much of derivatives trading will probably have to go exchange-based rather than point-to-point. All this means is that the derivatives market will catch up with the principle established for capitalism in seventeenth-century Amsterdam: that the exchange rather than the bilateral transaction is the best form of a market-based financial system.

As the crisis worsens, it is becoming commonplace for pundits to observe, while capitalism is collapsing, that nobody has thought of an alternative. This is not true. The Minsky alternative − a socialised banking system plus redistribution − is, I believe, the ground on which the most radical of the capitalist re-regulators will coalesce with social justice activists. And it may even go mainstream if the only alternative is seen to be low growth, decades of debt-imposed stagnation, or another re-run of this crisis a few years down the line. It is also possible that a socialised banking system, by allowing the central allocation of financial resources, could be harnessed to the rapid development and large-scale production of post-carbon technologies.

The problem is that there is a second dynamic that must shape the outcome, over and above the debate about structure and social justice in the West: it is the response of Asia, and above all China.

The great unwinding

We have seen that globalisation produced structural imbalances in the world economy: Asia produces, America consumes; Asia lends, America borrows; Asia exports, America imports. Before discussing how this situation might unwind, it is worth spelling out who gains from this yin-and-yang arrangement. The overwhelming beneficiaries have been US capitalists and Western consumers.

US capital profits from the situation in two ways: first, there is a mismatch in the type of investments that flow in each direction. Asian investors have generally put their money into long-term American debt, which provides a low rate of return; American investors have built factories and call centres in Asia, which provide a high rate of return. Second, there is the tendency of the dollar to decline against Asian currencies; so even where an Asian investor is earning a decent profit – say, on the US stock market – once that's translated back into the home currency in Japan or China, the profits don't look too good. Profits flowing back to the US, meanwhile, get an extra kick from this currency effect.

Western consumers have profited from the arrangement because a glut of Asian savings, offered through the banking system at low interest rates, allowed them to finance debt-driven lifestyles; meanwhile, until the mid 2000s the impact of Asia's export-led growth was to cheapen everything you wanted to buy, from training shoes to television sets and computers.

When they discussed the unwinding of these global imbalances, policymakers usually considered three broad options: the dollar falls dramatically; Asia develops a mass consumer market and invests more at home; or there is a 'controlled' switchover managed by the IMF, involving small tweaks in both directions over a long period of time.[17]

During the financial crisis, the initial moves have been contradictory. As US growth slowed, so too did its trade deficit with the rest of the world. But when the financial crisis erupted, the dollar strengthened against rival currencies, rather than falling. It is too soon to tell where this is going, but in the end the outcome is in the hands of Asia, and above all China.

Chinese policy is to peg its currency against the US dollar, allowing a microscopic rise in the value of the renminbi over time. To change that policy, and allow a massive fall of the dollar against the renminbi, would be a massive act of self-sacrifice by China and a massive signal that it intends to move away from an export-led strategy towards developing its home market.

Many academic discussions of the imbalances tend to assume that the US, or the IMF, would in some way dictate to China the course of rebalancing. It is now clear that the dictating will be done in the other direction. China has already unleashed the world's biggest state spending programme in response to the crisis, pitching 15 per cent of its GDP into a stimulus package in November 2008. But creating a mass consumer market in China to buy the goods that were once exported to the US and Europe would involve a massive social change in China. Put simply, it would involve turning Chinese workers from the low-paid wage slaves of the world into the consumer spenders of the world. That would mean redistributing wealth in China away from the new elite to the urban poor.

I have seen first-hand how ardently this change is hoped for on the Chinese factory floor. The second generation of migrant workers who staff the production lines of Shanghai, Shenzhen and Guangzhou are feisty, militant, modern people. Since 2003, when I first reported on Chinese workers' struggle for basic rights, a lot has changed. Despite the existence of half a

billion peasants just waiting to move off the land, there was –
on the eve of the world recession – a labour shortage in
Chinese factories. This is because the power of the local
bureaucrats and crony managers prevents the normal operation
of the Chinese labour market.

Managers who want to pay workers more are not allowed
to; the legal minimum wage is constantly chipped away by
food and accommodation charges on the workers who mainly
still live in dormitories; and to cap it all, billions of dollars of
owed wages are simply never paid. So Chinese workers vote
with their feet. The tactic of simply leaving sweatshops and
looking for a better job is the main tactic of resistance. And
when, in pursuit of 'social harmony', China's leaders imposed a
standard contract law early in 2008, many sweatshop bosses
responded by closing their factories.

Finally, at the end of 2008, it became clear that the downturn
in the US had hit China's remaining export factories hard: as I
write, the Pearl River Delta – the workshop of the world – is
wracked by closures, strikes and unpaid wage disputes.

All this makes the academic literature on the global imbalances
look a little bit otherworldly. Economists tend to say things like
'China will have to do X and America Y', as if it was all like
playing Sid Meier's *Civilization* computer game, where every
country is represented by a single player. Actually we live in a
world of classes as well as countries. The Chinese workforce is
getting stronger and more militant. Meanwhile the workforce of
the G7 countries is, for the first time in a generation, facing
unemployment and recession – and this time, unlike in the
1980s, the invisible restraints of social solidarity and stable
community are gone.

In short, it now looks likely that the unwinding of the global
imbalances will be disorderly rather than orderly. The $196
trillion dollars represented by the finance system represents a
claim on four times the world's output. It is a claim on future
profits which may well not materialise at all – and on future taxes

paid to service national debts. We know already that maybe a quarter of the world's financial assets have been wiped out in this crisis (see Chapter 3). But the way the rest of the wipe-out happens will be affected, above all, by currency and capital movements.

A 25 per cent fall of the dollar, envisaged in most academic studies of the global imbalances, would wipe out a quarter of China's foreign exchange reserves and turn the profits on all the capital invested by Asian savers into America into losses. But if the dollar is not allowed to fall against other major currencies, then China's workers have to become the new big spenders of the world, and a major redistribution of wealth is on the cards that will shatter the social harmony pursued by the Hu Jin Tao administration.

The second contradiction is the sheer scale of the national debts being accumulated by the Anglo-Saxon model countries: $10 trillion in the US; £1 trillion in the UK. Twice in post-war history, the US used aggressive devaluation of the dollar to transfer the cost of its national debt to other countries: in 1971, with the end of Bretton Woods; and the 1985 Plaza Accord, when Germany and Japan were persuaded to let their currencies rise against the value of the dollar. Any attempt to do this for a third time, unilaterally, will provoke an economic clash with China; it is more likely that Chinese, Middle East and Russian capital would demand new access and ownership rights in return for any such rebalancing.

A third problem concerns who will bail out the crisis-hit emerging markets. The IMF's $200 billion looks puny. China and Russia have the reserves, but they, together with much of Asia, have zero affinity for the IMF. It is likely that China will be called on to play a global financial role quite soon if the resources and influence of the IMF run out.

In short, the crisis has dealt China, together with the other emerging market giants, a strong hand. It is probably the only country that can power the world out of recession; yet to do so it must alter the balance of class forces and enrich its own workforce. Its willingness to advance capital – either by lending to governments or by buying up stricken banks – will depend on how far it thinks the US is prepared to let the dollar slide. Finally, China is in a position, on its own, to dwarf the IMF in the bailout of stricken economies in its diplomatic orbit, should it wish to do so.

It is not clear that the Chinese bureaucracy wishes to do any of these things; what it does wish for is for the West to get off its back on the issues of democracy, Taiwan, Tibet and climate change. A cynical view of history would suggest this is exactly what the West will have to do.

Lots of assumptions will have to be scrapped. It was at first thought that globalisation would create a more uniform economic model in the rapidly developing countries. Numerous investment bank reports were issued charting the path of the Chinese stock exchange towards transparency and maturity; bets were placed on the eventual transition of monopolies like Russia's Gazprom towards Anglo-Saxon levels of transparency and social responsibility. One of the most common uses of the arrow-drawing function in Microsoft's Powerpoint software has been to draw a line along which countries like South Korea and Venezuela must pass towards Anglo-Saxon norms of democracy and freedom as their economies mature. But it may not turn out that way.

The emerging market giants enter this crisis with more economic power and more political clout. They will face fewer calls to democratise. Meanwhile, their workforces are restless for better living standards. It is impossible to predict where all this will lead, but it certainly makes the phrase 'the end of history' sound laughable.

Social justice

Every new era in capitalism poses anew the question of social justice. It is not a question with a foregone conclusion, but the outcome of a struggle between contending interests. If you accept that we are at the start of a new, technology-driven upswing, then the current crisis looks set to raise the question of re-regulation once again. In fact, looking back, the last twenty-five years look a lot like the period between the invention of the factory system and the passing of the first effective factory legislation; from the opening of the first cotton mill at Cromford, Derbyshire in 1771 to the UK Factory Act of 1844.

For much of that period, the pioneers of industrial capitalism believed that any attempt at regulation would kill the dynamism of the new system. They too had their celebrity economist: Nassau Senior, the author of the theory that all profits were made in the last hour of the working day. Shorten the working day, said Senior, and – bam! – the profits go up in smoke. According to this theory, quipped reformer William Cobbett, the fate of capitalism depended on '300,000 little girls in Lancashire': 'for it was asserted, that if these little girls worked two hours less per day, our manufacturing superiority would depart from us'.[18]

The theory was wrong. Child labour was abolished; minimal standards of order and humanity were imposed on the factories. But capitalism did not die – it took off. It is no accident that 1844 was also the year that Britain, traumatised by recurrent financial panics, enshrined the gold standard and the powers of the central bank in law. This, too, laid the basis for mid-century stability and set the template for the new industrial economies that would emerge.

If the parallel is valid, then the re-regulation of global finance stands a chance of unleashing the information economy, not killing it. This, in turn, will form part of a wider reinsertion of the state into the economy; indeed, the first steps can be seen in the agreement to limit carbon emissions, the Millennium Development Goals, and the growing adoption of 'sustainable' business models. If I am right, then these tiny steps towards a more regulated capitalism will seem like the early Factory Acts in England: meagre. They will be eclipsed on a scale even social justice campaigners today can hardly imagine.

But it will not happen without a fight. And the key players will have to be the world's working poor. It is important to remember that the famous '300,000 little girls in Lancashire' did not stand quietly while somebody made things better for them. By the late nineteenth century they and their brothers, sons and daughters had formed a powerful movement for social justice that was present in every developed country. It was called the labour movement. And although it does not figure very high in the rebalancing schemes proposed by economists, to me organised labour looks set for a comeback.

If that happens, its renewal will challenge the assumptions of most of those who think of themselves as activists for social justice. Until now the various strands of the anti-globalisation movement have adopted the doctrine of non-socialist radical Saul Alinsky: 'think globally, act locally'. Increasingly this has become the model for union organising among the global trade unions, and it seems to have become the default mode of operation for social-justice activists everywhere. I have seen this tendency at work too often for it to be accidental: from slum-dwellers in Nairobi, to migrant workers in Shenzhen, to low-paid cleaners in the bank HQs at London's Canary Wharf, this low-level, non-ideological, anti-political culture of resistance is widespread.

However effective it has been in the fight to make corporations accountable, and to highlight the issues of poverty and global warming, 'horizontalism' does not look very relevant to the crisis that began in September 2008. You cannot reform the banking system branch by branch; even if you try to, your agenda will crash into the agenda of the most aggressive capitalist regulators. In conditions where the state has made the biggest intervention into the world economy in a century, it seems perverse to treat the state as irrelevant.

It seems likely to me that social-justice campaigners – again, probably against their inclinations – will now have to focus more on the state; that some form of big-picture narrative will emerge that describes how the state intervenes to deliver social justice. Just as with FDR's New Deal, what emerges will be the result of a tussle between top-down liberal reformists and bottom-up social activists. It will, of course, appal those who thought capitalism could only take a free-market form.

What next?

'Capitalism worked for two hundred years, but times change, and systems become corrupt.' That was the verdict of hedge fund boss Andrew Lahde in his now-famous 'fuck you' letter to the industry. It seems to me an unsophisticated judgement: capitalism has veered from stability to crisis with acute regularity over the past 200 years. There has been corruption in the system since the celebrated theft of intellectual property that allowed Arkwright to design the factory system: but corruption is not its biggest problem. Lahde's mistake was to see the free-market capitalism of the present as its only historically valid form.

Capitalism's tendency has been to expand the power of the market: to push for the maximum freedom for market forces and the destruction of all ties – family, clan, nation and class – not based on free exchange. But this has not been its only tendency. Hungarian philosopher Karl Polanyi famously described the rise of capitalism as a 'double movement': as the market destroyed the old social networks and reduced all human relationships to commercial ones, a counter-tendency arose to defend human values, community and security. Since 1989 we have seen the whole process happen again.

Nineteen-eighty-nine seemed like the start of a long neo-liberal era: history had come to an end, capitalism had assumed its pure and final form. Free markets and democracy would conquer the world. The story of organised labour was over. For those of us who lived through it – even those who regretted it – the claims seemed plausible. Now these claims seem utterly transitory.

The dominance of finance, derivatives and a debt-fuelled growth model is in reality only a little over ten years old. Likewise, the global imbalances really took off only in the wake of the 1997 crisis. There is, in other words, nothing permanent, nor even well entrenched about the current shape of the global economy – still less should it be sacrosanct. It was built aggressively by visionaries who innovated their way into rule-free spaces. It could be radically reshaped by human action, and in the timescale of a decade, not a lifetime.

The task of finding a better model confronts us in a period of economic recession and rising social unrest, and with the ideology of neoliberalism now lying shattered alongside that of Stalinist Marxism, which has been dead for twenty years. The magnitude of the crisis is much bigger than most of us yet imagine.

The dynamics of growth and crisis in the information age are hardly guessed at: they will be shaped not just by the ending of the super-bubble, but by the long-term ageing of populations, by climate change, by the rise of Asia, and by the coming decline of the carbon economy. But above all they will be shaped by the willingness of ordinary people to impose limits, standards and sustainability on capital – and the willingness of the state to take control where market forces lead to disaster.

The stakes are massive: info-capitalism has created the possibilities for limitless growth, yet the form it has taken is an abrasive, selfish, unequal society in which we've swapped repeated recession for repeated financial crisis. Whether the recession is short or long, whether it tips over into a slump or not, whether it solidifies the global economy or shatters it into rival fragments, whether the state bailouts lead to a new regime of stagnation and country bankruptcy – none of this is clear. But whatever the outcome of the crisis, it would be highly irresponsible to forget what caused it.

In the first week of October 2008 a deregulated banking system brought the entire economy of the world to the brink of collapse. It was the product of giant hubris and the untrammelled power of a financial elite. The crisis happened because the world was persuaded to forget the causes and consequences of 1929. It must never forget the events of 2008.

9. The Fatal Stimulus

From Global Slump to Euro Crisis

'WE WENT FROM a turnover of something on the order of £550,000 a month down to £200,000. Just overnight!' said Brian Yates, chopping the space in front of him with his hand. 'Everything was switched off for us.' After November 2008 it was all hand gestures in the manufacturing industry: sharp, decisive ones, indicating cut-off, switch-off, the end of things. From factory to factory I heard the same story.

I stood with Yates – the managing director of Berck Ltd, in West Bromwich in the English Midlands – in a room full of undelivered automobile parts still glistening with machine oil. He described how one big car manufacturer had simply turned the order away at the gates: 'Can't pay for them, don't want them.'

Across the world's industrial heartlands, in the first quarter of 2009, demand slumped. The famous 'just in time' supply chain of modern industry had, it turned out, been a fiction. There was months' worth of inventory piled on the factory floors at companies like Ford and Honda, but very few sales; in response, they shut down their production lines or slowed them massively. The backwash sank the weakest companies in the supply chain; among those that survived, short-time working became the norm. At Berck the workforce was slashed from 130 to 70 and the survivors went onto a three-day week.

The implosion of the banking system had triggered high-velocity economic collapse across the globe. Japan, the great export engine, had gone into reverse. Its industrial production in January 2009 was down 31 per cent year on year; its exports were down 46 per cent. America, the celebrated 'jobs machine', was destroying jobs at the rate of more than half a million a month. The Chinese export zones were shutting down, sending 20 million migrant workers back to their villages by the end of January.

This global output slump posed a new danger: when growth collapses so do wages, prices and the money supply. Deflation – if allowed to get out of control – would feed back into the financial crisis: people's incomes would fall, companies' turnover would fall, but the size of their debts would remain the same. Real interest rates would rise, nullifying the fact that official interest rates were close to zero. Consumers and firms would spiral into penury, just as they had after the Wall Street crash of 1929.

This 'debt-deflation spiral' was a real possibility in the first three months of 2009. The IMF's economists ran their model of the world economy and produced odds of 11 per cent that there would be a debt-deflation episode: 'Importantly, over 11 percent of the model runs over the next three years failed to solve: these simulations, which assume announced fiscal policies, have an ever-increasing deflationary spiral with rising real interest rates that prevent the economy from recovering.'[1]

Then, as the trade figures dribbled out, there was another stunning revelation: globalisation itself was in danger. In the depressions of the 1870s and 1930s the major economies of the world had been, at most, interlocked. Since 1989 they had become more like a single nervous system with extremely receptive sensors and highly conductive neural pathways. And the pathways were dying.

The multistep, transnational supply chain of modern manufacturing meant that one computer hard drive left unsold in London turned instantly into a hard economic signal in ten countries: cancel orders, lay off workers, put suppliers on credit-watch and demand cash upfront. This highly distributed model of production was undergoing its first crisis: we now discovered it could transmit collapse as effectively as expansion.

World merchandise exports declined at an annualised rate of 40 per cent in the last quarter of 2008. By this measure, China, South Korea, Japan and the United States all suffered huge double-digit falls in exports. But the world record holder was Germany, with an 80 per cent annualised rate of fall. The collapse, said Federal Reserve economist Kei-Mu Yi, 'has been sudden, severe and synchronised'.[2]

By March 2009 you could see the human cost of the slump at a factory like Berck, a Tier II supplier of finely honed metal parts to the car industry. Andy Jackson, the finance director, tugged apologetically at the waistband of his trousers: he'd lost so much weight with worry they would not stay up. Sarj, the firm's Sikh maintenance manager, who had personally set up every machine installed there since 1987, told me he felt 'ashamed, humiliated' by what had happened. The firm's two admin staff worked the phones, side by side: one stalling creditors, the other demanding money from customers, in the process shredding years of good-will from both. By mid-afternoon on most days there was only that sound fatal in a manufacturing shop: silence.

It was not like the 1930s yet, but it was unlike anything they had ever known. Now help was on the way – albeit from men who had no idea of what they were about to do.

Quantitative easing

By January 2009 central bank interest rates in the United States and Britain were close to zero, but growth was still collapsing. A massive stimulus would be required in the Anglo-Saxon coun-tries, and there were only two levers to pull: increased govern-ment spending and reduced taxation, known as fiscal stimulus, or a new, unconventional kind of monetary strategy known as quantitative easing.

I still remember the day I introduced the term into the editorial meeting at Newsnight. Several highly educated people sat scrunching their hair with their fingers at the prospect of using such impenetrable language on television. They were not alone: many senior politicians had no idea what it was.

In the world of central banking there was a different problem: they knew what it was but they didn't want to do it.

The central banks had begun to buy up the debts of distressed banks selectively and tactically. They had done this to the tune of tens of billions, but in their minds it belonged in the category of 'desperate measures to save the banks'.

Quantitative easing was something different: it was a desperate measure to save the whole economy – and it was a macro-economic strategy, not a tactic. It would involve pumping hundreds of billions of pounds and dollars into economic demand by 'printing money'. In the modern world this is easier than it used to be, since a printer isn't required. Instead, central banks start a new line in their spreadsheets and 'create' money there, using it to buy up not just the bad debts that have been troubling the system but also safe debt, and above all government debt.

To work, QE would literally target the quantity of money pumped in, not the quality of bad debt neutralised. The tactic had been adopted in Japan in 2002, after a decade of fiscal stimulus failed to halt deflation. But it had been originally conceived by John Maynard Keynes in the early 1930s and implemented in the United States in April 1932.

It was to this classic, elegant and (to them) wholly new strategy that the central bankers in Washington and London had to be dragged, kicking and screaming. In early January, UK Chancellor Alistair Darling said, 'Nobody is talking about printing money. There's a debate to be had about what you do to support the economy as interest rates approach zero, as they are in the United States. But for us that is an entirely hypothetical debate.'[3] On 13 January, Ben Bernanke travelled to London to make a speech at the London School of Economics against QE. The Fed would engage only in 'credit easing', he said, avoiding a pure QE strategy:

In a pure QE regime, the focus of policy is the quantity of bank
reserves, which are liabilities of the central bank; the compo-
sition of loans and securities on the asset side of the central
bank's balance sheet is incidental . . . In contrast, the Federal
Reserve's credit easing approach focuses on the mix of loans
and securities that it holds and on how this affects credit
conditions for households and businesses.[4]

But on 9 March the United Kingdom was forced to adopt 'pure
QE' to the tune of £150 billion, later expanded to £200 billion.
Ten days later Ben Bernanke swallowed his finely wrought
objections and pledged the Fed to print $1.25 trillion.

Supporters of pure QE had always warned that the combination of half-baked bank bailouts and neutralised toxic loans inside
the central bank would fail. Virtually nobody inside the financial
elite of Europe, the United States or the United Kingdom
accepted this argument. As with bank nationalisation, they split
the difference between what was necessary and what their
ideology told them.

When, on the eve of British QE, I met a group of investment
managers from the City of London, veterans of the Japanese crisis
who had been pushing for the measure, they told me glumly,
'We have no line of communication to the Bank of England or
the UK Treasury – they long ago sacked everybody who thinks
like us.' One, noticing I had Bernanke's book on the Great
Depression in my bag, leafed through to the index: 'Look,' he
said, 'there is no entry under Q.'

Once adopted, QE did what neither the bailouts, the interest
rate cuts nor indeed the tax and spend measures could: it pumped
demand into the system immediately. But between Bernanke's
speech at the LSE and his adoption of quantitative easing two
months later 1.5 million American workers had lost their jobs.
And the Dow had lost a quarter of its value.[5]

Fiscal stimulus

With fiscal stimulus there was a different set of problems. Printing money costs nothing in the short term; slashing taxes and boosting public spending, on the other hand, adds immediately to a country's budget deficit and, at year's end, to its debt. In addition, once you decide to pump demand into the economy in this way, the mechanisms for doing so involve political and ideological choices in a way that monetary stimulus does not.

The quickest and most decisive fiscal stimulus in history was launched in China. The State Council met on 9 November 2008 to approve a stimulus worth US $580 billion, or 14 per cent of China's GDP, to be rolled out over two years. By nightfall, local party committees were in session across China to discuss where the money could be spent. It was allocated broadly to four areas: welfare spending, infrastructure, urban sanitation and environmental projects, and relief for the Sichuan earthquake disaster zone. In the spring of 2009 I had the chance to see it working close up.

They were tired, dirty, slumped, huddled: a married couple from Gansu Province sipping water from a battered plastic beaker and cradling their possessions in raffia bags. They'd piled into the 'hard class' carriage of the train to Baotou in Inner Mongolia as part of a team of about fifteen workers, all from the same village.

They were going 'to build a tunnel' somewhere north. 'The boss knows us, he is bound to give us a job', said Shu Shing-Wei. 'We're used to this simple kind of work.' They had switched, like millions of Chinese factory workers, straight from the export industry to domestic infrastructure, in some cases without so much as a visit back home to see their kids. Those laid off from factories in the southern export zones told me of 5,000 renminbi ($730) salary agreements suddenly slashed to 3,000 ($440).

China's switch from export-led growth to massive investment in domestic infrastructure and job creation was already changing millions of lives. And the switch was more than just a spending spree: at the microeconomic level the Chinese state was pushing individual enterprises towards wartime levels of demand management.

At the King Deer cashmere factory in Baotou, the production manager, Eugene Tong, taught me the slogan of the Three No's: 'No layoffs, no wage cuts, no short time working.' That was an order you had to obey even if, as with King Deer – a major producer with 7,000 employees – you were technically in the private sector. Tong told me, 'Our real purpose in Chinese society is not to produce cashmere, it is to produce employment – and we're proud to fulfil it.'

At the height of the mid-decade boom, the city had been growing at 45 per cent a year, according to the official statistics; now it was down to 15 per cent. The city's propaganda chief proudly took me through another of the Communist Party's new slogans: 'Guarantee growth by boosting domestic demand. Accelerate development: benefit the people!'

But, for all the sloganeering and lever pulling, China faced two problems with its fiscal stimulus. First, the whole structure of the economy has been geared so that 'boosting domestic demand' can only be done through capital spending. Though long demanded by party slogans, the rise in consumer spending necessary to rebalance both China and the world economy was never going to come out of the barrel of a party directive. Chinese people, from the poorest factory workers to the middle classes, save more than a third of their income, because there is no welfare state: one sheep-farming family I met was spending 80 per cent of its disposable income on sending their daughter to college.

Thus, by the time I got to Inner Mongolia in April 2009, most of the money had been allocated to railways, tunnels, new rolling stock to replace perfectly adequate old rolling stock. I had already seen mile after mile of deserted six-lane pristine new highways, but more were planned. A huge amount of the stimulus money was – as it will do in any bureaucratic society – going to waste.

The second problem was more daunting. Though titled a 'fiscal stimulus', China's stimulus was in fact only one-third funded by taxpayers' money. The other two thirds would be coming from credit creation by the banks. Backed by an implicit guarantee from the Chinese state, they would lend on an unprecedented scale to projects good and bad – and in some cases to projects that did not exist.

Money had to be pumped into the economy at all costs, and it was. By the end of 2009 China's growth rate – which had slumped to 6 per cent – was surging back above its target 9 per cent, and at time of writing it is estimated at above 11 per cent. But it left China's banks with a pile of risky lending that as Phase Three of the crisis opened cast a long shadow over the world economy.

In the us the government took until February 2009 to agree on a fiscal stimulus package. President Obama's $787 billion plan, following a $100 billion tax cut from the Bush administration, was one third tax cuts and two thirds spending. It was passed without a single Republican vote in favour, amid the first wave of protests by the Tea Party movement – a grass-roots conservative campaign with its origins in the anti-bailout movement. The next challenge would be to spend the money, around 5 per cent of the country's GDP – and, as I discovered that summer, the United States is not really a country geared to spending taxpayers' money.

Christina Romer and Jared Bernstein, two left-leaning members of Obama's team, had laid out radical objectives for the stimulus plan. It would 'create or save' between three and four million jobs by the end of 2010, nine tenths of them private-sector, and boost the GDP by 3.7 per cent. And though construction and energy would account for a quarter of the jobs created, more than a million extra health, education and social care jobs would also be created, together with 800,000 public sector jobs 'saved' at state level. The implication was clear: the whole shape of America would begin to change. The stimulus would achieve the administration's social objectives as well as a raw macroeconomic boost. But by April 2009 this had run up against reality.

In the first place, the mechanisms for turning public money into private-sector jobs were as crumbly as the concrete that holds up America's freeways. There were myriad agencies to go through, many of which had no experience of spending money on this scale. I toured the state of Indiana armed with a precise list of the number of jobs to be created, district by district, issued by the Federal government. It had been generated by computer, based on demographics, but it bore no relationship to job-creation plans at the local level.

Then came the politics. 'Gary, Indiana is like an eagle poised to fly,' Mayor Rudy Clay told me. 'All we need is the air of the fiscal stimulus beneath our wings and we'll soar once again and make America proud.'

Clay, a Democrat, and like the majority of Gary's population African-American, had applied for $400 million out of the fiscal stimulus plan. Top of his wish list were automatic weapons and Kevlar vests for the police, and some more police to tote them: in 2008 – in this, the crime capital of the Midwest – he'd had to lay off police officers due to a shortage of funds.

For a city like Gary, surrounded by richer, whiter districts that levy their own local income taxes, redistribution is only possible if the state-level government plays ball. 'The only obstacle in the way', Clay told me, 'is the mindset of the folks who have the decision to make it happen.' This was code for Indiana's Republican governor, Mitch Daniels.

Some conservative governors refused to take any stimulus money on principle. In Indiana $1 billion would be taken grudgingly, in the teeth of opposition from the Republican Party. Privately, city officials in Gary told me they'd be lucky to get half the cash they asked for, and this in a buddleia-strewn urban wasteland where crime is a major lifestyle choice and well-paid work scarce. (In the end the city and its surrounding region were allocated $156 million, much of which went for education.)

The further I travelled in the American Midwest, the more I discovered the problem was not just high-level political opposition and the atrophy of state spending channels. There was a philosophical reticence about the fiscal solution even among its beneficiaries.

I met a group of laid-off automobile workers in Elkhart, Indiana, hard at work on the voluntary renovation of some social housing built by their church. All had benefited from a government dispensation that had extended the cut-off date for unemployment benefits, yet all they wanted from Obama and the federal state was that they 'get out of the way so's we can work'. They sensed the pointlessness of some of the schemes that federal money had been poured into. One told me, 'We don't want to be road construction workers, we're autoworkers. What will we do – hold the Stop-Go sign? We want to build automobiles again.'

By the spring of 2009 the big fiscal stimulus measures were under way: $600 billion in China, $786 billion in the United States, $153 billion in Japan. The European Union pledged a collective €200 billion fiscal stimulus – but here the so-called automatic stabilisers had already kicked in. Whereas in the United States you had to get new state spending through Congress, then persuade a reluctant local official to spend it, in Europe there were mechanisms superbly geared to spending taxpayers' money, through welfare benefits and industrial subsidies.

Across the G20 in 2009, there was a fiscal stimulus averaging around 2 per cent of GDP, with the ratio of spending increases to tax cuts about 2:1. Politicians congratulated themselves, and each other, at their speed of movement; their absence of doctrinaire attachment to the balanced budgets of yesteryear; their ability to avoid the mistakes of the early 1930s. Then, as the G20 London Summit approached, they ripped each other apart.

Arcane to the uninitiated, the backroom fighting in London was to prefigure a huge, competitive exit strategy battle later. Saving your favourite local auto factory, or paying its former workers to sit at home or throwing huge amounts of fictitious money at tunnel building allows you to compete in ways you never dreamed of in normal times. Fiscal stimulus marks the entry of the state into the national economy, and the results – from Indiana to Inner Mongolia – would inevitably distort the global marketplace that had been so carefully created.

London G20: Europe versus the rest of the world

'The delegates to the World Conference should assemble in sackcloth and ashes, with humble and contrite hearts.' So wrote John Maynard Keynes of the London Conference in 1933, a last-gasp attempt to prevent the Depression leading to a trade war. He continued: 'Fear and greed, duplicity and incompetence, but above all conventional thought and feeling, have brought their collective performance far below the level of the participants regarded as human individuals. But here is a last opportunity.'

Keynes's words were a chillingly accurate description of the situation on 2 April 2009, when inside a vast, soulless hangar, protected by a jumpy police force that had already killed one innocent bystander, the world's leaders were facing another last opportunity.[6]

Europe's recession had been mild compared to the global trend. Its bank bailouts, though large, had not involved massive direct exposure of the state to banking debts. Its fiscal measures, being largely 'automatic', provided a much bigger bang for the bucks than the improvised measures in China and the United States.

Led by French President Nicolas Sarkozy and Angela Merkel, the German chancellor, the EU approached the G20 summit in London with an agenda completely different from that of the Anglo-Saxon economies. Whereas both Obama and Gordon Brown wanted the summit to provide global validation for a second round of fiscal stimulus they wanted to unleash at home, the Europeans wanted a global commitment to a new round of regulation. As for a further fiscal stimulus, the Europeans wanted no part of legitimising it – indeed, they wanted a clear timetable for the ending of such stimulus measures as had been taken.

I had a ringside seat for this event, beginning with the arrival of Barack Obama for a press conference in the Foreign Office – a kind of marble mausoleum for British imperialism. Obama had, until now, basked in the glory of his election victory; he looked disoriented as the British press accused America of starting the crisis and pointed up the Europeans' opposition to any further fiscal moves. He replied, 'The fact of the matter is, is that almost every country that's participating in this summit has engaged in fiscal stimulus. The ones that are perceived as being resistant to fiscal stimulus have done significant fiscal stimulus.'

President Sarkozy had already threatened to leave an 'empty chair' at the summit if no serious progress was made on global regulation of the banks. That afternoon Sarkozy and Merkel called their own briefing in a cramped and stifling hotel dining room, the French president arriving flanked by a man in gold braid carrying a suitcase that turned out to contain the launch button for the French nuclear deterrent.

Sarkozy confirmed his threat to walk out of the summit: 'The time of useless summits has passed . . .' he muttered. German negotiators were, meanwhile, frantically trying to remove any mention of the word 'stimulus' from the communiqué. 'Such an impolitic press conference' the German magazine *Der Spiegel* commented, 'hasn't been seen at an international summit for a long time.'

By the next morning it was clear that the Europeans would not sign up for a new global fiscal stimulus. Likewise the Americans, supported by the British, were not prepared to move against derivative markets and hedge funds – indeed, at this point the United States even wanted to defend the old model of investment banking.

So the London Summit produced a kind of minimum programme. Instead of a fiscal stimulus, the countries agreed to pledge $1.1 trillion of new borrowing facilities via the IMF. Crucially, this was not to be actual money spent, but a loan facility created. That did not stop Gordon Brown calling it a stimulus.

Instead of a global crackdown on the root causes of the banking crisis – the conflict of interest at the heart of investment banking – they cracked down on a series of island states whose main function is to provide brass-plate addresses for hedge funds and channel the private wealth of political leaders. Brown, in a valedictory press conference, announced the end of the neo-liberal era:

> The old Washington Consensus is over. Today we have reached a new consensus that we take global action together to deal with the problems we face, that we will do what is necessary to restore growth and jobs, that we will take essential action to rebuild confidence and trust in our financial system and to prevent a crisis such as this ever happening again.

With hindsight we can see that the G20 was the last possible chance to create a united strategy between the three great economic blocs. They recognized the problem: that competitive exit strategies would tear the world economy apart and that rival, unilateral crackdowns on the banks could tear global finance into pieces. But they limited their actions to a common denominator, not a strategy.

At the ill-fated 1933 London Conference, Keynes had urged delegates: 'Our plan must be spectacular, so as to change the grey complexion of men's minds. It must apply to all countries and to all simultaneously.' Not one of the political leaders assembled in London on 2 April 2009 had the nerve even to conceive of such a call, let alone make it. The die was cast for the competitive exit strategies that would begin less than a year later.

A short, sharp, v-shaped slump

In the days after the London G20 Summit, economists Barry Eichengreen and Kevin O'Rourke published a series of graphs that sent shivers through the finance ministries of the world. They had compared the data from the modern meltdown to data from the crash that had begun in 1929.

On industrial production, the slide from an April 2008 peak over the ten months that followed mirrored almost exactly the shape of the slump after June 1929. After the 1929 crash it had taken the world's equity markets twenty-seven months to lose half their value; this time, it had taken just ten. On world trade the story was the same: the modern world had seen exports decline to 80 per cent of peak in just ten months, a point it had taken Depression Era exports more than two years to reach. Eichengreen wrote: 'The world is currently undergoing an economic shock every bit as big as the Great Depression shock of 1929–30 . . . The good news, of course, is that the policy response is very different. The question now is whether that policy response will work.'

One glance at the same charts a year later shows that it did work. By March 2010 industrial production had recovered up to 95 per cent of its pre-slump total; world trade had recovered half its losses, reaching back to around 90 per cent of its peak. Only the equity markets looked more fragile, hovering below 80 per cent of their April 2008 value.[7]

What is less clear is how the stimulus measures worked, and why.

On the Eichengreen–O'Rourke charts, the trade and stock market curves bottom out in February 2009, whereas March 2009 is the bottom point of the V for industrial production. According to their figures, then, the turning point had been reached in advance of any material impact by the major stimulus measures.

With China, the data is fairly clear – showing an almost symmetrical switch from exports to domestic investment. By the autumn of 2009, exports were down 23 per cent but fixed investment up 33 per cent, driven by a 28 per cent increase in the money supply.[8] By the first quarter of 2010, growth had surged back into double digits. Importantly, China's trade had also bounced back with an eye-catching 85 per cent surge in imports in January 2010, compared with a year earlier. All of these figures are commensurate with a one-year economic turnaround led by a combination of fiscal and monetary stimulus. This in turn produced a mini-surge in neighbouring Asia, from South Korea to Australia.

In the United States the response was much more anaemic. Economic growth returned in the third quarter of 2009 and was projected to top 3 per cent in both 2010 and 2011. However, the unemployment rate doubled between July 2008 and January 2010, peaking at 10.1 per cent and then flattening out. President Obama claimed the fiscal stimulus 'created or saved' up to 3 million jobs to the end of 2010 – but that still left 15 million Americans unemployed.[9] To date the US recovery has been a high-profit, low-employment story, with company profits up 20 per cent year on year but unemployment static at around 10 per cent.

However, there are doubts as to how much the fiscal stimulus contributed to this recovery. Economists Joshua Aizenman and Gurnain Kaur Pasricha plotted the sharp rise in federal government spending during the crisis against the collapse in state-level spending that had predated it. They concluded that throughout the whole of 2009 the US government had achieved just $49 billion worth of demand 'bang' for about $330 billion stimulus 'bucks':

> So far, the federal fiscal expenditure stimulus has mostly compensated for the negative state and local stimulus associated with the collapsing tax revenue and the limited borrowing capacity of the states. While this is a significant accomplishment, the net effect is that the consolidated fiscal expenditure stimulus is small relative to the sharp fall in private aggregate demand.[10]

If this calculation is correct, and the United States' fiscal actions have had a negligible stimulus effect, then the tangible turnaround in demand in the United States must be due to a mixture of currency effects, microeconomic intervention, healing of the credit system and quantitative easing.

For all Bernanke's reticence about the theory of QE, the fact that he had already begun to do it on as small scale after the collapse of Fannie Mae and Freddie Mac in the autumn/winter of 2008 probably led to its early impact in the second quarter of 2009.

In addition, the mix of bonds bought with printed money in the United States was different than in the United Kingdom and Japan. Bernanke bought $1.25 trillion of the so-called agency mortgage backed securities issued by Fannie and Freddie, but only $300 billion of US government bonds. Because Fannie and Freddie had already been effectively nationalised, this hardly mattered in the national accounts, but as a means to pump money into the banking system it seems to have been particularly effective. Taken together, the Fed's bond purchases allowed the equivalent of 12.5 per cent of GDP to be pumped into the system in a matter of months.

Now, as they say, do the math: 12.5 per cent of GDP in the form of monetary stimulus plus 3 per cent in the form of fiscal stimulus produces a 3 per cent growth rate. The scale of the slump averted was clearly huge – and this is by no means academic. For both fiscal and monetary stimulus measures were one-offs. The only way to unwind them without producing a further slump would be to restart the banking system and sustainable growth. Yet, as we will see, this is not so easy.

Meanwhile in Europe both the recession and the anti-crisis response was patchy. The twenty-seven-country EU saw growth collapse by 4.7 per cent in 2009, but that figure masked an economic catastrophe at the periphery: Estonia, Lithuania and Latvia experienced a true slump, losing 14 per cent, 15 per cent and 18 per cent of GDP respectively. Ireland's growth collapsed by 7 per cent. Excepting Poland, much of Eastern Europe experienced falls of about 6 per cent. Of the large industrial economies, France did best, powering back into growth in August 2009 and losing only 3 per cent of GDP overall.

When it came to fiscal stimulus, the EU powers were technically constrained by the Maastricht Treaty criteria, which stipulated that member states had to hold debt at 60 per cent of GDP and borrowing at 3 per cent. But they now flagrantly broke the rules: over 2009–2010, states launched discretionary fiscal stimulus measures that would be judged small compared to America's and China's, but which, combined with the 'automatic stabilisers', pushed their budget deficits way above the Maastricht limits. French borrowing was 8 per cent of GDP in 2009, Britain's 11 per cent, Italy 's 5.3 per cent.[11]

Basically, some EU countries could afford the fiscal hit of falling revenue plus discretionary stimulus; others could not, and a few would now struggle to balance the books. As a result, the gross national debts of the major Maastricht signatories are now way above target and set to be significantly higher by 2015. Yet their actual stimulus measures were smaller than elsewhere (see Table 1). This contradiction would be a storm signal for Europe.

Table 1 **Fiscal cost of the crisis per cent gdp**

	2-year fiscal stimulus	2009 budget deficit	Gross debt 2010	Gross debt 2015 (est.)
Germany	3.6	3.3	77	81
France	1.5	8	84	95
UK	1.8	11	78	91
Italy	0	5.3	115	124
US	4.7	12.5	83	110
Japan	5	10.3	235	250
China	5.8	3	20	17

Source: IMF *May 2010*

In Europe too, the path of quantitative easing ran in different directions. Britain's 'pure' QE strategy saw it inject around 12 per cent of GDP into the economy. The Bank of England estimates this should, over a period of three to four years, filter through into a 12 per cent increase in the money supply and thus in demand. But they are not really sure how it works.

When I and other journalists questioned the bank's economists at a 'deniable' briefing in the dingy basement at Threadneedle Street in late 2009, they declined to say how much had already filtered through, nor how much would in each of the subsequent years. By implication, because UK money-supply growth actually fell during the first 12 months of QE, the Bank of England must believe the main impact will be felt in later years.

If you look at the British government's projection for growth – never above 2.9 per cent over the next five years - you would have to say that, according to the bank's theory, QE is accounting for almost all of the increase in GDP over the medium term. Britain's fiscal stimulus was puny in 2009, and was withdrawn by the Labour government in its March 2010 budget, paving the way for the Conservative/Libdem coalition to launch a £113 billion spending cuts package in its emergency budget in June.

Without a return to self-sustaining growth, Britain – as the result of its meagre stimulus, massive deficit and stringent emergency budget – is in danger of a double-dip recession or prolonged stagnation, with only the two bullets left in the clip to fight it: sterling devaluation and more QE.

Britain's June 2010 emergency budget set the bar for G20 countries in the rapidity and severity of its deficit reduction plan – but the whole project was based on cuts of a severity not seen since 1945 and a rapid switch to export-led and private sector growth that has never been attempted before.

However, for the rest of Europe the European Central Bank had rejected QE on principle, as a threat to the stability of the eurozone monetary arrangements. Instead it expanded its role as provider of liquidity to the market, extending it well beyond the size and timescale offered by similar operations in Washington and London. Technically the ECB was simply expanding the availability of existing money to banks in the eurozone, accepting AAA-rated bonds in return for euros and not boosting total money supply or demand.

Practically, the quality of the bonds was questionable. However, for more than a year this action made the ECB look like the calmest and steadiest central bank on earth. All was well. Or so it seemed.

Before coming to any synthetic judgment about what drove the global bounce-back that began in the third quarter of 2009, we have to look at the micro-economic measures and continued support for stricken banks.

Cauterising the Banks

By the time of the April 2009 G20 summit the bank crisis had been effectively cauterized, with multibillion-dollar equity stakes in the stricken banks: Citigroup, Bank of America, RBS and Lloyds Group, ING, UBS and many more, smaller bailouts. In the United States, Obama's incoming treasury secretary, Tim Geithner, turned the original $700 billion allocated to TARP (see Chapter 2) into a plethora of initiatives. In addition to the original plan – buying up the bad debts of US banks – money would be thrown at automobile companies, and at homeowners via a scheme to reduce repossessions, and, as with the British bailout, the US government would 'guarantee' losses on the bad loans of specific banks.

The advantage of this approach – apart from the natural attractiveness to politicians of anything complicated and opaque – was that it shared the burden of saving the system with the Fed, and allowed a more micro-targeted approach to crisis. It also allowed the US government to assume much larger liabilities for much lower nominal costs: if you guarantee the losses on $300 billion, then estimate the losses at 10 per cent, only $30 billion shows up in the government accounts.

Altogether about half of the TARP money was spent. But by March 2010 the biggest net outlay under TARP had been the purchase of shares in 707 failing banks. Of the $205 billion laid out, the US Treasury was carrying a loss of $70 billion. A further $70 billion used to bail out AIG looked impossible to recover. On top of that the next biggest loss-line was the money used to bail out the stricken auto industry firms General Motors, Chrysler and GMAC in June 2009, totalling $77 billion; on top of that there was a $36 billion expected loss on a programme to help 50 major mortgage lenders refinance or modify stricken mortgages to prevent default and repossession.

Much of the money laid out in specific guarantees to banks – above all to Citigroup and Bank of America – had been paid back by early 2010. For all the sound and fury over TARP in September 2008, it had worked – on paper at least – and at half the expected price.

But TARP by now was a minute portion of the US government's real exposure to the crisis. The US Treasury had issued loan guarantees totalling $1.6 trillion, including $600 billion to underwrite losses on money market funds, $400 billion to nationalise losses at Fannie and Freddie and $200 billion on student loans.[12] In addition, the US Federal Deposit Insurance Corporation (FDIC) was exposed to $1.4 trillion of guarantees in its role of lender of last resort to the commercial banking system. If you add in the US government's exposure to mortgage debt through quantitative easing ($1.25 trillion), and the $5.5 trillion of liabilities taken on board when nationalising Fannie and Freddie, by one calculation the total exposure of the US government comes to $3.6 trillion in outlays and $16 trillion in guarantees (this latter number being two trillions more than the US GDP).

By throwing – literally – everything at the banking crisis, the system had been saved. But in the process huge losses had been nationalised. The US budget deficit would spiral to $1.4 trillion in 2009 and US debt to $13 trillion. Meanwhile the gains had remained with the private sector. The only reason so little of the TARP money had been lost was that quantitative easing allowed the investment banks, in the soar-away summer of 2009, to fill their boots.

At a macro level the deal was simple. Governments all over the world had reduced the cost of borrowing, for banks, to near zero; in fact technically it was below zero. Yet for real-world companies, like Berck in the English Midlands, which was struggling to refinance a massive overdraft, the risks were high. Consequently, Berck's borrowing costs – even on an ordinary overdraft – would be ramped up to double-digit interest rates and company directors would be asked for the first time in living memory to pledge their homes and cars as collateral against business loans. It was the same story with consumers and homebuyers: all over the world credit criteria became tight, lending slowed to a trickle, and real interest rates soared.

Investment banks, which had trained tens of thousands of the world's best minds to the task of finding high-profit opportunities in a low-profit world, leapt at the chance to do it risk-free.

Banks like Goldman Sachs and JP Morgan Chase, who had survived the 2008 meltdown, reaped record profits: $3.3 billion in the first three months of 2010 for Goldman. Even Citi and Bank of America, still haemorrhaging losses from subprime and CDOS, could offset them with soaring profits from trading stocks, commodities and currencies.

In addition to the creation of a risk-free banking environment, government policies now provided the investment banks with two key tactical opportunities. Though the aim of quantitative easing is to flush money into the economy via the banking system, while that money is going through the banking system it can boost the price and trading volume of the key financial markets: thus, partially as a result of QE money and partially as a result of returning growth, the global stock markets recovered 50 per cent of their losses. As they did, the cash registers of the investment banks swelled.

On top of this, the growing debts that had been created by fiscal stimulus now increased the cost of borrowing for states themselves. Both directly and − through credit default swaps − indirectly, the banks could now make money from a whole new high-risk lending opportunity: government bonds. And if the chaos in the banking system had created a backwash of instability in the foreign exchange markets, that was just one more opportunity for the investment banks to make money.

By September 2009 three things were clear: that most countries' economies would recover as a result of the fiscal and monetary stimulus; that the moral hazard problem in the banking system had worsened; and that elements of a new financial bubble were emerging as a result of the large amount of stimulus money 'trapped' in the financial markets and failing to trickle through into demand in the real economy.

This set the stage for a rethink in Washington over the scope of bank regulation and a renewed push for the goal the Europeans had fought for in April: global financial regulation.

Pittsburgh: A New Financial Order?

There was something medieval fortress-like about the security arrangements that ringed the Pittsburgh G20 Summit: at the centre, the powerful and their bodyguards; around them, the broadcast media and NGOs, like courtiers; then a ring of battlements topped with razor wire – all protected by armour-clad riot police with dogs, shotguns and a sound laser.

What would emerge from the Pittsburgh convention centre was equally medieval: a power-sharing deal akin to that made by Frederic Barbarossa with his feudal lords at the foundation of the Holy Roman Empire. Sink your political differences and legal claims on each other inside a new economic system; implement a commonly agreed rule of law; accept a kind of collective despotism to replace the old international order, which had descended into chaos.

The G20, it was promised, would formally replace the G8. Much more importantly, as it issued orders, directives and advice to the IMF, World Bank and WTO, it would move the global management of the crisis away from these treaty-endowed bodies set up in 1944 and into the hands of the G20 itself. Only two years before, the United States had threatened to expel Russia from the G8 over its war with Georgia. Now, before our eyes, an ad hoc global body was being created that included the one-party state of China and the religious dictatorship in Saudi Arabia. Such were the powers now claimed by this self-selected body that it was impossible to imagine any state being expelled from the G20 for any reason short of an all-out trade war.

Inside the conference chamber a major shift was going on in the thinking of the world's big powers. Confronted with the reality of huge bank bonuses and profits, even as cash drained from their own treasuries to pay for the stimulus, they were forced finally to address the issue of moral hazard.

Ever since the AIG rescue it had been clear that some banks were too systemically important to be allowed to fail. Now the banks were operating on the entirely logical principle that should they fail again the state would bail them out again. But the states assembled in Pittsburgh knew their finances were in no condition to do so. And even if they were, the banks were effectively getting a free 100 per cent–money-back guarantee deal from the taxpayer. Thus, to those minded to work this out with philosophical logic, the entire system was operating on a false premise.

It fell to the head of financial stability at the Bank of England, Andrew Haldane, to spell out the consequences. While the G20 met, Haldane addressed a Federal Reserve conference in Chicago with a paper that had already begun to shape the thinking of both the Brown and Obama administrations.

Haldane pointed out that over the past 100 years the banking system has become more and more dependent on state guarantees. Each time there is a banking crisis, the state bails out the system and introduces new regulations to prevent the crisis recurring. But Haldane produced data to show, convincingly, that after each episode of crisis the banks have managed successfully to 'game' the new regulations.

Haldane showed, mirroring the argument presented in Chapter 4 of this book, how the banking system's profits had leapt after the 1970s, when banks were allowed to progressively slash the amount of capital they needed to hold. He showed, too, how in the three years before the current meltdown, specific UK banks had massively hiked the ratio of loans to capital: banks whose ratio of loans to capital had been clustered around 25/1 had rocketed to, on average, 40/1 and in one case 70/1. The entire golden age of British banking, as Gordon Brown once called it, had been achieved through catastrophic leverage. As Haldane put it: 'Higher leverage fully accounts for the rise in UK banks' returns on equity up until 2007. It also fully accounts for the subsequent collapse in these returns. The high-leverage strategy pursued by uk and European banks rather effectively privatised gains and socialised losses.'

Across the Atlantic, in the rehearsal rooms of Britain's National Theatre, the radical socialist playwright David Hare was putting the finishing touches to an anti-capitalist play that said just this: that the bailout process had been 'socialism for the rich'. Now here was the same sentiment being expressed out of the distinctly non-leftist Bank of England.

In a few elegantly argued pages Haldane had demolished the arguments against the radical reform of banking. As the bankers recovered their poise in the summer of 2009 it had become common to hear them purr that the whole system could be put right with a 'higher capital cushion', preferably imposed many years hence and only then if implemented on a global scale.

Now the logic of the situation was spelled out: only structural reform would prevent another banking crisis from bankrupting major states. Not only had states to demand an explicit fee or levy from banking profits to pay for this crisis and deter others, they had to confront the problem of what to do with banks that were 'too big to fail'. Haldane's boss, Mervyn King, had already hinted at the answer:

> If some banks are thought to be too big to fail, then, in the words of a distinguished American economist, they are too big. It is not sensible to allow large banks to combine high street retail banking with risky investment banking or funding strategies, and then provide an implicit state guarantee against failure. Something must give . . . Privately owned and managed institutions that are too big to fail sit oddly with a market economy.[13]

In the face of blatant opposition from their own government, and in defiance of the nostrums of the bankers, the United Kingdom's central bankers had quietly outlined the case for a new Glass–Steagall act.

Haldane's paper concluded with a backhanded swipe at the changes to banking regulation achieved in the year since Lehman: 'Reversing direction will not be easy. It is likely to require a financial sector reform effort every bit as radical as followed the Great Depression. It is an open question whether reform efforts to date, while slowing the swing, can bring about that change of direction.'[14]

The change of direction would begin at Pittsburgh. In a toughly worded communiqué, the world's major powers agreed to four principles they had resisted in London – indeed, which had then seemed impossible to agree on:

First, a co-ordinated global macro-economic policy, designed to keep growth sustainable and smooth out the global imbalances over time. Second, a move to 'macro-prudential regulation' – where central banks would have the duty to burst financial bubbles before they inflated. Third, regulation and if necessary dismantling of big systemic banks and hedge funds. Finally, a macro-economic policy that was itself counter-cyclical; that is, one that committed all 20 states not only to interest-rate policies designed to slow down booms and mitigate busts, but also to the rest of the economic policy.

It was one of those 'motherhood and apple pie' declarations that had most people in politics and banking sniggering quietly into their post-Pittsburgh cocktails. Nevertheless it did close a chapter in the crisis response. From now on the banks knew that they would face some form of direct levy or tax on top of new capital adequacy rules. And it opened the way to a major policy debate in Washington.

On 21 January 2010 President Obama lined up for a White House press conference alongside a figure hardly seen in public for decades, Paul Volcker. In the months since Pittsburgh, the Carter-era economist had been pushing for a new, structural separation within investment banking. The 'Volcker rule' would ban proprietary trading within regulated US banks – so that firms such as Goldman and JP Morgan could no longer, as FDR had once put it, 'speculate with other people's money'. Direct involvement in hedge funds and private equity groups would also be off-limits. Though not exactly a Glass–Steagall Act, the Volcker rule did embody the same principles. Hovering in the background, Tim Geithner – who had actively opposed any attempt at structural reform on Wall Street – looked cowed. But not for long.

As this book goes to press, the 2,000-page Dodd–Frank Act has passed through the US House of Representatives. It contains measures to limit banks' proprietary trading and hedge fund ownership to 3 per cent of their capital. The principle of the Volcker Rule has survived in just the same way as the coccyx of a human being, the vestigial remnant of a monkey's tail; the whole evolutionary process from radical measure to pointless gesture taking, in this case, just six months. The *Atlantic* magazine sumarised the outcome in its headline: 'Dodd–Frank Bill's Volker Rule a Win for Big Banks'.

Meanwhile in Europe, tentative moves towards an EU-wide banking tax were first stonewalled by Gordon Brown's government (which insisted it be done globally or not at all) and then by the incoming Conservative/Libdem coalition, which favoured a small (£2 billion) banking levy, but not of the kind advocated by Brussels.

In summary, though the world's politicians were able to make a conceptual breakthrough at Pittsburgh, promising co-ordinated action at every level, they were unable to achieve it even on the pressing issue of bank reform. Their unilateral moves have been meagre; their multilateral moves exist only as commitments in principle. In the key Anglo-Saxon countries the shift towards re-regulation at the top has not survived resistance within the legislature and the electoral cycle, resistance driven by relentless lobbying from the banks themselves.

The former IMF economist Simon Johnson explained this situation as a form of regulatory 'capture' by a political and banking elite too intermeshed with each other to see beyond their own material interests:

The people in charge of our strategy towards big banks are not fools and they are not corrupt; they are also not doing things just because someone on Wall Street calls them up. Our top policymakers are simply convinced that what is good for the biggest and most dangerous element on Wall Street is good for the American economy. This is cultural capture in its purest and most extreme form . . . Unfortunately, the White House and Treasury may be the last to realize this.'[15]

Johnson had long warned that the failure to rapidly re-regulate the banks, breaking up those too big to fail and separating the key functions that create the conflict of interest within the business model, could fatally weaken the world economy if a new crisis were to break out. In a doomsday scenario he envisaged the collapse of the banking sector in East Europe feeding back into the system and causing a new tremor of global crisis.

In the end it was not some obscure *Sparkasse* in a corner of Europe that detonated the crisis but a whole country. By April 2009 the euro itself was facing collapse.

The Euro crisis

When it gets dark, Exarchia Square in Athens comes alive with the murmur of drug dealers. Students wander past them, deep in argument and abstract thought. Posters denounce capitalism; graffiti denounces police harassment. Small shops and bars ply their trade in the neon gloom. Riot cops lounge, exhausted, against street corners.

It is an archetypical scene from a place called Europe: layered, tribal, intensely urban, sporadically violent, intellectual, tolerant and until now resilient: this is the civilisation the European Union was set up to build after 1945 – and the eurozone was set up to 'harmonise'.

But by May 2010 it was facing its biggest challenge: Europe had become the weak link in the world economy. Though individual economies in Europe could bear the cost of the fiscal stimulus and bank bailout, the eurozone could not. It would now face the prospect of deep austerity or breakup, or both.

The trigger was the Greek fiscal crisis. In October 2009 the social-democratic party Pasok, headed by Prime Minister George Papandreou, came to power and immediately discovered that the country's budget deficit – hiked from 3.7 per cent to 6 per cent as a result of the downturn – was in fact 12.7 per cent. That put Greece at the top of the borrowing league for developed countries and created two immediate problems.

First, the credibility of Eurostat – the EU agency required to audit the national accounts in line with the euro currency arrangements – was shattered. Second, because of the short-term way Greece had financed its €210 billion national debt on the global markets, a quarter of the debt would become due for repayment in 2010. Greece would need a highly draconian austerity package to prevent its borrowing costs soaring to unsustainable levels in the second quarter of the year.

On 12 January 2010 the Papandreou government published its plan: an aggressive combination of tax raising and public sector pay and pension cuts. On 2 February the European Commission would approve that plan. Unfortunately, on the same day, Eurostat published a report excoriating the former right-wing government of Greece for its failure to report its rising deficit:

> Inappropriate governance, with poor cooperation and lack of clear responsibilities between several Greek institutions . . . diffuse personal responsibilities, ambiguous empowerment of officials, absence of written instruction and documentation, which leave the quality of fiscal statistics subject to political pressures and electoral cycles.[16]

Greece, in plain English, had cooked the books. Not only that, it had done so legally with the help of Goldman Sachs – which had helped the Greek government move some of its debt 'off balance sheet'.

Suddenly it was not just the Greek government under fire but the whole of the eurozone. The continent had avoided quantitative easing, exposed its governments to far less bad banking debt than in the United States and Europe, and had adopted only a mild discretionary stimulus. Now it had a credibility problem, a sovereign debt problem and a currency devaluation problem rolled up into one.

Europe had got to the end of Phase One of the global crisis – marked by the April 2009 G20 Summit – with its nerve and systems intact. Italy's barely modernised banking sector had borne up well; Spain – where tough banking regulations had kept iconic groups like Santander financially robust – had survived the test. If Ireland was the continent's basket case, with its key banks nationalised and a severe austerity programme slashing the pay of public sector workers, it also gave assurance that Europe's social model could withstand the rigours of austerity.

If there were worries in Europe, they lay outside the eurozone: Iceland, hubristically bankrupt; Latvia's politicians leading it defiantly into depression to maintain their dream of EU-entry; the wannabe countries of Eastern Europe with their idiotic housing booms and corrupt governments. Plus of course the Brits with their busted banking system and disgraced regulators.

But it turned out the eurozone was based on just the same kind of systemic flaw as Wall Street and that the flaw had been hidden by just the same kind of 'social silence' among a political elite of bankers and policymakers as was discovered in Wall Street. Only this time it concerned states and social classes, not banks.

The eurozone is a currency and a central bank without a government. But a currency is only as sound as the public finances of the state that issues it. In the eurozone, fiscal discipline was supposed to be enforced through treaty obligations and common oversight. But it was not.

To understand why, you have to go back to the 1992 Maastricht Treaty. Maastricht wrote the principles of neoliberalism into a political constitution. History will see this as all the more remarkable because, even at the time, that economic doctrine was heavily disputed. Now that neo-liberalism is dead, the provisions of the Maastricht and successive EU treaties seem all the more arcane.

Under Maastricht, the mission of the European Central Bank was to be price stability. This was logical, since 'inflation targeting' was being adopted in Washington and London and would underpin the long period of low-ish, stable growth described in Chapter 4. But in Europe there was an added imperative for monetary discipline: countries on Europe's periphery would boom on entry, boosting inflation. To pursue the long-term goal of harmonising Ireland and the Mediterranean with the industrialised countries of northern Europe, the monetary policy of the ECB would have to be temperamentally austere.

The ECB's inflation target was set at a maximum figure – 2 per cent – at a time when the UK's central bank was already moving to a more flexible 'symmetrical' target around the same number. The ECB's 'independence' from politics – and therefore from democracy – was absolute in a way that never happened at the Bank of England or the Fed. It had no growth target. Crucially – unlike the Bank of England – it set its own inflation target. And, though it ruthlessly protected itself from political influence, it was always prepared to exert it – for example, insisting on writing the goal of price stability into the Lisbon Treaty.

Since its foundation, then, the ECB has followed a rigid, doctrinal monetarism. It exerted perennial downward pressure on growth in northern Europe as the price for 'harmonising' southern Europe into the system, raising interest rates in the face of the global downturn at the start of the twenty-first century.

The Maastricht Treaty decreed strict rules: all countries must keep budget deficits below 3 per cent and debt below 60 per cent of GDP; no bailouts would be available to states facing deficit problems; even state aid to failing banks was technically disallowed; and the ECB would never intervene in the bond markets to prop up the currency arrangement. But – as the Greek budget crisis showed – this was, by the mid-2000s, an arrangement based on falsehood. Eurostat had put Greece under 'intense scrutiny' after 2004, with ten separate visits to check the accounts. The problem, though, was not an accounting issue; it was political.

When a Greek guy calmly tells you that his country is systemically corrupt, that you have to pay a bribe to jump the hospital queue or to pass your driving test; that politics, too, is corrupt, geared to patronage and incapable of cleaning up the system – that's a moment of frankness. But when the man in question is George Papaconstantinou, the Greek finance minister, it illustrates the scale of the problem.

When I interviewed Papaconstantinou in late February 2010 it was in an office surrounded by striking public-sector workers. On the shelf behind his desk one book in English stood out among the volumes on Greek statistical data: *Nice Capitalism*, by Greek consultant Kostas Cataras. Cataras's book claims that Europe, with its 'human ethos' and social solidarity, is about to surpass and replace the US model of capitalism. Published in 2008, the book had enjoyed a brief flurry of popularity as Europe indulged in schadenfreude over the Lehman collapse.

But the Greek finance ministry now had a problem: nice capitalism was no longer an option. The eurozone's conditions for bailing out Greece would signal the suspension of the social model. And for Greece – and across southern Europe – the welfare state and the large, well-paid public sector workforce were of historic political significance.

Greece, Portugal and Spain are, as the euphemism has it, 'young democracies'. Both Greece and Portugal lived through anti-militarist revolutions in 1974, and Spain's route out of fascism saw shots fired by army officers in the parliamentary chamber as late as 1981. To those who remember southern Europe in the 1970s and 80s, it is a region transformed. Eurozone entry gave impetus to the rapid growth, marketisation and modernisation that had begun in 1989. If, in the process, a rising middle class enriched itself – taking advantage of property speculation and tax avoidance – it was not exactly kicking against the spirit of the age.

The Greek conservative newspaper *Kathimerini* spelled out the implicit deal the political class had offered to the working class since the 1980s:

> At last, all those who had been shut out by the right-wing establishment which triumphed in the Civil War in 1946-49 – and which was thoroughly discredited by the dictatorship of 1967–74 – would get to share in the wealth of the nation. The fact that this new middle class was founded on wealth that the country was not producing meant that the economy broke free from all logic and went into its own orbit.[17]

To the extent that it was known about or suspected, the systemic scam going on in Greece was tolerated because the sudden appearance of Prada outlets, the sudden ubiquity of four-wheel-drive automobiles, the urgent completion of all those half-built seaside villas all signalled 'harmonisation'. In countries scarred by the living memory of fascism and civil war it was, the politicians noticed, harder to remember that your grandfather fought my grandfather if we both now own suvs.

And it was never just about the private sector. During democratisation Portugal, Ireland, Spain and Greece had granted generous pension schemes, job security rules and rising real wages to the public sector workforce – again, to guarantee social peace. Now that it had all gone wrong, the German press took the lead in blackening the whole southern European arrangement: 'Are we the schmucks of Europe?' the tabloid magazine *Bild* would ask its readers.

In fact, the whole arrangement suited Germany, lying at the heart of its strategy to utilize the eurozone arrangements to its own competitive advantage. On entry, the exchange rates for all countries thought to be at risk of high inflation had been set in

Germany's favour. However, as the austere monetary policy of the ECB bore down on the eurozone economy, a new battle for competitiveness would break out: whoever could impose cuts in real wages and social benefits fastest would win. The winner was Germany.

After 2003 Germany introduced a series of labour reforms that would suppress any rise in labour costs. Meanwhile a combination of rising social benefits, higher growth and political pressure delivered a real rise in unit labour costs in Ireland and southern Europe. The graph of German unit labour costs since 1995 is flat, but for the peripheral countries it rises at a 45-degree angle.

With wages falling as a component of GDP in Germany, and rising on the periphery, there was an inevitable outcome: Germany became a giant export machine to the rest of Europe, exporting goods and capital. As the soas-based Research on Money and Finance (RMF) network put it: 'The eurozone has become an area of entrenched current account surpluses for Germany, financed by current account deficits for peripheral countries. Monetary union is a beggar-thy-neighbour policy for Germany, on condition that it beggars its own workers first.'[18]

We will not know to what extent the eurozone authorities suspected fiscal duplicity in Greece until the memoirs are written. But the arrangement was a win-win, just like Gordon Brown's reliance on booming financial profits to pay for the UK's public spending spree and America's addiction to property and cheap credit in the 2000s. Germany's financial and political elite profited massively from the eurozone arrangement: wages boomed in the south; Germany's trade surplus also boomed. Everybody won. Or seemed to.

When I met Mr Papaconstantinou the situation in Greece looked containable. The civil service strike that had brought reporters flocking to Athens passed off without trouble; the conditions imposed by the eurozone authorities on a Greek bailout looked not simply doable, but doable without the need for massive public service cuts. A crackdown on tax evasion, plus

real cuts in pensions and pay, looked like enough to tackle the
deficit without permanently depressing private-sector growth.

How it spiralled from this into a continent-wide fiscal crisis is a
story of blind adherence to neo-liberal and monetarist norms – at
the ECB and in Berlin.

On 3 March the Greek government produced a revised,
harsher cuts plan: again, it was approved by the European
Commission. On 15 March the EU leaders agreed 'in principle'
to bail Greece out. Greece needed access to cheap money to roll
over the €50 billion of debts becoming due in 2010. On 11 April
European finance ministers agreed to a €30 billion bailout
package – then failed to deliver a single cent.

With the German press and the Free Democrat party up in arms
at the 'profligate' Greek lifestyle, Angela Merkel pressed persistently for harsher conditions. The Bundesbank, Germany's central
bank, warned the ECB against any retreat from its monetarist rules.
The euro governments railed against 'speculators'.

But the failure to deliver a bailout now opened the door to 28
days of speculation. As the interest rate on Greek debt spiralled
into unpayable territory, the cost of insuring against a Greek
default began to signal that the default was likely. Then, in the
last week of April, came the week of 'contagion'.

Bond investors, who mainly represent pension funds, began to
fear that the Greek crisis would lead to 'restructuring' – that is,
partial default – of Greece's debts; that the bailout would, in
other words, inflict pain on them as well as on the Greek public
sector. Once established, this precedent of partial default would
be used to solve the fiscal crises in Portugal and Spain.

A crisis point in confidence was reached not because Portugal
and Spain were facing imminent fiscal crisis but because their
deficit-reduction plans looked unrealistic, based on overly opti-
mistic growth plans and a refusal to confront their own public-
sector workers. It was at this point, in late April, that the cost of
borrowing for Portugal – its 'spread' against Germany's bond

interest rate – took off, and that of Spain also ticked upwards. OECD Secretary General Angel Gurria, in an emotional outburst, warned Europe's leaders: 'It's not the danger of contagion. Contagion has already happened. This is like Ebola. When you realise you have it, you have to cut your leg off in order to survive.'[19] Now began a massive speculative attack on the euro. Bets were placed on its rapid depreciation, on its breakup, and on a new banking crisis.

According to analysts at rbs, the European banks were exposed to around €500 billion of potentially bad government debt from Spain, Portugal and Greece. In addition, they were holding €1 trillion of bad debt from the southern European banking system – and this on top of whatever toxic debt still remained from the domestic banking crisis in northern Europe. With small banks in Spain now going under, and the danger of partial debt-default at country level, the contagion looked set to spread to the heart of the northern European banking system. The vix Index – that reliable Geiger counter of market volatility back in 2008 – reached the levels it had attained during the Bear Stearns collapse and on the brink of the Lehman debacle.

In order to prevent Greece becoming the prelude to a Lehman-scale event with Spain, the European governments acted. During frantic negotiations on 9 May they binned their objections to IMF involvement in the EU, to ECB intervention in the bond markets, to bailouts, to bad collateral at the ECB. With the aid of the US Federal Reserve they once again opened up 'swap lines' so that European banks could borrow and lend in dollars, preventing a new retreat by global capital to the safe haven of currency blocs.

The ECB's move was not in itself quantitative easing, because the money injected would be removed in short order once the crisis was over. But it was a psychological Rubicon. The euro was no longer the 'deutschmark in disguise': it was a currency whose authorities had left themselves the option of printing money on a massive scale and, if necessary, of allowing inflation to erode the value of bad debts.

But the price northern Europe demanded for the deal was austerity: austerity and fiscal truth across southern Europe – and, by implication, a new concept of fiscal sovereignty to back the euro. Jean-Claude Trichet, ECB's chief, said:

> Surveillance of budgetary policies, of eurozone economies' competitiveness, and of structural reforms must be radically improved. We are a monetary federation. Now we need the equivalent of a budgetary federation in terms of the control and surveillance of the application of public finance policy.[20]

New, draconian rules would be drawn up to enforce budget discipline. As with the Greek deal, parliaments in bailed-out states would lose effective sovereignty over their budget decisions.

To achieve this deal, President Sarkozy at one point banged the table and threatened to take France out of the euro. By the morning of 10 May they had abandoned almost every tenet of the Maastricht orthodoxy. In the process, northern Europe had, effectively, seized control of the fiscal policy of southern Europe.

To view any graph of the southern European borrowing costs in April–May 2010 is to see a picture of spiking risk. After the bailout of 9 May the graph line falls again – and a new question emerges: where had the risk moved to?

The clue is in the name given to the €440 billion European loan facility designed on 9 May: it was a 'special purpose vehicle', or SPV. Just like the London Tube PPP, Enron's off-balance sheet companies and the jointly owned hedge funds that triggered the 2008 credit crunch, the SPV is designed to obfuscate the risk – to make its ultimate size and ownership hazy.

But logic dictates that if the €440 billion is borne pro rata by the twenty-seven EU countries, it is France, Germany, Italy and the United Kingdom – the taxpayers of northern Europe – who bear the risk of southern European default. Likewise, as members of the IMF, the industrialised countries of Europe are additionally exposed to the fund's €250 billion loan.

In return for this, northern Europe demanded that the countries of southern Europe impose austerity at levels that would push them into stagnation for at least half a decade. The Greek economy was set to shrink by 8 per cent of GDP as part of their austerity plan. Spain, tipped into deflation, and with unemployment at 20 per cent, faced several years of downward adjustment. Its parliament passed a €15 billion emergency austerity package by just one vote, with the Catalan nationalists abstaining. The country's reward was a new debt downgrade, the very next day, by the Fitch ratings agency, which now claimed the resulting Spanish recession would lessen its ability to repay debt. Meanwhile in Ireland core deflation already stood at minus 3 per cent even before next phase of austerity kicked in.

It slowly dawned on these countries that the economic surge that came with the eurozone was over. The Gucci lifestyle for the middle classes that had bandaged the scars of fascism, civil war and clerical reaction for a generation would also be curtailed.

Austerity means low growth or recession. Few now believe these countries on the eurozone periphery can grow their way out of deficit, and they cannot stimulate their way back to growth. They had, by May 2010, become the first potential victims of the debt-deflation spiral that had haunted the world since the meltdown began, and which will impose unprecedented strains on the social truce that has prevailed in these countries. It also has global ramifications.

Globally the danger was spelled out by UK central bank boss Mervyn King and, in the run-up to the Toronto G20, by Barack Obama. Unless the world's big exporters stimulate their own domestic demand, to allow countries in fiscal crisis to export their way back to growth, Europe faces a double-dip recession. And the second dip could be prolonged because there are no bullets left in the clip when it comes to stimulus.

Though relevant for South Korea, China and the United States, King's plea was above all targeted at Germany. Its consumers have to learn to borrow; its voters have to learn to rubber-stamp bailout plans for southern Europe, was the implication. There is little chance of that.

When he was still an academic, Ben Bernanke codified the data from the 1930s into one big lesson: that it was adherence to the Gold Standard, an international currency peg, that had pushed America into the monetary rationing that triggered the Depression. Bernanke showed that, conversely, those who came off gold first, and devalued their currencies first, recovered first.[21]

This is what, quietly, modern governments have been trying to do: Britain's authorities silently rejoiced at sterling's 25 per cent depreciation, hoping – vainly, it turned out – that it would boost the export economy. The US authorities spent half their waking hours during 2009 trying to devalue the dollar against the Chinese RMB. Now the euro's collapse against world currencies would change the game again: analysts believe the euro is headed for parity with the dollar in 2011. According to a model run by the OECD, the 10 per cent drop in the euro's value between November 2009 and the euro bailout should boost eurozone GDP by somewhere between 1 per cent and 2 per cent a year for the next five years – offsetting the impact of the tax rises and spending cuts expected across the eurozone, and exporting the austerity somewhere else.

But competitive devaluation has its limits. Once your reach them there are few options left: either your own population bears the cost of the crisis or you force it onto somebody else.

Since 2008, the overwhelming risk to the global economy has been the debt-deflation spiral. Now, from Washington to London to Frankfurt, all that stands in the way of debt-deflation is the state – in the form of massive state money-printing exercises through central banks; in the form of states underwriting the banking system; and in the form of big states agreeing to stand behind small states.

The euro bailout did not make the risk disappear. It simply transferred the risk in southern Europe to the governments and taxpayers of northern Europe. Its geo-strategic and moral implications are clear: the eurozone is either on a path to becoming a supra-national state-like entity, or it will fragment.

But because every step of the EU project has been taken by elites, with the populations left to work out what was happening months and years later, we can now trace very accurately where the risk was transferred. It has been transferred to the streets: streets like that narrow warren around Exarchia Square, with its disgruntled students, angry workers and exhausted riot cops.

The eurozone staved off crisis by ripping up its rules, defying its own ideology on the promise of a future consolidation into a fiscal super-state. Yet the path to that super-state cannot lie through electoral consent: it never has, even in the good times, and with voters from Athens to Dusseldorf rejecting it, it does not look like a winner now.

So Phase Three of the global crisis poses the following danger for Europe: that the fiscal stimulus of the past eighteen months produces country-level default, that the markets demand austerity to prevent it and that in the process they create the debt-deflation scenario and massive social unrest. This will test Europe's distinctive social model — recognisable on the streets of Galway, Oviedo and Perugia as well as Athens — to breaking point.

The coming global crisis

In the summer of 2010, any attempt to predict the future would be pointless. However, the fault-lines of the global recovery are clear. In the space of twenty-four months the risk has moved from housing to banking to states and now, in southern Europe, to social cohesion.

In searching for a metaphor to illustrate what's happened, I am drawn to the image of tank armour. When a depleted-uranium dart hits the armour of a tank its energy is diffused into layer-upon-layer of complex materials: metals, fabrics, ceramics. If you are lucky, the round never penetrates the final layer and the crew survives. But take a look at the armour plate: it is mangled, defabricated, and can never be used again. What you need to avoid at all costs is being hit by a second shot.

The anti-crisis measures improvised by the political elites during 2009 always fell short of being decisive but somehow worked: the sheer complexity of the TARP as implemented; the chutzpah of Chancellor Alistair Darling in underwriting stricken loans the size of Britain's GDP; the Mao-era heroism of the Chinese government, instructing banks to create money on the basis of a state guarantee. Only the eurozone's armour failed, making it the clear target now for the next shell.

Yet at a macro level nobody is completely out of the mire. A second stimulus in the United States is politically impossible; the stimulus in China has stored up massive problems for the banks there; Britain and Spain stand too close to the Greek contagion for comfort; Japan stands condemned to the prospect of a 250 per cent debt-to-GDP ratio by mid-decade and is destined to remain a stagnant economy until long after today's manga comics turn up in on the vintage shelves.

If the recovery fails to become self-sustaining into 2011, it is hard to see how the world can avoid a double-dip recession. In that situation, the massive overhang of debt – in the banks, among states, among consumers – would pull the weakest economies towards the deflation whirlpool. Once started, this second downturn could no longer be stopped by monetary and fiscal stimulus at the levels already achieved. It would have to be stopped by measures involving direct competition with rival states or economic blocs.

The options include, first, the conversion of the QE strategies of 2009 into outright 'monetization' – that is, where the central bank simply prints money to finance the government debt. Second, the acceleration of exchange-rate rivalry into outright trade rivalry,

with import quotas and devaluations used to boost exports. Third –
the inevitable result of both these policies – the active encourage-
ment of domestic inflation. High and sustained inflation – not seen
in the developed world on any scale since the early 1990s – has the
advantage of imposing silent wage cuts on the workforce while
whittling away at the value of the national debt.

Once you are into a combination of any of these three –
monetization, trade rivalry and inflation – you are into the final
phase for the meltdown that started on 15 September 2008.

Long before you get there, however, you are into the realm of
social unrest and class conflict – but social unrest is also a pressure
that can be relieved by competition between states. One obvious
option for Greece and other eurozone members that come under
pressure is to leave the euro and/or default on their debts. There
are serious market commentators who believe Greece will be
forced to do both.

What the world's rulers cling to, as they move from summit to
summit, is the idea of global solidarity, the belief that the spectre
of the 1930s will prevent a slide into rival exit strategies. In the
best-case scenario, the Chinese recovery does not falter but pulls
Asia into a more consumption-led and stable pattern of growth.
America's banks survive any second global downturn, while the
eurozone hits the bottom of its austerity drive sometime around
2013 and bounces back, writing off €230 billion of outstanding
toxic subprime loans in an orderly rather than chaotic way.

The stakes are massive, because many of the givens of the
global situation militate against this best-case outcome. China's
one-party dictatorship is determined to unleash the new model
of consumption-driven growth at a pace commensurate with
maintaining its own power and privilege – that is, slowly.
America's banking elite will cling on to the hard-fought dominance it attained during the Clinton–Bush era. And Europe's
working class, swelled by a new generation of disgruntled
graduate youth, will not lightly give up the social gains that
brought peace after the downfall of dictatorships.

Above all, any orderly rebalancing of the economy and re-regulation of the banking system must come through the multi-lateral forums. Once we are into serious unilateral re-regulation we are well down the route towards the breakup of the globalised economy. The danger is not, as the bank lobbyists often put it, that such action drives financial services elsewhere; it is that capital itself retreats to national and continental pools, permanently limiting the dynamism of the global economy.

The future, then, depends on the complex interplay between the interests of die-hard political elites and the interests of the salariat, the urban youth, the manual working class and the elderly.

For me, the abiding images of the months between Lehman and the euro crisis involve the forbearance shown by these plebeian social groups. The Chinese workers patiently transfer-ring from factory to building site on the orders of macro-economic policy makers; the finance director of the Midlands component factory thin with worry; the autoworkers in Elkhart, Indiana; the dockers of Piraeus, Greece, who told me – despite the bloodcurdling Communist slogans on their canteen wall – 'We're family men, we don't do social explosions.'

They have been patient. The question is, how long will their patience hold out?

10. The Return of Political Economy

Who Pays for the Crisis?

ON 20 DECEMBER 1954 a Michigan housewife called Marian Keech called together a group of followers to await an event that had been revealed to her by aliens. The world would be destroyed the next day in a great flood – but Keech and her friends would be rescued by flying saucer. Members of the cult left their jobs and spouses and as midnight approached divested themselves of all metal objects. When the flying saucer failed to appear, following a few tearful hours, Keech received a new message from outer space: God had spared the world thanks to the cult's unwavering belief in aliens.

This was the first major case study of a phenomenon known as cognitive dissonance. Leon Festinger, a social psychologist who infiltrated the cult, observed that the total disproof of a theory could be counteracted by a) strong peer pressure and b) the equally strong importance of the theory to a person's social existence. If the theory underpinned some key relationship for the cult member, then all facts contradicting it would simply be incorporated into a new version of the theory.

So it was with the nutjobs of 1950s America; so it would be with the elite of neo-liberal economics after Lehman Brothers. Alan Greenspan, having publicly admitted his ideology was flawed, set about reconstructing it to encompass the new reality.

In a series of Congressional grillings, newspaper articles and academic papers, Greenspan rejected the charge that the Fed's low–interest rate policies had stoked the housing boom: it would have happened anyway, he said. He rejected the idea that regulators could have stopped the crisis happening. Nor should they have tried.

At the core of his argument were two related propositions: that it was the global savings glut resulting from the rise of China and other developing countries that had dictated low interest rates after 1989, and, therefore, that a boom-bust cycle had been inevitable:

> Unless there is a societal choice to abandon dynamic markets and leverage for some form of central planning, I fear that preventing bubbles will in the end turn out to be infeasible. Assuaging their aftermath seems the best we can hope for. Policies, both private and public, should focus on ameliorating the extent of deprivation and hardship caused by deflationary crises.[1]

A purer vindication of Hyman Minsky's critique of financially complex capitalism is hard to imagine.

Greenspan admitted that crises on the scale of Lehman Brothers, previously thought to be a 'once in a hundred years event', now seem likely to recur. But nothing can be done. Regulation remains blind compared with the partial sight of the risk control managers at investment banks – so it is pointless trying to regulate systemically, Greenspan argued in a paper titled 'The Crisis'.

At most, he said, the capital cushion held by banks should be lifted to somewhere close to 14 per cent – higher if the bank in question is too big to bail. Banks should get used to lower profits and higher capital requirements in order to make ready for the inevitable re-runs of September 2008 that lie in store.

The critics clustered around the stricken giant, picking holes in his logic, his algebra, his motivation. Yet at one level Greenspan's intervention was correct. Given that high savings and low interest rates are a global fact, the excess capital accumulated by humanity will slosh around from one asset class to another, creating catastrophic financial manias. If you wish to prevent this outcome you must alter the plumbing of capitalism, not tinker with its thermostat.

But Greenspan remained blind to the human, social causes of the meltdown. As to the admitted central weakness of his ideology – that it failed to explain why bankers acted against the interest of the banks – he proposed an econometric solution, a more complex risk management model: 'If we could adequately model each phase of the cycle separately and divine the signals that tell us when the shift in regimes is about to occur, risk management systems would be improved significantly.'[2]

For the problem of herd behaviour, which flies in the face of such warning signals, Greenspan also had a technocratic fix. Herd behaviour could be modelled just as easily as credit risk, and should take its place in a new, more complex set of tools available to the bankers.

The only downside of such risk analysis tools, wrote Greenspan, is that they would tend to prolong the up phase of the cycle and smooth its ending rather than allow contradictions to resolve themselves through crash and destruction.

Thus, at some point, crashes are inevitable, Greenspan admitted: inevitable, more frequent and more devastating as the free-market system conquers the world. The only thing we can do, he concluded, is prevent re-regulation inhibiting 'our most reliable and effective safeguards against cumulative economic failure: market flexibility and open competition.'[3]

Just like Marian Keech, who concluded that the non-appearance of her extra-terrestrial saviours was proof of their existence, the Lehman crisis proved to Alan Greenspan that his theory was right: devastating crashes caused by low interest rates and absent regulators are a lawful outcome of the free-market economy.

Joe Stiglitz and the radicalised third way

The onset of the crisis jolted another giant of economics into action. Professor Joseph Stiglitz took to haunting the fringe events of the G20 summits, firing off radical proposals for global curbs on capital: in the short term, a more aggressive fiscal stimulus and immediate re-regulation of the banks; at the strategic level, the creation of a global reserve system to demand-manage the world economy, the democratisation of the IMF and World Bank and the creation of a global financial regulator.

The proposals Stiglitz drafted for UN Secretary-General Ban Ki-Moon going into the April 2009 G20 contained a coherent and strategic vision for what capitalism would look like if any part of the political and financial elite were serious about trying to make it stable.

So if anybody was going to produce a new economic theory and vision to guide the left beyond the financial crisis, it was going to be Joe. But he has not managed it yet.

His book *Freefall: America, Free Markets and the Sinking of the World Economy* is about politics, hubris and the failure of the Obama administration. It is a manual for action for the next twelve to eighteen months, linked to a plea for a wider rethink about power structures and values in modern capitalism. It is also a vivid demonstration of the author's inability to escape from the confines of the doctrine he helped create: the Third Way.

The book begins with the story of the crisis and what caused it. Stiglitz's account places him firmly in the camp of those who identify consumption, not finance, as the source of the problem. The finance system may have amplified the collapse, but for Stiglitz the collapse originated in an overblown housing market, which itself was the creation of America's addiction to consuming when it should be saving, and its politicians' determination to stimulate lending when they should not.

The core of the book lies in Stiglitz's account of the US policy response, which he believes to consist of a string of disasters. Disaster number one was Obama's instinctive conservatism. He chose a 'muddle through' strategy which, though it may have seemed low risk politically, has turned out to be high risk for the 15 million Americans who have no job, and the two million families whose homes have been repossessed.

Stiglitz criticises Obama for refusing to formulate a vision, a target end state for the US economy after the recession: 'While the risks of formulating a vision were clear, so were those of not having one. Without a vision the whole reform process might be seized by those in the financial sector, leaving the country with a financial system that was even more fragile than the one that had failed.'[4]

And so, as we've seen, it came to pass. Disaster number two was the decision to maintain most of the Bush administration personnel who had fuelled the boom-bust cycle, supplementing them with a team of right-wingers from the Clinton years with whom Joe himself had once sparred and lost.

Disaster number three was the maintenance of the revolving door between Wall Street and Washington, which put former bankers in charge of regulating for the crisis. Disaster number four was the meagre scale of the fiscal stimulus, which, Stiglitz argued, would fail to make an impact and would have to be followed by a second stimulus.

It is to Stiglitz's lasting credit that while other economists moved back into the realm of algebra and Greek letters, he remained in the trenches of policy. He predicts a Japanese-style recovery in America, with the economy facing a prolonged period of below-potential output and none of the problems of excess borrowing, high consumption and low wages sorted out.

At the centre of the policy response he advocates is the state. The state should have forced the banks to restructure financially at the height of the crisis, wiping out their shareholders and handing ownership and control to those who held their debts, large parts of which would have been state-owned in any case. He correctly identifies what stopped Obama doing this, over and above the influence and personnel of Wall Street: the belief that the banks were too big either to fail or to be restructured: or to put it another way, that the state was too small.

With the chance for that now gone, Stiglitz advocates a forcible breakup of the major banks and a comprehensive set of regulations and statutory protections for the consumers of financial products. This, he argues, has to be done alongside a restructuring of the US economy, and a rethink of America's world role.

America, he writes, saves too little, consumes too much and is failing to address the long-term problems that will define the twenty-first century: aging, climate change and the shambolic sectoral and regional mismatches within the US. He writes:

> The big question in the 21st-century global economy is what should be the role of the state. Achieving the restructuring . . . will require government taking a greater role . . . if we are to restore sustained prosperity we need a new set of social contracts based on the trust between all elements of society, between citizens and government, between this generation and the future.

The problem for Stiglitz – as for all Third Way economists and politicians – is how this should be achieved. And it is here that the author runs into the barrier his intellect has been running into, and bouncing off, for the best part of two decades: the assumption that state ownership, state provision, socialised enterprise and state-led economies must be stagnant, that they could never work better than the regulated market economy.

Thus, though the question of the state's role is boldly posed, it is only tentatively answered. The state 'may have to become more central', he suggests, in shaping research priorities, or regulating to achieve macroeconomic stability.

The tone throughout is apologetic. To America's plebeian right wing – sections of which already fantasise about a crisis during which they will simply lock their gates and load their guns – he can only plead: 'There is no choice but to have some forms of collective action.'

Because Stiglitz's intellectual framework is bounded by the belief that there is no alternative to a market-driven economy, his critics – both on the left and right – have noticed the existence of 'two Joes'. One is a fiery critic of modern capitalism, the other teaches students at Columbia University that capitalism could be made to work if only its institutions were more effective and the powerful could be persuaded to abstain from abusing their power.

Freefall, though written in haste and fury by Joe Number One, comes to the same conclusion that Joe Number Two always does. Reform the institutions, moderate the excesses, leave behind economic fundamentalisms in favour of a middle way.

The problem is, laudable though the sentiments are, the theory can never explain why this best-of-all-possible economic systems keeps on producing regulators like Alan Greenspan, bankers like Dick Fuld, hedge fund managers like Bernie Madoff – and why a political-economic elite goes on showering them with honours and attending their cocktail parties.

In addition, it leaves the author bereft of an explanation for this curious fact: on both sides of the Atlantic the course to the boom-bust cycle was actually plotted by Third Way politicians, Clinton alumni like Tim Geithner in New York; Blair and Brown in London. And that Europe, a whole continent based on Third Way economics, stands on the brink of its own catastrophe.

In a brilliant final chapter, Stiglitz takes apart the theorists of market fundamentalism – for their abstractness, and for their failure to see where economics should stop and sociology should begin. But his own economics seems shorn of a social and political dimension: whether you choose Foucault, Marx or C. Wright Mills, if you are a critic of the capitalist system you must have some explanation of why it goes on producing power elites. You must explain why these elites are able constantly to prevent capitalism from achieving its potential to be humane, measured and controlled. This is the missing piece in Stiglitz's framework.

So, in the end, despite the brilliance of *Freefall*, Stiglitz, too, remains locked within his prior doctrine: the market economy is intrinsically more dynamic than the state-led economy. Yet he intuits – far more clearly than in his work in the 1990s on the Russian transition or the Asian crisis – that the state-led economy is what we're about to get.

A return to state capitalism?

One author who has challenged the accepted wisdom on the state-led economy is Ian Bremmer. Bremmer is a business thinker who coined two buzzwords of the 2000s boom: the 'fat tail' and the 'J-curve'. With the boom over, he argues, the financial crisis has given strategic momentum to a new form of state capitalism:

> Public wealth, public investment and public ownership have made a stunning comeback. Governments dominate key domestic economic sectors. The oil companies they now own control three quarters of the world's crude oil reserves. They use state owned and favoured privately owned companies to intervene in global markets . . . They own enormous investment funds that have quickly become vitally important sources of capital.[5]

In the post-Soviet model of state capitalism, ruling elites use control of national oil companies and national champions in the sphere of resource extraction to build a powerful and, for now, dynamic alternative to free-market capitalism. They use trade protectionism and currency manipulation to stimulate rapid growth and urbanisation; then they deploy the country's excess wealth – public and private – into the acquisition of strategic corporate assets in the West. Finally, Bremmer predicts, they will use the present crisis to alter their terms of trade with free-market economies – in the process winning an ideological battle.

There is no single ideology of state capitalism: in La Paz it is a kind of social-democratic indigenism; in Caracas it is the modern incarnation of of Bolivarianism; in Tehran it is Shi'i Islam; in Riyadh a sort of playboy Wahhabism; in Beijing, clay-heavy Confucian Marxism manured with the ramblings of Jiang Zemin.

However, there is a common practice, and its textbook version is the practice of the Chinese Communist Party. In China there is a direct and overt trade-off made between the communist princelings and the people: we get rich, you get rich. To observe the glitter and haze of a city like Shanghai or Shenzhen is to understand the deep ideological advantage the model gives to ruling elites. It is almost impossible to lament the rise of one's own country, under whatever political conditions.

As to the argument, which seems so unchallengeable in American universities, that 'the market is always more dynamic than the state', the rulers of these countries can point to double-digit growth rates and real rises in disposable income for the masses as disproof.

Though Bremmer's book is not a work of theory, its strength lies in his ability to see that the state-capitalist moment has arrived. And that free-market capitalism is not the default condition of the twenty-first century, against which state capitalism is simply some kind of temporary distortion.

State capitalism and the fractured form of free-market capitalism that has emerged from the meltdown are, in fact, different expressions of the deep imbalances between saving countries and borrowing countries discussed in Chapter 4. Though Asia's resilience during this crisis has created new patterns – a surge in Chinese imports, a reduction in China's dollar and euro holdings – it will take a macro-economic revolution on both sides of the divide to rebalance the global economy. This, fundamentally, is the task of states, not supra-national bodies, because it poses the question of routes out of poverty, social justice, and the dominance of political elites.

We can see now, far more clearly than in September 2008, that the global imbalances can't be resolved by the existing power-elites in China and the West, nor without big changes in patterns of consumption across the globe. If the imbalances remain unresolved there is a strong chance that the strategic outcome of the whole post-1989 period is the decline of several advanced countries into Japan-style stagnation, a process that then collides with the two 'exogenous' crises of this century: ageing and resource scarcity.

The return of political economy

The absence of any brilliant new contribution from the mainstream suggests that the theoretical challenges posed by the meltdown are not resolvable on the terrain of professional economics. We need a return to the discipline of political economy. Smith, Marx, Keynes and Kondratieff were all essentially *political* economists whose insights were eviscerated by academia.

It is no accident that political economy has been twice defeated by 'pure' econometric models, which discounted social forces, randomness and corruption. Both moments of defeat coincided with a global upturn, in the 1880s and 1950s, which legitimised the existing form of capitalism so thoroughly that it seemed only a closed and timeless algebra could explain it.

We are now at the opposite kind of moment: a moment of theoretical collapse for mainstream economics. The algebraic jottings of the mainstream economists begin to look like the workbook of some aging *kapellmeister* trained in Baroque counterpoint trying to work out what's going on in a late Beethoven quartet: nothing fits the old theory, no matter how much crossing out you do.

The sources of political economy go beyond data; they involve speculation, deductive logic, insight — even intuition. Keynes's friend Oswald Falk once told him that, for all the veneer of theory, all he had really done was codify 'the moral feeling of an age, floating around us and ready for apprehension by the most sensitive minds, by other than reasoning processes'.[6]

In this spirit I will avoid the usual formula for ending books on the current crisis: a list of bullet points to be enacted now, and a list of long-term measures that would be nice to have if there were a benign world government. Instead I offer the following observations:

1. *Moral hazard*. This is the central problem raised by the crisis, and looms larger now than it did eighteen months ago. Whereas right after the meltdown it was implicit for a generation that the state stood behind all banks, it is now explicit. The solution proposed by Andrew Haldane of the Bank of England is intellectually elegant: impose a cost for this explicit indemnity in the form of a bank levy, higher capital requirements or even a transaction tax. However, even at the conceptual level this breaks down: the US federal government has put $3 trillion at risk to save the banks. For a tax to be both sufficiently punitive to deter speculation, and to raise enough money to insure the system against future bailout costs, it would have to be so heavy that it suppressed the dynamism in the system.

Logically there is an alternative, which is to refuse to indemnify the banks and socialise their losses, either now or in future: to let them fail. And, by way of deterrence, to do what Greenspan has half-jokingly suggested and make bank failure a criminal offence for the executives, ensuring personal bankruptcy and imprisonment for the next Fred Goodwin.

A third alternative, not considered in mainstream economics but long ago suggested by Minsky, would be to accept socialising the losses but to socialise the banking system too.

This, as explained in Chapter 8, might not mean simply the outright nationalisation of the banks but the creation of a mixed economy of finance, with credit unions, non-profit banks, mutuals and industrial banks providing a transparent utility service to businesses and individuals. To make that happen you would have to restructure capitalism – but it is being restructured, chaotically, in any case.

2. *Financialisation.* Post-Keynesian economists have theorised the emergence of a new relationship between capital and labour in the era since 1989, labelled 'financialisation'. Costas Lapavitsas argues that with the decline of commercial banking as a source of business finance, and its replacement by the capital markets, banks turned increasingly to the workforce as the source of profits.

The rate of profit available to banks through services such as credit cards, personal loans, student loans, auto loans and, of course, mortgages outstrips that which characterised the wage relationship between worker and boss during the post-war boom.

Though the worker–boss relationship involves degrees of power and powerlessness, the relationship between borrower and lender is always individual and one-way. It is not possible to strike against your credit card lender – and not often possible to understand the effective rate of interest at the heart of the transaction. Basically, any factory owner making a cool 18 per cent return on capital would consider that doing well; any credit card company making that amount would consider it barely worthwhile.

Lapavitsas lamented not only the altered power structure, but also its ideological impact on the salariat:

> Financialisation, finally, has allowed the ethics, morality and mindset of finance to penetrate into the deepest recesses of social and individual life. Social values have been affected by the outlook of the financier (calculating, distant from produc-tion, always looking for the main chance, constantly worried about liquidity) . . . Waves of greed have been released by the transformation of housing and pensions into 'investments', dragging individuals into financial bubbles.[7]

Lapavitsas allows that this phenomenon varies, being more pronounced in the Anglo-Saxon countries. I would argue it is global but varies across generations. Anecdotally, people who grew up during the 70s and 80s wince when they see young salaried workers in their twenties and thirties pay for drinks and snacks by credit card. The former are residually aware of the credit risk and astronomic interest rates involved in such transactions; the latter, if aware at all, see it as the overhead cost of living in an instant-access retail-driven economy.

The financialisation thesis allows us to understand the extreme reluctance of policymakers this time to go down the route of austerity and unemployment advocated by neo-liberalism in the 1980s. At no stage has any political elite – either in the West or in Asia – been prepared to impose mass unemployment; conversely, much of the private-sector workforce has agreed to impose upon itself levels of short-time, unpaid work and extreme flexibility unthinkable during the downturns of the early 1980s and 90s.

At a micro level it seems as if by blurring the distinctions between work and leisure time, the financialised model made job flexibility easier to accept. What for many workers was impossible to accept was the loss of status associated with outright unemployment, and with it the loss of access to financial services.

There is a political and ideological dimension here as well. After the British miners' strike, when communities lost everything, there was at least the promise of a new lifestyle. It seems to me that if the salariat of the 2010s were to be put through the traumatic destruction of business models, the breakup of workforces and the immediate loss of access to the trappings of salaried work – mobile telephony, Internet access, downtime in Starbucks, cheap international travel and instant credit – the psychological impact would be worse. Losing your mobile phone and credit card, for today's workforce, might feel worse than losing the coalmines felt for the miners.

If these observations are valid, then any turn to austerity in the third phase of the crisis may provoke far more unpredictable social reactions than the austerity programmes of the 1980s.

3. *Britain*. Britain did not feel like the epicentre of the crisis, even during those days of ashen faces and cold coffee in subterranean Downing Street, when its banks were being nationalised. But one glance at the data reveals the UK is an outlier when it comes to future risks.

First, quantitative easing has left the Bank of England holding government debt to the value of 15.2 per cent of GDP. Japan, eight years into QE, holds less, and the United States about 5 per cent. Unwinding that position is going to be tricky.

When it comes to the amount pledged by government to support the banks, Britain again sticks out: 12 per cent of GDP in direct support to banks; 40 per cent of GDP pledged to guarantee bad loans; a further 28 per cent of GDP used in asset swaps and QE. Now while much of this money is notional, it is, in each line of the spreadsheet, massively larger in percentage terms than for any other stricken country, including the United States and Japan. This means Britain has more to lose than any other country from a global double dip.

Yet Britain is the first of the major economies to have embraced austerity. Once the Greek crisis blew up into a system-wide run on sovereign debt, it is hard to see what choice it had, other than the final mix of tax raising and spending cuts – and the choice between severe and super-severe. The Conservative/Libdem emergency budget stands a good chance of flattening the incipient recovery – but this only expresses a more strategic problem.

Britain, alone of the major economies, has allowed financial services to 'crowd out' innovative productive industry. It suffered the earliest conventional bank run (Northern Rock), and then, simultaneously, the biggest bank collapse (RBS/HBOS/Lloyds) and a massive drop in revenue. During the British general election the Conservative party indicated its desire for a 'new economic model', moving away from reliance on finance. Yet without finance it is left with the rapid onset of the 'old' economic diseases: low growth, high inflation, sterling depreciation, public sector-led recession. The June 2010 budget was based on projections implying a rapid, three-year shift from an economy based on credit, consumption and government spending to one based on exports and business investment. Even if this were achievable through micro-economic policy, welfare reform and tax breaks, the UK is still faced with the problem of who's going to buy the exports. For the Eurozone is also playing the austerity game.

4. *Institutional crisis.* One of the most striking features of this recession has been the inability of political systems to cope with the scale and speed of economic crisis. If Greenspan is right, and catastrophic financial slumps are endemic to modern capitalism, this bodes ill for the institutional framework. Central banks missed the onset of the financial downturn, they pared interest rates when it would have been more logical to slash them, they quibbled about QE; governments split the difference between decisive action and the pre-existing idea-set.

Again and again I have heard policymakers quietly mutter about other policymakers, 'he does not know what he's doing; we've never been here before and nobody knows what to do, there is no playbook' and so on.

The central problem here was identified before the crash by Nasim Nicholas Taleb, who wrote that globalization

creates interlocking fragility, while reducing volatility and giving the appearance of stability. In other words it creates devastating Black Swans. We have never lived before under the threat of a global collapse. Financial Institutions have been merging into a smaller number of very large banks. Almost all banks are interrelated. So the financial ecology is swelling into gigantic, incestuous, bureaucratic banks – when one fails, they all fall.[8]

We've begun to understand the implications of this for banking, but probably not yet for politics. Central banks and financial regulators who become captivated by the euphoria of bubbles or elite-club mentality cannot be effective problem solvers in this world of fragile, rapidly collapsible networks. Politicians, too, have to ask themselves what the key attributes of economic crisis management should be if they want future stewardship of the system. I would suggest that speed, vision and decisiveness are three qualities we could have done with more of during the financial meltdown.

5. *The moral feeling of the age.* From the streets of a Kenyan slum to the back-channels of Chinese cyberspace I think there is what Oswald Falk called a 'moral feeling' infusing the present age: the task of political economy, and policy, is to capture it and act on it.

The first truth is self-evident: everywhere the network is more powerful than the hierarchy: from Iran's green revolution to China's quiet social network insurrection. Yet in finance and regulation two dysfunctional hierarchies confront each other.

The second component is the feeling that some degree of social justice is an inalienable right for everybody on the planet. Having seen the once callous corridors of power soften towards this position, in numerous G8 summits and through the Millennium Development Goals, I doubt that this moral right can be clawed back.

The third element is the sense that we are on the brink of an upturn in human productivity, technology and civilisation – not a downturn. This, above all, is what makes the present 'feel' different from the early 1930s. Having handed out cheap cell phones to the peasant poor of Africa and watched them leapfrog into the world of digital money transfer, we cannot imagine taking it all away again.

The old neo-liberal model of capitalism is discredited and physically broken, yet the personnel of the political elites – in Germany and Japan just as much as in Britain and the United States – grew up with it. But in the search for a new vision, and a new model, we run into a deep, almost psychological complacency that the political class actually shares with the mass of consumers and workers. It appears – because it has been the case for twenty years – that every problem is solvable; that every solution is immediate; that we can always avoid severe choices and severe negative impacts.

During the past fourteen months the illusion has been sustained that no matter how badly the world economy slumps, there is always a pain-free way out of it. Once the realisation dawns that there is not, and that the pain will be severe, the question is posed that has not really been posed for twenty years: who should feel it?

Notes

Introduction

1 A. Barr, 'Goldman charged with fraud over Paulson cdo Trade', Marketwatch, 16 April 2010.

2 A Valukas, 'Lehman Brothers Holdings Inc. Chapter 11 Proceedings Examiner's Report', United States Bankruptcy Court Southern District of New York, p.740. Online. Available HTTP: http://lehmanreport.jenner.com/

3 Hopkins, K. and J. Treanor, 'Bank of England reveals secret £62 billion loans used to prop up RBS and HBOS', Guardian, 24 November 2009.

1. Midtown Meltdown

1 There is a glossary of financial terms at the back of this book.

2 http://www.newsmeat.com/ceo_political_donations/John_Thain.php.

3 http://fundrace.huffingtonpost.com/neighbors.php?type=name&lname=mack&fname=john&search=Search+by+Name; David Weidner, '(S)Mack Talking', Marketwatch.com, 4 December 2007, http://www.marketwatch.com/news/story/macks-knife-cuts-both-ways/story.aspx?guid={513FEDA5-2392-4AE6-A7C6-6D493BEEBE99}

4 http://fundrace.huffingtonpost.com/neighbors.php?type=name&lname=blankfein&fname=lloyd&search=Search.

5 The Firing of an SEC Attorney and the Investigation of Pequot Capital Management, August 2007, Senate Finance Committee.

6 'Ultimatum by Paulson Sparked Frantic End', Wall Street Journal, 15 September 2008.

7 Kate Kelly, 'Bear CEO's handling of crisis raises issues', Wall Street Journal, 1 November 2007.

8 William D. Cohan, 'The Trials of Jimmy Cayne', *Fortune*, 4 August 2008.

9 *Schiff's Insurance Observer* 12:1, September 2000.

10 AIG press release, 30 March 2005.

11 'Spitzer Sues AIG, Greenberg, Smith', CFO.com, 27 May 2005, available at http://www.cfo.com/article.cfm/4028469.

12 Chapter 5 explains this in depth.

13 'FBI Watched Spitzer Before February Incident', *Washington Post*, 12 March 2008.

14 M. Lewitt, 'Wall Street's Next Big Problem', *New York Times*, 16 September 2008, A29.

15 Research note, Sandy Chen, Panmure Gordon, 16 September 2008.

16 CNBC, *After The Bell* 1640, 16 September 2008, available at http://www.cnbc.com/id/26747318/?__source=aol%7Cheadline%7-Cother%7Ctext%7C&par=aol.

17 'Hank's Last Stand', *Fortune*, 7 October 2008.

18 'S&P cuts HBOS plc to "A+" from "AA–" ', Reuters, 16 September 2008, available at http://www.tradingmarkets.com/.site/news/Stock%20News/1884826.

19 'Shock Forced Paulson's Hand', *Wall Street Journal*, 20 September 2008.

20 All TED spread prices taken from http://www.bloomberg.com/apps/cbuilder?ticker1=.TEDSP%3AIND.

21 'Bailout of money funds seems to staunch outflow', *Wall Street Journal*, 20 September 2008.

22 'A Joint Decision to Act: It Must Be Big and Fast', *Washington Post*, 20 September 2008.

23 Ibid.

24 David Wighton, 'A sickening slump gives way to euphoria in rollercoaster week', *Times*, 20 September 2008.

2. Hyperdrive Blitzkrieg

1 'Bailout Debate Spawns High-Stakes Lobbying Scramble', *Washington Post*, 24 September 2008.

2 'Text of Draft Proposal for Bailout Plan', *New York Times*, 20 September 2008.

3 http://www.bunning.senate.gov

4 'A Grilling on the Hill', *Washington Post*, 24 September 2008.

5 'The Financial Crisis: Bernanke, Paulson Face Skeptics On the Hill', *Wall Street Journal*, 24 September 2008.

6 Willem Buiter, 'The Paulson Plan – a useful first step but nowhere near enough', voxeu.org, available at http://www.voxeu.org/index.php?q=node/1706.

7 Henry Paulson, BBC *Newsnight*, 23 September 2008.

8 Ben S. Bernanke, 'The Financial Accelerator and the Credit Channel', 15 June 2007, available at http://www.federalreserve.gov/newsevents/speech/Bernanke20070615a.htm.

9 'Paulson and Bernanke savaged over bailout plan', *Independent*, 24 September 2008.

10 'US Commercial Paper Slumps Most Since August 2007', Bloomberg, 25 September 2008.

11 'Constituents Make Their Bailout Views Known', *New York Times*, 25 September 2008.

12 'The Financial Crisis: An Inside View of a Stormy White House Summit', *Wall Street Journal*, 27 September 2008.

13 'German Min: US to Lose Super Financial Power Status', Dow Jones, 09:28 GMT, 25 September 2009.

14 ' "Laissez-faire" capitalism is finished, says France', *EU Observer*, 26 September 2008, available at http://euobserver.com/9/26814.

15 United States Bureau of Economic Analysis, *National Accounts*, Table 1.1.5. Gross Domestic Product, 1929–41, available at http://bea.gov/national/nipaweb/TableView.asp?SelectedTable=5&ViewSeries=NO&Java=no&Request3Place=N&3Place=N&FromView=YES&Freq=Year&FirstYear=1929&LastYear=1941&3Place=N&Update=Update&JavaBox=no.

16 http://www.analyzeindices.com/dowhistory/djia-100.txt.

17 Ben S. Bernanke, 'A Crash Course for Central Bankers', *Foreign Policy*, September 2000.

18 Ibid.

19 Ben S. Bernanke, 'Deflation: Making Sure "It" Doesn't Happen Here', 21 November 2002, available at http://www.federalreserve.gov/boardDocs/speeches/2002/20021121/default.htm.

20 J. K. Galbraith, *The Great Crash, 1929*, London, 1992: 116.

21 Ben S. Bernanke, 'On Milton Friedman's Ninetieth Birthday', 8 November 2002, available at http://www.federalreserve.gov/BOARDDOCS/SPEECHES/2002/20021108/default.htm.

22 John Zavesky, *Los Angeles Times*, 29 September 2008.

23 R. Frank, *Times-Picayune*, 29 September 2008.

24 'Leaders plead for a yes today', *Boston Globe*, 29 September 2008.

3. Financial Krakatoa

1 Paul Mason, 'This is an economic Krakatoa', *Idle Scrawl*, 15 October 2008 http://www.bbc.co.uk/blogs/newsnight/paulmason/2008/10/this_is_an_economic_krakatoa.html.

2 G. Pararas-Carayannis, 'Near and far-field effects of Tsunamis . . . in Indonesia on August 26–27 1883', *Science of Tsunami Hazards*, vol. 21, no. 4, 2003: 191; P. J. Gleckler, T. M. L. Wigley, B. D. Santer, J. M. Gregory, K. AchutaRao and K. E. Taylor, 'Volcanoes and climate: Krakatoa's signature persists in the ocean', *Nature* 439, 675, 9 February 2006.

3 Budget Speech, 5 October 2004, available at http://eng.fjarmalaraduneyti.is/Minister/GHH/nr/2905.

4 N. Roubini, 'The World Is at Severe Risk of a Global Systemic Financial Meltdown and a Severe Global Depression', *Huffington Post*, 11 October 2008.

5 'G7 Finance Ministers and Central Bank Governors Plan of Action', 10 October 2008.

6 L. Armistead and P. Aldrick, 'The inside story of a dramatic week', *Sunday Telegraph*, 19 October 2008.

7 http://www.world-exchanges.org/statistics/ytd-monthly.

8 McKinsey Global Institute, *Mapping Global Capital Markets: Fifth Annual Report*, October 2008.

9 W. H. Auden, 'September 1, 1939', available at http://www.poets.org/viewmedia.php/prmMID/15545.

4. White Shoes

1 Senator Phil Gramm, statement, 12 November 1999, available at http://banking.senate.gov/prel99/1112gbl.htm.

2 'Clinton Signs Financial Services Bill Into Law', *Dow Jones News Service*, 12 November 1999.

3 'Clinton Signs Legislation Overhauling Banking Laws', *New York Times*, 13 November 1999.

4 P. Kiesel, 'The subprime mess and Phil Gramm: an experiment in deregulation', *Los Angeles Injury Board*, 24 July 2008.

5 'Nokia and Samsung have 54% of the mobile phone market', *Mobile Monday*, 28 October 2007, available at http://www.mobilemonday.net/news/shares.

6 O. Jeidels, *Das Verhältnis der deutschen Grossbanken zur Industrie mit besonderer Berüchsichtigung der Eisenindustrie*, Leipzig, 1905; quoted in V. I. Lenin, *Imperialism, the Highest Stage of Capitalism*, Moscow,

1963, Chapter II.

7 R. Morck M. and Nakamura, 'The history of corporate ownership in Japan', ECGI Working Paper 20/2003, available at http://www.ecgi.org/wp/f2003.pdf.

8 J. K. Galbraith, *The Great Crash: 1929*, London: Penguin, 1992: 32.

9 Franklin D. Roosevelt, Inaugural Address, 4 March 1933, in Samuel Rosenman, ed., *The Public Papers of Franklin D. Roosevelt, Volume Two: The Year of Crisis, 1933*, New York 1938: 11–16.

10 Joseph Kahn, 'Former Treasury Secretary Joins Leadership Triangle at Citigroup', *New York Times*, 27 October 1999.

11 W. L. Megginson, 'The International Investment Banking Industry', Swiss Banking Institute, 24 June 1999.

12 Bank for International Settlements, 'Triennial Central Bank Survey: Foreign exchange and derivatives market activity in 2007', December 2007.

13 Bank for International Settlements 'OTC Derivatives Market Activity In the Second Half of 2007', May 2008: 7.

14 'Gross domestic product 2007, PPP', World Bank Statistics, available at http://siteresources.worldbank.org/DATASTATISTICS/Resources/GDP_PPP.pdf; S. S. Roach, 'Green China', Morgan Stanley Research, 9 March 2007.

15 Berkshire Hathaway, Annual Report 2002.

16 Hoover Institution, 'Facts on US Policy: Savings Rate', 10 October 2006.

17 M. Wolf, *Fixing Global Finance*, Baltimore, 2008: 59.

18 G. Moec and L. Frel, 'Global imbalances, saving glut and investment strike', Banque de France Occasional Paper 1, February 2006.

19 Arnab Das, 'Russia in 2008', Dresdner Kleinwort Research presentation, 15 April 2008: 12.

20 Robert Solow, *New York Review of Books*, 12 July 1987.

21 'SEC Settles Enforcement Proceedings against J.P. Morgan Chase and Citigroup', 23 July 2003.

22 http://www.sec.gov/litigation/complaints/comp18115b.htm.

23 http://www.sec.gov/litigation/litreleases/lr18111.htm.

24 'Ten of Nation's Top Investment Firms Settle Enforcement Actions Involving Conflicts of Interest Between Research and Investment Banking', Securities & Exchange Commission, 28 April 2003.

25 See Chapter 5 for an exploration of the subprime system.

26 P. Augar, *The Greed Merchants: How the Investment Banks Played the Free Market Game*, London, 2005: 29.

27 Alan Rappeport, 'A short history of hedge funds', CFO.com, 27
   March 2007, available at http://www.cfo.com/article.cfm/
   8914091/2/c_2984367.
28 Letter from Andrew Lahde, *Financial Times*, 17 October 2008.
29 David Reilly, Carrick Mollenkamp and Robin Sidel, 'Big banks
   like Citigroup face risks from conduits', *Wall Street Journal Europe*, 6
   September 2007.

5. Subprime

1 City of Detroit Neighbourhood Stabilisation Plan, available at
   http://www.ci.detroit.mi.us/Portals/0/docs/planning/pdf/NSP/
   City%20of%20Detroit%20NSP.pdf.
2 'Labor Day Report: Many Workers Lag Behind in New Economy', Michigan League for Human Services, September 2007.
3 See above, Chapter 4.
4 Tom Wolfe, *Bonfire of the Vanities*, London, 1989: 71.
5 Apu Sikri, 'JP Morgan brings novelty to derivatives', *Wall Street
   Journal Asia*, 31 December 1997.
6 David X. Li, 'On Default Correlation: A Copula Function Approach', Risk Metrics Working Paper 99–07, April 2000.
7 'How a Formula Ignited Market That Burned Some Big Investors',
   Wall Street Journal, 12 September 2005.
8 'Re-invention puts market on course for $1 trillion', *Financial News*,
   17 January 2000.
9 J. Tavakoli, *Structured Finance and Collateralized Debt Obligations*,
   Hoboken, 2008: xiii.
10 G. Tett, 'Derivative Thinking', *Financial Times*, 30 May 2008.
11 'Subprime Debacle Traps Even Very Creditworthy', *Wall Street
   Journal*, 3 December 2007.
12 S. Kirchoff and J. Keen, 'Minorities hit hard by rising costs of
   subprime loans', *USA Today*, 25 April 2007.
13 Gretchen Morgensohn, 'Inside the Countrywide Lending Spree',
   New York Times, 26 August 2007.
14 Gregg Krupa, 'Detroit aims at predatory home lending', *Detroit
   News*, 26 November 2002.
15 Richard H. Neiman, State of New York, press release, 29 May
   2007.
16 Source: Annual Reports, author's calculation.
17 Tavakoli, *Structured Finance*: xvii.
18 Bank for International Settlements Quarterly Review, December

2008, available at http://www.bis.org/statistics/otcder/dt1920a.pdf.

19 'SEC slams credit-rating agencies over standards' *USA Today*, 11 July 2008.

20 Committee on Oversight and Government Reform, 22 October 2008, available at http://oversight.house.gov/documents/20081022112325.pdf.

21 http://oversight.house.gov/documents/20081022112154.pdf.

22 http://oversight.house.gov/documents/20081022111050.pdf.

23 http://oversight.house.gov/documents/20081022112307.pdf.

24 *The Simpsons*, 'Lisa's First Word', series 4, episode 10, 3 December 1992, Fox Broadcasting Company.

25 'The Financial Crisis Blame Game', *Business Week*, 18 October 2008.

26 http://www.federalreserve.gov/releases/Z1/Current/z1.pdf; http://www.monthlyreview.org/docs/0506tbl1.pdf.

27 http://www.sifma.org/research/pdf/SIFMA_CDOIssuanceData2008q3.pdf.

28 'The Economic Outlook', Federal Reserve, 28 March 2008.

29 'Bernanke believes housing mess contained', Forbes.com, 17 May 2007.

30 City of Detroit Neighbourhood Stabilisation Plan, available at http://www.ci.detroit.mi.us/Portals/0/docs/planning/pdf/NSP/City%20of%20Detroit%20NSP.pdf.

31 Geoffrey Cane, 'The Great Panic', Porfolio.com, 8 August 2008, available at http://www.portfolio.com/news-markets/top-5/2008/08/08/Birth-of-the-Credit-Crunch.

6. The Big Freeze

1 G. Soros, *The New Paradigm for Financial Markets: The Credit Crisis of 2008 and What It Means*, London, 2008: 81.

2 'Mortgage Crunch', *San Francisco Chronicle*, 9 August 2008.

3 J. Daníelsson, 'Blame the Models', *Journal of Financial Stability*, June 2008, available at http://risk.lse.ac.uk/rr/files/JD-33.pdf.

4 Gary Duncan, 'Governor warns careless lenders: the Bank will not bail you out', *The Times,* 9 August 2007.

5 AP Newswire, 8 August 2007, 'Bush: Economy will make soft landing'.

6 ESF Securitisation Data Report Q3, 2008, available at http://www.europeansecuritisation.com/Market_Standard/2008-08%20ESF%20Q3.pdf.

7 Ibid.

8 Stephen Labaton, 'Agency's '04 Rule Let Banks Pile Up Debts', *New York Times*, 3 October 2008.

9 Erik Holm and Stephanie Luke, 'AIG's Losses Lead Insurers as Tally Nears $1 Trillion', Bloomberg.com, 11 November 2008.

10 www.rgemonitor.com, 'Financial Writedowns Reach Nearly $1 Trillion: Are We Half-Way Through?' 20 November 2008.

11 http://futures.tradingcharts.com/chart/RI/M.

12 'Of Froth and Fundamentals', *Economist*, 9 October 2008.

13 http://seekingalpha.com/article/77282-a-commodity-hedge-fund-in-every-pot.

14 Testimony of Michael Masters, 20 May 2008, Homeland Security Committee, available at http://hsgac.senate.gov/public/_files/052008Masters.pdf.

15 'The Silent Tsunami', *Economist*, 18 April 2008.

16 Frank Carlson, 'Are hedge funds to blame for rising food prices?' Medill News Service, Windycitizen.com, 3 June 2008.

17 HM Treasury, Speeches, 20 June 2007, available at http://www.hm-treasury.gov.uk/2014.htm.

18 Labaton 'Agency's '04 Rule Let Banks Pile Up Debts'.

19 Ibid.

20 M. K. Brunnermeier, 'Dechiphering the 2007–08 Liquidity and Credit Crunch', *Journal of Economic Perspectives* (draft), May 2008, available at http://www.princeton.edu/~markus/research/papers/liquidity_credit_crunch_WP.pdf.

21 Eurostat, 14 November 2008 'Euro area and EU27 GDP down by 0.2%'.

7. Helping Is Futile

1 C-SPAN Video Library 281958, available at http://www.cspanarchives.org/library/index.php?main_page=product_video_info&products_id=281958-1.

2 Ibid.

3 John T. Woolley and Gerhard Peters, *The American Presidency Project*, online, Santa Barbara, CA: University of California, available at http://www.presidency.ucsb.edu/ws/?pid=14890.

4 Ayn Rand, *Atlas Shrugged*, London, 2007: 1,069.

5 Ibid.: 1,052–9.

6 Ibid.: 14.

7 H. van der Wee, *Prosperity and Upheaval: The World Economy 1945–1980*, Harmondsworth, 1987: 225.

8 R. Reich, *Supercapitalism*, Cambridge, 2008: 107.

9 Van der Wee, *Prosperity and Upheaval*: 240.

10 A. Greenspan, letters to the editor, *New York Times*, 3 November 1957.

11 A. Greenspan, 'Gold and Economic Freedom', *The Objectivist*, 1966.

12 M. Friedman, *Capitalism and Freedom*, New York, 1962: Chapter 1.

13 http://www.reclaimdemocracy.org/corporate_accountability/po-well_memo_lewis.html.

14 'Entre los métodos de tortura identificados por esta Comisión, los más utilizados durante este período fueron los golpes y la aplicación de electricidad', *Report of the National Commission on Political Imprisonment and Torture*, Chilean Ministry of the Interior, Chile, June 2005: 217, available at http://www.comisiontortura.cl/filesapp/06_cap_iv.pdf.

15 William Safire, 'Economy in Meltdown', *New York Times*, 8 October 1979.

16 K. Joseph, *Monetarism is Not Enough*, Centre for Policy Studies, 1976.

17 L. Von Mises, 'Economic Calculation in the Socialist Commonwealth', 1920, in F. A. Hayek, ed., *Collectivist Economic Planning* London, 1935: 87–130.

18 J. Williamson, 'What Washington Means by Policy Reform', in J. Williamson, ed., *Latin American Adjustment: How Much Has Happened?*, Washington, 1990.

19 Reich, *Supercapitalism*: 106.

20 'The State of Working America 2008/2009', Economic Policy Institute, 2008, available at http://www.stateofworkingamerica.org/tabfig/03/SWA06_Fig3D.jpg.

21 Economagic.com, http://www.economagic.com/em-cgi/data.exe/var/togdp-householdsectordebt.

22 D. M. Kotz, 'Neoliberalism and Financialisation', Conference Paper, Political Economy Research Institute, University of Massachusetts Amherst, May 2008: 5.

23 D. Farrell, 'Asia and the Global Capital Markets', McKinsey Global Institute, May 2007.

24 R. Puttnam, *Bowling Alone: The Collapse and Revival of American Community*, New York, 2000.

25 R. Reiner, 'Neoliberalism, crime and justice', *Social Justice and Criminal Justice*, King's College London, 2007.

26 'International trade statistics 2007' World Trade Organisation, available at http://www.wto.org/english/res_e/statis_e/its2007_e/its07_charts_e.htm.

27 World Bank, available at http://siteresources.worldbank.org/DA-TASTATISTICS/Resources/table2-7.pdf.

28 J. K. Galbraith and H. Kum, 'Inequality and Economic Growth: A Global View Based on Measures of Pay' CESifo Economic Studies 49: 527–56.

29 R. Freeman, 'What Really Ails Europe (and America): The Doubling of the Global Workforce', *Globalist*, 3 June 2005, available at http://www.theglobalist.com/DBWeb/printStoryId.aspx?-StoryId=4542.

30 UNIS, 24 March 2004.

31 'Global Mobile Phone Users Top 3.3 Billion By End-2007 – Study', *Agence France-Presse*, 24 May 2008.

32 *The Simpsons*, series 4, episode 2, 1 October 1992, Fox Broadcasting Company.

33 Jeffrey Sachs, 'The IMF Is a Power Unto Itself', *Financial Times*, 11 December 1997.

34 J. Stiglitz, 'What I Learned at the World Economic Crisis', *New Republic*, 17 April 2000.

35 Ibid.

36 R. Wade, 'Showdown at the World Bank', *New Left Review* 7, January–February 2001: 125.

37 Speech by National Security Affairs Presidential Assistant Anthony Lake, 21 September 1993.

38 C. Wright Mills, *The Power Elite*, Oxford, 1956.

39 R. Shelp, op cit: 161.

40 John Nichols, 'Enron: What Dick Cheney Knew', *Nation*, 15 April 2002.

41 David Rothkopf, *Superclass: The Global Power Elite and the World They Are Making*, New York, 2008; and David Rothkopf, 'This Is What Power Looks Like', *Newsweek*, 14 April 2008.

42 Lisa Kassenaar, 'Wall Street's New Prize: Park Avenue Club House With World View', Bloomberg.com, 15 December 2005.

43 A. Ghiridaras, 'Indian to the core and an oligarch', *Wall Street Journal*, 15 June 2008.

44 Kassenaar, 'Wall Street's New Prize'.

45 Reich, *Supercapitalism*: 134.

46 Richard Wachman, 'This transforms the financial system. Forever', *Observer*, 21 September 2008.

8. The Disrupted Wave

1 A discussion of so-called New Growth Theory is beyond the scope

of this book, but for a basic outline see 'Post Scarcity Prophet: Economist Paul Romer on growth, technological change, and an unlimited human future', Reasononline, December 2001, available at http://www.reason.com/news/show/28243.html.

2 N. D. Kondratiev, 'The Long Waves in Economic Life', *Review of Economic Statistics* XVII, November 1935: 105–15.

3 Kevin Kelly, 'New Rules for the New Economy', *Wired*, issue 5, September 1997.

4 http://www.internetworldstats.com/emarketing.htm.

5 International Telecommunication Union Internet Usage 2008, available at http://www.itu.int/ITU-D/icteye/Reporting/Show-ReportFrame.aspx?ReportName=/WTI/InformationTechnolo-gyPublic&RP_intYear=2007&RP_intLanguageID=1.

6 ITY Mobile Cellular Telephony 2008, available at http://www.i-tu.int/ITU-D/icteye/Reporting/ShowReportFrame.aspx?Re-portName=/WTI/CellularSubscribersPublic&RP_in-tYear=2007&RP_intLanguageID=1.

7 R. Freeman, 'What really ails Europe (and America); The doubling of the global workforce', *Globalist*, 3 June 2005, available at http://www.theglobalist.com/StoryId.aspx?StoryId=4542.

8 Ben Bernanke, 'The Great Moderation', 20 February 2004, available at http://www.federalreserve.gov/BOARDDOCS/SPEECHES/2004/20040220/default.htm.

9 G. Magnus, 'Have We Arrived At A Minsky Moment?' *UBS Economic Insights*, March 2007.

10 H. P. Minsky, *Stabilising an Unstable Economy*, New York, 2008: 320.

11 Though Ponzi schemes are technically illegal in the US, Minsky pointed out that not all Ponzi schemes in his theory had to be. I echo this: I am not suggesting that the US mortgage industry was intentionally in breach of the law in this sense.

12 H. P. Minsky, 'The Financial Instability Hypothesis', Levy Institute Working Paper 74, May 1992, available at http://www.levy.org/pubs/wp74.pdf.

13 G. Magnus, 'Have We Arrived At A Minsky Moment?'

14 H. P. Minsky, *John Maynard Keynes*, New York, 2008: 164.

15 S. Roach, 'Pitfalls in a Post-Bubble World', *Morgan Stanley Research*, 1 August 2008.

16 Ibid.

17 G. Moec and L. Frel, 'Global imbalances, saving glut and investment strike', Banque de France Occasional Paper 1, February 2006.

18 Hansard's Parliamentary Debates, 3rd Series, vol. XIX, 18 July 1833: 912.

9. The Fatal Stimulus

1 J. Decressin and D. Laxton, 'Gauging the risks for deflation' IMF Staff Position Note, 9 January 2009.

2 Kei-Mu Yi, 'The collapse of global trade: the role of vertical specialisation' in *The Collapse of Global Trade: Murky Protectionism and the Crisis*, R. Baldwin and S. Evernett, eds. 5 March 2009, VoxEU.org.

3 *Financial Times*, 9 January 2009.

4 Ben Bernanke, 'The Crisis and the Policy Response', speech for the Federal Reserve delivered at the London School of Economics, 13 January 2009.

5 G. Turner, *No Way to Run an Economy: Why the System Failed and How to Put it Right*, London, 2009: 85.

6 *New Statesman*, 6 November 2008.

7 Barry Eichengreen and Kevin O'Rourke, 'What Do the New Data Tell Us?' Available http://www.voxeu.org/index.php?q=node/3421.

8 'FACTBOX-China's August economic data, charts and analysts' views', Thompson-Reuters, 11 September 2009. Available at http://www.forbes.com/feeds/afx/2009/09/11/afx6873997.html.

9 Bureau of Labor Statistics figures for April 2010. Available at http://www.bls.gov/news.release/pdf/empsit.pdf.

10 Joshua Aizenman and Gurnain Kaur Pasricha, 'The net fiscal expenditure stimulus in the US 2008-2009: Less than what you might think', 3 March 2010. Available at http://www.voxeu.org.

11 'Navigating the Fiscal Challenges Ahead', IMF Fiscal Monitor, 14 May 2010.

12 31 May 2010. Available http://www.usfederalbailout.com/program_details.

13 Mervyn King, 'Mansion House Speech',17 June 2009. Available at http://www.bankofengland.co.uk/publications/speeches/2009/speech394.pdf.

14 Andrew Haldane and P. Alessandri, 'Banking on the State', 25 September 2009.

15 Simon Johnson, 'The Consensus on Big Banks Shifts, but Not at Treasury' 30 May 2010. Available at baselinescenario.com.

16 'Report on Greek Government Debt and Debt Statistics'. Available at http://epp.eurostat.ec.europa.eu/cache/ITY_PUBLIC/COM_2010_REPORT_GREEK/EN/COM_2010_REPORT_GREEK-EN.PDF.

17 Editorial page, *Kathimerini*, 8 March 2010. Available at http://

www.ekathimerini.com/4dcgi/_w_articles_columns_1_08/03/
2010_115465.

18 C. Lapavitsas et. al., 'Eurozone Crisis: Beggar Thyself and Thy
   Neighbour', RMF Report, March 2010.
19 Bloomberg TV, 28 April 2010.
20 Jean-Claude Trachet, Le Monde, 31 May 2010.
21 Ben Bernanke, 'Essays on the Great Depression', Journal of Money,
   Credit and Banking, Vol. 27, No. 1, February 1995.

10. The Return of Political Economy

1 Alan Greenspan, 'The Crisis', 9 March 2010.
2 Alan Greenspan, 'We Will Never Have a Perfect Model of Risk',
   Financial Times, 16 March 2008.
3 Ibid.
4 Joseph Stiglitz, Freefall: America, Free Markets and the Sinking of the
   World Economy, New York, 2009, p. 36.
5 Ian Bremmer, The End of the Free Market: Who Wins the War Between
   States and Corporations, New York, 2010.
6 R. Skidelsky, Keynes: The Return of the Master, London, 2009: 192
7 Costas Lapavitsas, 'Financialised Capitalism: Direct Exploitation
   and Periodic Bubbles', Historical Materialism, May 2008.
8 Nassim Nichols Taleb The Black Swan: The Impact of the Highly
   Improbable, New York, 2007.

Glossary

The jargon used by bankers, politicians and journalists can be exasperating. Here are just a few definitions you might want to bear in mind as you grapple with the details of the banking crisis.

Anglo-Saxon model

Capitalism as practised in the USA, Britain, Australia, New Zealand and Canada. Institutional arrangements designed to maintain social harmony are minimised. Instead the emphasis is on maximum economic freedom. In finance, the Anglo-Saxon model describes the separation of control and ownership in stock market listed companies. Proponents of this model value, above all, transparency and a supposedly level playing field for all participants in the market. Contrast this with the European Social Model, based on social partnership and often privately owned companies; or the state-capitalist model in China, where the government will openly attempt to manipulate markets and avoid transparency.

Asset

1. Anything you can buy or sell in a financial market. In the housing market a home counts as an asset; in the stock market it is a share certificate.
2. In banking, the word asset has a specific and slightly perverse meaning. To a bank, its loans are assets because they generate interest.

Asset bubble

A situation where an asset trades in large volumes at prices higher than its intrinsic value. In seventeenth-century Holland this happened with tulip bulbs. During an asset bubble it becomes illogical for people in the market not to participate. Eventually there is too much money in the market to sustain the bubble and it bursts. The first decade of this century saw asset bubbles in dotcom stocks, housing, credit derivatives and finally commodities.

Basel II Accord

An international treaty signed in 2004 which forms the template for banking regulations in the developed world. Its most important provision is that banks have to balance the risks on their books with a certain amount of capital, held in the form of cash or easily cashable IOUs. Before the current meltdown, this capital adequacy requirement was set at 4 per cent. Much of the shadow banking system was created to get around the treaty, a process known as 'gaming' Basel II.

Bond

An IOU for a long-term loan, usually paying the bearer a regular rate of interest over its lifetime. Both governments and companies issue bonds, often to finance long-term investments. In a stable market, bonds are a key investment for anyone who wants to generate a stable income (such as for a pension fund) rather than a rise in the value of their investments.

Bretton Woods System
At the 1944 Bretton Woods Conference the Allied powers agreed a system of exchange rates fixed against the dollar, which was pegged to gold. They also designed an economic management system to help rebuild the world: the International Monetary Fund and the World Bank. In 1971 President Richard Nixon unilaterally cancelled the currency agreement, inaugurating the present system of free-floating exchange rates, in which currencies have no intrinsic relationship to reserves of gold.

Broker-dealer
A bank that operates both as a broker, buying and selling shares on its clients' behalf, and as a dealer, using its own money to invest in the stock market. As a dealer, such a bank is potentially in competition with the customers it represents as a broker. All the Wall Street investment banks were broker-dealers, but many of the big failed commercial banks incorporated broker-dealing arms.

Buy side
The part of financial markets that specialises in buying and selling shares to make money on what then happens to the shares. Another side makes money out of the act of buying and selling; this is called the sell side. Inside a broker-dealer (see above) there are both sell-side and buy-side departments, which is where the trouble started during the dotcom boom.

Capital
1. Karl Marx's definition is unparalleled: self-expanding money. Any money that you don't need to cover your living expenses, or owe to somebody else, and can be thrown into the financial markets in the hope of making a profit, or invested in a business, is capital. Most people, on that definition, don't own any capital.
2. For a bank there's a different meaning. The capital is the sum, consisting of cash or easily cashable bonds, that is kept handy in case the loan book goes bad.

Capital adequacy
The amount of capital that, under Basel II, a bank must maintain to cover its potential losses from bad loans. A complex formula calculates the exact amount. Capital adequacy is more than just a regulatory requirement – it makes economic sense too: if investors think a bank has too little capital they will generally start selling their shares in it, signalling to the bank that it needs to raise more capital, usually through a 'rights issue'.

Cognitive dissonance
A mass psychological state in which a group committed to an ideology fails to adjust that ideology to changing events. In the first scientific paper on this phenomenon, the subjects were a 1950s alien abduction cult who, on the non-appearance of the aliens, resisted the conclusion that the aliens did not exist, deciding instead that they, the believers, had been spared from abduction.

Collateralised Debt Obligation (CDO)
Bonds wrapped up together, often issued only for the purpose of being wrapped up and sold, in chunks, with the risks inside not immediately obvious to the credit rating agencies that gave them a risk rating.

Commercial paper
Short-term loans taken out by companies on the financial markets, by issuing IOUs that are then not only bought but traded. The loan often lasts three months.

Commodity Price Index
An index that weights and averages various commodities traded on the world market to create an overall theoretical price for the most commonly traded raw materials, from pork to silver. There are two main commodity indexes, the Dow Jones AIG and the S&P Reuters. When commodities became the subject of an asset bubble, the value of these two indexes shot up rapidly.

Conduits
A vehicle for off-balance sheet bank lending. Conduits were a key part of the shadow banking system and differ from SIVs (see below) in that their losses are theoretically borne by the bank that sets them up.

Credit default swap
An insurance policy that pays out in the event that somebody else goes bust. Pat thinks Mac is going to go bust. He buys a CDS on Mac from Joe. He is technically obliged to tell Mac about it. CDSs are typically bought by banks or finance companies. As a result of a technical innovation the volume of this kind of finance, which is in part speculative, grew from less than £1 trillion in 1998 to $58 trillion by 2008. The unwinding of this tangled web of default bets drove the markets towards catastrophe in October 2008.

Credit rating
1. A personal creditworthiness rating, such as those issued by Experian or Equifax, which banks and other lenders use to assign rates of interest, the size of a loan, the need for collateral etc. Often expressed as a three-digit number.
2. Banks, companies, governments and even individual products are given credit ratings on a standardised scale by the credit ratings agencies.

Credit rating agency
Three credit rating agencies dominate the market: Moody's, Standard & Poors and Fitch. Their job is to perform a standardised risk measurement exercise on financial assets, companies and governments and produce a label that allows investors to assess the risk of losing their money. The safest rating is AAA. Anything below BBB is known as 'junk' – or high risk – and must generate a high rate of interest to compensate investors for the risk they are taking. As outlined in Chapter 6, the credit rating agencies are alleged to have systematically failed to perform their role in the run up to the meltdown of 2008.

Debt–deflation theory
An explanation of the 1930s Depression which says that the primary accelerator was that prices fell but debts didn't shrink with them. First outlined by Irving Fisher in the 1930s, the debt–deflation theory was adopted by Ben Bernanke. This heavily influenced Bernanke's initial design of the TARP in September 2008.

De-leveraging
Withdrawing from investment positions in order to pay back money borrowed for investment purposes (i.e. leveraged); usually done under conditions of stress.

Federal Reserve

The US central bank, set up in response to the financial panic of 1907. Responsible for financial stability and monetary policy, its chief in 2008 was Ben Bernanke. There are twelve city-level Federal Reserve Banks and a committee that sets interest rates.

Fiscal stimulus

The policy of boosting economic growth using government finances: a tax cut counts as a fiscal stimulus, releasing money into the economy; so does a rise in public spending. Unless the government has large reserves, it leads to growth in both the annual overdraft and long-term debt of the state in question.

Hedge fund

An investment fund open only to rich people, but increasingly used by pension funds to generate high returns on investments. Hedge fund managers make their money through fees; investors make their money from the high-risk investments they authorise the manager to make. Hedge funds typically run a 'strategy' relying on the superior market knowledge, mathematical skill or trading skill of the manager. The hedge fund also has the right to lock in the investor, to prevent them taking their money out when times are hard. Many hedge funds use leverage. This creates the argument that, though they are speculating with their own money, they pose a systemic risk to other people's.

Ideology

1. Any comprehensive idea-set describing or justifying the state of the world.
2. Used by philosophers and economists, from Hegel and Marx to Weber and Mannheim, to describe an idea-set that reflects a false view of the world, often associated with the material interests of a social group.

Kondratiev Wave

A fifty-year cycle of capitalist development first theorised by Soviet economist Nikolai Kondratiev, in which a twenty-five-year upswing is followed by a twenty-five-year downswing, ending in a slump.

Leverage

Borrowing money to amplify the power of your investment decisions. If you had $100 to invest and borrowed another $1,000, you would be considered 10x leveraged.

Margin

1. Shorthand for profit, as in 'profit margin'.
2. For investors, investing 'on margin' is slang for the practice of leveraging an investment – or borrowing to increase its value. Typically investing on-margin involves borrowing up to 50 per cent of the value of the shares you buy, doubling your potential winnings. Your stockbroker takes the shares as collateral and charges interest, so it's a win-win. Until you lose, then the losses are also amplified for you. And if everybody loses at once, the losses are amplified throughout the system.

Minsky Moment

US economist Hyman Minsky described the dynamics of a modern financial crisis, as asset prices collapsed, lenders rapidly reduced their exposure to bad debt, and many high-risk investors were forced to sucker in new investors simply to pay their old investors. When this moment loomed in March 2008, UBS economist George Magnus asked, 'Have we reached a Minsky Moment?'

Money market fund

A financial innovation aimed at individual savers. The fund invests in shares and bonds, aiming to keep the value of initial investment constant. Therefore investors do not benefit from a rise in the value of their capital, but from any interest or dividends. MMFs grew to become alternatives to bank savings accounts for many middle-class Americans; they were seen as a very conservative way to participate in financial markets, until the silent run on MMFs of 17 September 2008.

Off–balance sheet

An approach to accounting which moves risks, liabilities or other commitments off the balance sheet of a company or government. The UK's Private Finance Initiative has been described as off–balance sheet; the creation of the shadow banking system was a spectacular development of this approach. It is not illegal per se.

Ponzi scheme

A scheme, such as that alleged to have been run by Bernie Madoff, where losses on speculative investments are covered by new money raised from unsuspecting investors. Though technically illegal, Minsky (see above) argued that Ponzi finance was a logical outcome of the dynamics of financial capitalism. Named after Boston businessman Carlo Ponzi, who practiced deception on a spectacular scale in 1920, ruining thousands of investors.

Proprietary trading

Trading undertaken by investment banks using their own money rather than that of their investors. Prop trading is said to generate high but volatile profits, and creates an inherent conflict of interest, since the bank is in competition with its customers. Much of hedge fund activity grew out of the proprietary trading activities of the banks in the 1980s and '90s.

Quant

A quantitative analyst, usually a mathematician working for a bank or big investor who calculates the amount of 'value at risk' on a given day, according to complex models. The meltdown of 2008 revealed that many quants were working with inadequate models.

Recapitalisation

In general, adjusting the proportion of a bank's capital to its risks, which can be done by voluntarily getting rid of some of the risks (selling them on to someone else) or by pulling new capital into the business from investors. The bank recapitalisations of 2008 were attempts to do the latter: at first funded by private investors, who then lost a portion of their money, and then by the state, which at time of writing, is also in the process of seeing its money burn.

Rights issue

The issuing of new shares by a stock market–listed company in order to raise capital, allowing existing shareholders the 'right' to buy in proportion to their old shareholding. Anybody who does not buy sees their holding diluted, and their allocated shares sold off to new investors. A series of rights issues by UK and US banks in 2007–8 failed, indicating the existing shareholders believed this would be pouring away good money after bad.

Sell side
The part of the financial markets where money is made on the buying and selling of shares rather than on the investment decisions themselves (which is the buy side of operations). In the analyst scandals of the early 2000s, sell-side analysts were found to have used knowledge of the buy side to fool investors.

Short selling
A three-stage process: 1) the investor borrows shares from an institution that does not need to trade them; 2) he sells the shares in the hope that their price will fall; 3) once the price falls, he buys the shares back, returns them to their rightful owner and pockets the difference between the two prices.

Structured Investment Vehicle
A vehicle for off–balance sheet accounting crucial to the shadow banking system created after 2000. An SIV differs from a conduit in that it is technically independent of its sponsoring banks. Many SIVs were recognised as not independent at all, once they went bust, and their liabilities were absorbed by the parent banks, which were crippled in the process.

Structured finance
The practice of bundling bonds or other loans into complex investment vehicles, where the investor can pick and mix the risks on offer. Key to structured finance is the amount of risk judged to be involved. Assessments have been done by credit agencies, in many cases inaccurately.

Subprime
Lending to a borrower who has a high risk of defaulting on the payments or going bust. Generally done at a higher than normal interest rate and a high upfront fee.

TARP
Troubled Assets Relief Program. Introduced into the US Congress in late September 2008 to buy up the bad debts of banks at prices advantageous to the banks. Radically revised in November 2008.

TED-Spread
The difference between what it costs the US government to borrow money and what it costs banks to borrow from each other, expressed as a percentage. Normally 0.3 per cent, it hit 4.8 per cent in October 2008.

Tier I Capital Ratio
The actual measure of capital a bank needs to hold under Basel II, as interpreted by their national regulator. Was 4 per cent but reinterpreted in many Western countries as 9 per cent in the aftermath of the credit crunch.

Index

Page numbers in bold refer to glossary entries.